BLOOD AND STEEL 2

Other Books by Donald E. Graves

Ready, Aye Ready: The History of The Royal Regiment of Canada, 1861–2014 (The Regiment, 2015)

Blood and Steel: The Wehrmacht Archive: Normandy 1944 (Frontline, 2013)

And All Their Glory Past: Fort Erie, Plattsburgh and the Last Battles in the North (Robin Brass Studio, 2013)

First Campaign of an A.D.C.: The War of 1812 Memoir of Lt. William Jenkins Worth, U.S. Army (Old Fort Niagara Press, 2012)

Dragon Rampant: The Royal Welch Fusiliers at War, 1793–1815 (Frontline Books & Robin Brass Studio, 2010)

Fix Bayonets! A Royal Welch Fusilier at War, 1796–1815 (Robin Brass Studio & Spellmount Publishing, 2007)

Century of Service: The History of the South Alberta Light Horse (The South Alberta Light Horse Regiment Foundation & Robin Brass Studio, 2005)

More Fighting for Canada: Five Battles, 1760–1944 (Robin Brass Studio, 2004)

Another Place, Another Time: A U-boat Officer's Wartime Album (with Werner Hirschmann; Robin Brass Studio, 2004, 2011)

In Peril on the Sea: The Royal Canadian Navy and the Battle of the Atlantic (Canadian Naval Memorial Trust & Robin Brass Studio, 2003)

Quebec, 1759: The Siege and the Battle (by C. P. Stacey; edited and with new material by Donald E. Graves; Robin Brass Studio, 2002)

Guns Across the River: The Battle of the Windmill, 1838 (Friends of Windmill Point & Robin Brass Studio, 2001, 2013)

Fighting for Canada: Seven Battles, 1758–1945 (Robin Brass Studio, 2000)

Field of Glory: The Battle of Crysler's Farm, 1813 (Robin Brass Studio, 1999)

The Incredible War of 1812: A Military History (by J. Mackay Hitsman; updated by Donald E. Graves; Robin Brass Studio, 1999)

South Albertas: A Canadian Regiment at War (South Alberta Regiment Veterans Association & Robin Brass Studio, 1998, 2004)

Where Right and Glory Lead! The Battle of Lundy's Lane, 1814 (Robin Brass Studio, 1997, 2013)

Soldiers of 1814: American Enlisted Men's Memoirs of the Niagara Campaign (Old Fort Niagara Press, 1996)

Redcoats and Grey Jackets: The Battle of Chippawa, 1814 (Dundurn Press, 1994)

Merry Hearts Make Light Days: The War of 1812 Journal of Lieutenant John Le Couteur, 104th Foot (Carleton University Press, 1993; Robin Brass Studio, 2012)

Normandy 1944: The Canadian Summer (with W. J. McAndrew and M. J. Whitby; Art Global, 1993)

BLOOD AND STEEL 2

The Wehrmacht Archive:
Retreat to the Reich,
September to December 1944

Donald E. Graves

Frontline Books, London

Blood and Steel 2: The Wehrmacht Archive:
Retreat to the Reich, September to December 1944

This edition published in 2015 by Frontline Books,
an imprint of Pen & Sword Books Ltd,
47 Church Street, Barnsley, S. Yorkshire, S70 2AS
www.frontline-books.com

ISBN: 978-1-84832-851-8

CIP data records for this title are available from the British Library

For more information on our books, please visit
www.frontline-books.com, email info@frontline-books.com
or write to us at the above address.

Printed and bound by CPI Group (UK) Ltd, Croydon, CR0 4YY

Typeset in 10.8/13.5 point Minion Pro Regular

Contents

Goebbels Scrapes the Barrel 2; Message from Field Marshal Model 4;
The Siegfried Line 6; Orders to Hold the Scheldt Estuary 7; October
1944: Field Marshal Model Exhorts 9; Creation of the *Volkssturm*,
October 1944 11; Goebbels Sums Up the General Situation, 27 October
1944 13; Order of the Day by Field Marshal Walter Model, 9 November
1944 16; The Goebbels Grenadiers 18; The High Command Discusses
Surrender 19; Major Eberhard Furst von Urach 24

'Führer Words' and Battle Songs 29; To the Last – Well Almost 31;
Behaviour of Officers 33; Festung Walcheren 35; Battle Creed of 2nd
Parachute Division 36; Special Awards for Snipers 37; Analysis of
Mail 38; A Propaganda Company Officer Reports on Morale on the
Western Front 40; Hunger at Dunkirk 42

Extracts from the Diary of a German Officer captured by Belgian
Partisans 44; Experience of an Officer of the 17th SS Panzer Grenadier
Division Götz von Berlichingen, June–November 1944 46; Calais
Calling 50; A German Account of the Arnhem Battle, September
1944 52; Life on Walcheren in the Autumn of 1944 59; The Thinking
Sergeant 62; Morale of Pilots 64

List of Plates

German prisoners, August 1944. *(U.S. Army)*

Dolle Dinsdage ('Mad Tuesday') was the Dutch term for 5 September 1944 when amazed civilians watched the Wehrmacht's panic-stricken flight through their country in a variety of vehicles.

Allied airpower. By the autumn of 1944 the Allied air forces ruled the skies over western Europe. *(U.S. Army)*

Map of the Western Front, September 1944. *(Canadian Army Historical Section)*

'For Freedom and Life': German poster extolling the *Volkssturm*.

Feldmarschall Walter Model (1891–1945). *(Author's collection)*

A *Volkssturm* unit prepares for battle. *(U.S. Army)*

Map of the Siegfried Line, 1944. *(1st Canadian Army Intelligence Summary)*

'Front and Home Front – the Guarantors of Victory': a German propaganda poster of the late-war period.

Page from a manual for the *Panzerfaust*, the hollow-charge weapon that was deadly at close range to Allied armour *(Author's collection)*

German paratrooper, 1944. *(Author's collection)*

Destroyed bridge over the Albert Canal, Belgium, 1944. *(U.S. Army)*

Generaloberst Kurt Student (1891–1978). *(Author's collection)*

Flooded polderland, October 1944. *(Library and Archives of Canada)*

Feldmarschall Gerd von Rundstedt.

Canadian armour advances east of the Scheldt, October 1944. *(Library and Archives of Canada)*

The first ship to enter Antwerp, November 1944. *(Library and Archives of Canada)*

Canadian armour knocked out in Holland. *(Author's collection)*

Dead German, Holland 1944. *(Author's collection)*

Introduction

In the summer of 1944 the Third Reich was pummelled by a series of catastrophes. On 4 June, Allied armies took Rome and two days later landed in Normandy. On 22 June, the Soviet Union launched Operation BAGRATION against Army Group Centre and over the next two months followed it with a series of major offensives that totally or partially destroyed eighty-three German divisions on the Eastern Front. Germany's allies, sensing that the tide of war had shifted against her, began to drop away – in short order, Bulgaria, Rumania and Finland either negotiated peace with the Soviet Union or switched sides and Hungary teetered on the brink. On 20 July a conspiracy of army officers attempted to assassinate Hitler and, although they failed, the event sent shock waves throughout the Nazi state. Three days later the United States army began Operation COBRA, the breakout from Normandy, which eventually caused the near-collapse of the German forces on that front. On 15 August, the Western Allies landed in southern France and, on 25 August, Paris was liberated. Brussels followed on 3 September and Antwerp the following day. The German retreat from France showed no signs of stopping and threatened to become a panic-stricken migration. The Dutch would long remember 5 September 1944 as *Dolle Dinsdage* ('Crazy Tuesday') as long columns of German soldiers, sailors and airmen, mounted on a bewildering variety of transport piled high with loot and lady friends, drove through their towns day and night. By the first week of September, it appeared to many Allied soldiers and Europeans that the war would soon be over.

During early September, Allied armies came very close to breaking the back of the Wehrmacht in the west. The problem was that as the American, British and Canadian armies moved away from Normandy, their supply lines grew longer and logistical concerns began to dominate Allied planning. Field Marshal Montgomery ordered First Canadian Army to take the ports

of Dieppe, Dunkirk, Boulogne and Calais on the Channel coast to help ease
supply difficulties while Second British Army advanced on the right flank
into Belgium. To the south the three armies of General Omar Bradley's 12th
U.S. Army Group also pushed east through Alsace and Lorraine toward the
German frontier. The Allied supply problem would have been eased if the
great port of Antwerp could have been used but, unfortunately, the British
troops that captured it did not see fit to advance a few miles and cut off the
Beveland Peninsula on the north side of the Scheldt Estuary. This omission
not only permitted a large part of the German Fifteenth Army to escape, it
also left both sides of the estuary in German hands, preventing the use of
Antwerp's facilities.

Montgomery, however, was not concerned about this as he had a plan
in mind. He convinced General Dwight D. Eisenhower, the Supreme
Allied Commander, to approve a daring operation, codenamed MARKET-
GARDEN, using airborne troops to seize bridges on the major waterways
in Holland that would create a corridor along which Second British Army
could advance over the Rhine and into the Ruhr. Eisenhower approved
MARKET-GARDEN but also stressed to Montgomery the importance of
clearing the Scheldt and opening Antwerp. Determined to get across the
Rhine, Montgomery gave the job of besieging the Scheldt to First Canadian
Army which was miles back and just beginning the task of clearing the
Channel ports, even as Second British Army moved away from the Scheldt.
This was a very dangerous deployment but in the heady days of September
1944, it seemed a risk well worth taking.

Unfortunately, Allied plans did not take into account the enemy, and
as September wore on, the Third Reich managed to make a remarkable
recovery from the summer disasters. On the Eastern Front, the Red Army
was forced to pause on the banks of the Vistula because of logistical
difficulties. Hitler appointed two of his most trusted lieutenants, Josef
Goebbels and Heinrich Himmler, as Plenipotentiary for Total War and
commander of the *Ersatz Heer* or Home Army respectively. They initiated
a series of emergency measures which combed out all available manpower
from the Reich's civilian population, created the *Volkssturm* or home guard,
curtailed all activities that were not essential to the war effort, provided
labour for war industries and constructed fixed defences in the east and
west. In the last six months of 1944, these measures procured more than a
million men for the German armed forces but this only replaced the losses
suffered in the same period.

With the Russian armies pausing before Warsaw and in the Carpathian

Mountains, the greatest single threat was on the Western Front. The same day that Antwerp fell, *Feldmarschall* Gerd von Rundstedt was appointed commander in the west and, with the energetic efforts of his subordinate, *Feldmarschall* Walter Model, the commander of *Armeegruppe* B and a master of improvisation, the two were able to stop the panicky flight through Belgium, Holland and eastern France. Collection points were created to round up stragglers who were formed into *ad hoc* battlegroups and placed in good defensive positions behind the many canals and waterways. By dint of an extreme effort, 135,000 men were taken out of training establishments and the rear services, and sent west. The Luftwaffe – overwhelmed by Allied air superiority – alone contributed 30,000 men who were formed into the First Parachute Army to be commanded by *Generaloberst* Kurt Student, the father of the German airborne forces. Rundstedt planned to halt the Allies along the *Westwall*, the German counterpart to the French Maginot Line, but he needed six weeks to put its defences in order. To gain this time, he ordered *General* Gustav-Adolf von Zangen, commanding the Fifteenth Army, to hold a bridgehead in the Breskens area of the south shore of the Scheldt Estuary and sent all available armoured forces to the Moselle area to slow the advance of General George Patton's Third U.S. Army. After Model had defeated Montgomery's plan to seize a bridge over the Rhine at Arnhem, military operations on the Western Front degenerated into two slow, grinding battles of attrition to seize the German border city of Aachen and clear the approaches of Antwerp. These objectives were only attained in early November after considerable effort and high Allied casualties. Rundstedt had gained the time he wanted and it became clear that the war would not be over – as many Allied leaders had thought in early September – by Christmas.

   Blood and Steel 2: Retreat to the Reich, the second volume of the *Wehrmacht Archive*, depicts the German experience on the Western Front from September to December 1944. It is not a history of the military operations during this period but an attempt, based on translations of period German documents and the observations of German eyewitnesses, to depict the 'other side' of the war in the west. This material is taken from the daily intelligence summaries of First Canadian Army, which provide a wealth of information on the Wehrmacht in the last year of the Second World War.[1] They also contain contributions from the five American and two British armies that fought in the European theatre.

---

1. The Daily Intelligence Summaries of First Canadian Army are located in Record Group 24 of the Library and Archives of Canada in Ottawa.

Retreat to the Reich begins with an examination of the extraordinary efforts of senior Nazi party and military leaders to prevent Germany's war efforts from collapsing. We read the words of Hitler, Goebbels, Himmler, von Rundstedt, Model and von Zangen calling for greater effort and sacrifice. It continues with an examination of just how effective these measures – some very impractical – actually were. The experiences of German soldiers and civilians, as revealed in their diaries and letters, constitute the subject matter of Chapters 3 and 4.

The next five chapters primarily contain documents of military subject matter. They reveal the desperate attempts made to provide manpower for the Western Front: the creation of *ad hoc* battle groups, the creation of units composed of men with medical disabilities and non-German soldiers but, overall, reveal the remarkable recuperative powers of the Wehrmacht even in last year of the war.[2] Shortage of men, weapons and equipment – not to mention Allied air superiority – led to changes in tactics with emphasis on defensive warfare, camouflage and night attacks.

Chapter 9 examines the Wehrmacht's internal problems including acts of indiscipline and a high rate of desertion, despite extreme measures used to correct these weaknesses. It also examines food shortages and dire difficulties with motor transport. It is followed by a chapter which contains examples of Nazi propaganda distributed to the military and measures taken to prevent the widespread dissemination of Allied propaganda. Ironically, despite serious defeats at the hands of the Western Allies, the Wehrmacht was not that impressed with its enemies' effectiveness. Chapter 11 contains several German assessments of their enemies' capabilities. The final two chapters examine German treatment of Allied prisoners and the conduct of German prisoners in Allied captivity, and provide some examples of humour – such as it was and it was pretty black – during the period.

As one historian has commented, during the summer of 1944 the Third Reich had seemed to 'teeter close to the edge,' but as autumn arrived, it 'had stabilized the military situation and redoubled its energies at home to galvanize an often reluctant or truculent population into action to shore

---

2. I have made no attempt to analyze or discuss at length the bewildering variety of German military units in service during the autumn of 1944. The reader interested in those details is advised to consult Georg Tessin's magisterial *Verbände und Truppen der deutschen Wehrmacht und Waffen-SS im Zweiten Weltkrieg, 1939–1945* (17 volumes, Bissendorf, 1979–86) or the specialist websites concerned with German military history during the Second World War.

up defences and provide manpower for the front and armaments industry'.[3] *Blood and Steel 2: Retreat to the Reich* examines the nature of that recovery.

The leaders of the Third Reich, however, were planning more than a recovery. Late in November 1944, a German order dated 30 October was captured by British troops. It requested that all unit commanders inform their men that volunteers who were physically fit, had combat experience and a knowledge of English, 'especially the American dialect', were needed to form a new two-battalion unit for 'reconaissance and special tasks' on the Western Front. Men interested were ordered to report immediately to 'HQ Skorzeny' at Friedenthal near Berlin. The same order also directed units to turn in all captured American vehicles, weapons, uniforms and equipment. This document puzzled Allied intelligence officers who thought that not enough men meeting the requirements could be found in the ranks of the Wehrmacht, although if such a unit was created, they insisted that the threat it posed for 'infiltration' needs 'no stressing'.[4]

That done, the western Allied armies settled down for the winter, which all hoped would be quiet. As the next volume of the *Wehrmacht Archive* will show, these hopes would not be met.

Donald E. Graves
'Maple Cottage',
Valley of the Mississippi,
Upper Canada

3. Ian Kershaw, *The End. The Defiance and Destruction of Hitler's Germany, 1944–1945* (New York, 2011), 91.
4. Circular letter, 86th German Corps, ISUM 152, 1 December 1944.

A Note to the Reader

The First Canadian Army Daily Intelligence Summaries, from which most of the documents below were taken, were the product of many different hands working under extreme pressure (and perhaps the occasional artillery round or aerial bomb). The result is that there was little consistency in format and terminology from one summary to the next. Some translators and typists retained the original German document format; others simply transcribed everything as they thought best. Even the translations of words or titles can vary from document and, thus, the 12th Waffen SS Panzer Division can be referred to as the *Hitlerjugend*, *Hitler Jugend* or Hitler Youth Division.

This lack of consistency made the task of editing the following manuscript not only laborious but also very difficult. There was also the consideration that the imposition of a strict but artificial consistency on the documents would have, in some cases, adversely affected their period 'flavour'. Therefore, editorial work was kept as minimal as possible. Obvious mistakes in times, names and dates were silently corrected. The titles and identifications of formations and units were anglicized in the document titles and preliminary comments but left as they appeared in the text of the original document. German words and phrases that appear in the text were italicized except for such words as Luftwaffe, Panzer and Wehrmacht that have become so common in English that they are near part of the language. I should mention that Wehrmacht is used below – as, indeed, it often was during the war – to indicate German land forces although it actually encompassed all three German services.

Editorial or prefatory comments by wartime intelligence officers have been put in italics as have comments by the present editor – the latter being titled 'Editor's Comments'. Wartime editorial intrusions are enclosed within round brackets () while those of the present editor have been placed within square brackets [].

One final point is that the Wehrmacht identified corps by Roman numerals, divisions and regiments by Arabic numerals, battalions by Roman numerals and companies by Arabic numerals. Thus, the 5th Company of the II Battalion of the 979th Infantry Regiment of the 271st Infantry Division was part of the LVIII Panzer Corps.

D. E. G.

Acknowledgements

I must acknowledge the assistance given to me by Christopher Johnson and Brian Reid and, as always, particular thanks to my wife, Dianne, my editor and translator.

D. E. G.

German Ranks and their Equivalents

German Army	Waffen SS	British/American
Generalfeldmarschall		Field Marshal/ General of the Army
Generaloberst	*Oberstgruppenführer*	General
General der Infanterie*	*Obergruppenführer*	Lieutenant-General
Generalleutnant	*Gruppenführer*	Major-General
Generalmajor	*Brigadeführer*	Brigadier/ Brigadier-General
Oberst	*Oberführer*	Colonel
	Standartenführer	Colonel
Oberstleutnant	*Obersturmbannführer*	Lieutenant-Colonel
Major	*Sturmbannführer*	Major
Hauptmann	*Hauptsturmführer*	Captain
Oberleutnant	*Obersturmführer*	First Lieutenant
Leutnant	*Untersturmführer*	Second Lieutenant
Stabsfeldwebel	*Sturmscharführer*	Sergeant-Major Master Sergeant
Oberfeldwebel	*Hauptscharführer*	Technical Sergeant
Feldwebel	*Oberscharführer*	Staff Sergeant/
Unterfeldwebel	*Unterscharführer*	Sergeant
Unteroffizier	*Rottenführer*	Corporal
Stabsgefreiter	*Sturmmann*	Lance-Corporal/PFC
Obergefreiter	*Sturmmann*	Lance-Corporal/PFC
Gefreiter	*Sturmmann*	Lance-Corporal/PFC
Obersoldat/Obergrenadier	SS-*Oberschütze*	Private
Soldat/Grenadier	SS-*Schütze*	Private

* Or *der Artillerie, der Panzertruppen* etc.
Source: War Department, *Handbook on German Military Forces* (Washington, 1945).

List of Abbreviations and Acronyms Used in Text and Notes

AA	anti-aircraft
ADMS	Assistant Director, Medical Services
AP	armour-piercing
APCBC	armour-piercing, capped ballistic cap (shell)
AV (Tech)	Armoured Fighting Vehicles (Technical)
BDM	*Bund Deutscher Mädel* (League of German Maidens)
C of S	Chief of Staff
CG	Commanding General
CGS	Chief of the General Staff
CO	Commanding Officer
COS	*See* C of S
Coy	Company
CP	Command Post
CRA	Commander Royal Artillery
DAAG	Deputy Assistant Adjutant General
DAF	*Deutsche Arbeitsfront* (German Workers' Front)
DAQMG	Deputy Assistant Quartermaster General
DF (SOS)	Defensive Fire (SOS)
DSD	Director, Staff Duties
DTD	Directorate of Technical Development
flak	anti-aircraft
FAO	Forward Artillery Observer (US)
FEB	*Feld Ersatz Bataillon* (Field Replacement Battalion)
FDL	Forward Defence Line
FOO	Forward Observation Officer (UK)

FPN   *Feldpostnummer* (Field Post Number)

GAF   German Air Force, *Luftwaffe*
GHQ   General Head Quarters
GS 1 (A)   General Staff Officer 1 (Armour)
G.v.H.   *Garnisonsverwendungsfähig Heimat* (a soldier only physically
       capable of garrison duty)

HE   high explosive
HF   harassing fire
HJ   *Hitlerjugend* (Hitler Youth)
HKL   *Hauptkampflinie* (*see* MLR, q.v.)

i/c   in charge or in command, depending on context
Int   Intelligence
ISUM   First Canadian Army Intelligence Summary

KIA   Killed in action

MDS   Main Dressing Station
MG   Machine-gun
MLR   Main Line of Resistance
MT   Motor Transport

NAAFI   Navy, Army and Air Force Institutes
NSF   *Nationalsozialistischer Führungsstab des Heeres* (National
       Socialist Leadership Staff of the Army)
NSFO   *Nationalsozialistischer Führungsoffizier* (Nazi Indoctrination
       Officer)
NSKK   *Nationalsozialistisches Kraftfahrkorps* (Nazi Motoring
       Organization)

OB West   *Oberbefehlshaber West* (Commander-in-Chief West)
OC   Officer Commanding
OKH   *Oberkommando des Heeres* (army high command)
OKL   *Oberkommando der Luftwaffe* (air force high command)
OKW   *Oberkommando der Wehrmacht* (armed forces high command)
OP   observation post
ORs   Other Ranks (i.e. NCOs and enlisted men)

pdr.   pounder
pdv   Probability Directional Value

PIAT	Projector, Infantry, Anti-Tank
POL	Petrol, Oil and Lubricants
PW	Prisoner of War, both singular and plural
Q.	Quartermaster
RAD	*Reichsarbeitsdienst* (State Labour Service)
RdF	*Reichs-Rundfunk-Gesellschaft* (German Radio Broadcasting Service)
REME	Royal Electrical and Mechanical Engineers
RM	Reichsmark
RP	rocket projectile
RSO	*Raupenschlepper Ost* (a tracked truck)
R/T	Radio/Telephone
SA	*Sturmabteilung*
SD	*Sicherheitsdienst* (Nazi Party Security and Intelligence Agency)
SFH	*Selbsfahrlett-Feld-Haubitze* (self-propelled gun)
SHAEF	Supreme Headquarters Allied Expeditionary Force
SMG	submachine-gun
SP	self-propelled
SS	*Schutzstaffel*
VD	Venereal Disease
WIA	Wounded in action
WO	Warrant Officer or War Office, in context
WT	Wireless Telegraphy
z.b.V.	*zur besonderen Verwendung* (for special purpose or special employment)

Chapter 1

Stemming the Flood

Preparing to Defend the Reich, August–November 1944

Editor's Comments

As the Allies begin to approach the borders of the Reich in the west, east and south, the Nazi government makes a tremendous effort to bolster the nation's defences. Two of Hitler's most faithful lieutenants, Josef Goebbels and Heinrich Himmler, are given responsibility for the raising of new formations for the final battle (Documents 1/1, 1/6, 1/7 and 1/9). It comes as no surprise that Hitler orders the Westwall or Siegfried Line 'to be held to the last round' (Document 1/3) while Feldmarschall Model tries frantically to stop his retreating forces (Document 1/2) and exhorts them to greater efforts (Documents 1/5 and 1/8). In contrast, General der Infanterie von Zangen calmly explains to the men of his Fifteenth Army why they must hold the Scheldt and deny the Allies the use of the great port of Antwerp. In Document 1/10, instructions are given to the German officer corps not to 'sacrifice themselves' as they will be needed for a future 'trial of strength for leadership of the world'. Unfortunately, some junior officers – to be nominated by divisional commanders – must be prepared to die 'the hero's death' for 'the maintenance of the troops' morale'. Following this grim and cynical document, the views of a sensible and realistic German officer, Major Eberhard von Urach (Document 1/11), make for refreshing reading.

Document 1/1[1]

Goebbels Scrapes the Barrel

Wartime Intelligence Officer's Comments

A new announcement from Goebbels on 24 August 1944 gives details of a further comb-out to provide manpower for the Army and the war industries. The following are extracts from the announcement:

(a) The whole of Germany's cultural life has been maintained, even in the fifth year of the war, to an extent which the other belligerents did not reach even in times of peace . . . The total war effort of the German people now necessitates far-reaching restrictions in this field as in others. In future it will be mainly by film and radio that relaxation will be provided for a cultural value conveyed to the soldiers at the front and the working homeland.

   All theatres, music halls, cabaret shows and schools of acting are to be closed by September 1st. Private lessons in the arts will be suspended. All circus enterprises will be closed down except for a few needed to preserve the valuable animals. All orchestras, schools of music and conservatories, with the exception of a few leading orchestras urgently required, for instance, by the radio for its programmes will discontinue their activities. Academies, art colleges, private schools of art and painting, and art exhibitions, will be closed down. Only scientific and technical literature, armament and school books, as well as certain standard political works will be published; all other types of literature will be suspended. The daily press will be further curtailed and far-reaching amalgamation must be effected. Many tens of thousands of high-class skilled workers will be released for work of war importance or for the Forces by closing down and restrictions in these fields.

(b) The welfare work for the troops carried out by the NS Community RdF[2] will be suspended. About 200 touring companies, concert agencies and theatrical companies can thus be closed down, the RdF

---

1. ISUM 72, 4 September 1944.
2. RdF, an abbreviation for the *Reichs-Rundfunk-Gesellschaft*, the German radio broadcasting service controlled by Goebbels's propaganda ministry.

offices in the occupied territories, all artists' homes and all tours suspended, and the welfare work for armament workers confined to the communal camps.

(c) The Reich Minister for Learning, Education and Adult Education has drawn up a comprehensive programme for the curtailment of activity. Trade schools of no direct war importance, e.g. domestic and commercial colleges, will be closed. At the universities male and female students who are studying subjects which are not of direct importance to the war will be available for employment in the armament industry. These measures will make available a total of several hundred thousand persons.

(d) A new combined food ration card will be introduced on 16 October, saving about 300 million ration cards in each rationing period. Apart from saving a substantial quantity of paper, many workers will be released for other purposes of war importance.

(e) In order to fully utilize all labour, working hours in public administration and offices in industry and trade have been fixed uniformly at a minimum of 60 hours per week. Those sectors where considerably more hours are worked to deal with vital war contracts will not be affected by this measure. Every head of an authority or factory will be responsible for seeing that no workers are idle. Any staff made redundant by the increased working hours must be released immediately. The afternoon of one day per week can be left free for shopping and other personal needs, provided that the prescribed total number of working hours per week is maintained and the work in hand is done.

(f) In order to bring civilians in line with the soldier, a universal temporary ban on holidays is ordered with immediate effect. Women who will be 50 and men who will be 65 or over on 31 December are exempt from this ban. Short leave may be granted in accordance with strict but just standards to people who are bereaved or have serious illness in their family.

Goebbels concludes: 'Our joint endeavours for the war are not only a matter of voluntary effort. Care will be taken that the burdens involved are fairly distributed.'

Document 1/2[3]

Message from Field Marshal Model

Wartime Intelligence Officer's Comments

The following message from the Commander-in-Chief West, Field Marshal Model,[4] was delivered on Sunday 3 September 1944:

To the Soldiers of the Western Army

With the enemy advance and the withdrawal of our front, a great stream of troops has been set in motion. Several hundred thousand soldiers are moving backwards, Army, Air Force and tank units, troops which must reassemble and form new strongpoints or lines according to a plan and the orders they receive.

Among them there stream along, together with headquarters now superfluous, columns which have been routed, which have broken out from the front and which for the moment have no firm destination and could receive no clear orders. Town Major's offices and headquarters of rearward towns are often taking on tasks which would not overtax a corporal and three men. So, while closely packed columns turn off the road to get themselves sorted out, the stream of the others pushes on. With their vehicles travel idle talk, rumours, haste, inconsiderateness, unnecessary disorder and short-sighted selfishness. They may bring a feeling into the rear areas and into the fully intact bodies of the fighting troops which must be prevented at this moment of extreme tension with the severest measures.

As your new Commander-in-Chief I direct this call to your honour as soldiers. We have lost a battle, but I tell you, we will win this war! I cannot say more now, although I know that there are many questions burning on the troops' lips.

Despite everything that has happened do not allow your firm confident faith in Germany's future to be shaken one whit.

---

3. ISUM 77, 8 September 1944.
4. *Generalfeldmarschall* Walter Model (1891–1945) was the commander of *Armeegruppe* B, which defended the Low Countries against the Allied advance. He was known both for his success in defensive battles and his ruthlessness.

I must however make known to you the gravity of this day and hour. This moment will and should separate the weaklings from the real men. Every single man carries now the same responsibility: when his commander falls out, he must take his place and carry on in his spirit.

I demand of you categorically:

(1) Report without any hesitation to the nearest headquarters or collecting point. In your statements there about your withdrawal, about orders given, your destination and your tasks, stick precisely to the facts.

(2) Do not expect that headquarters or collecting points can deal with you and your affairs and fix you up as quickly and as suitably as is now necessary. Think over to yourself what is best and most right in the situation.

(3) Don't sit back with your hands folded! Stand up and get about actively, and don't rely on luck. Above all don't give yourself up to the feeling that luck would never come to you. It comes to every man who has his heart in the right place. A quiet word, a sensible thought, a steady word of advice at the right moment will give to countless others the necessary support, confidence, self-reliance, self-belief and the right demeanour.

(4) Show increasingly to the outside world a flawless discipline. I have satisfied myself that your inward spirit is flawless. Do not forget that even the slightest gesture, each word, every good proof of honour, shows the population that the spirit and cohesion of the German Army are intact. So let your inward feelings be fully demonstrated outwardly: your head high in all difficulties: your body erect: your salute smart and confident. With the French and Belgians too the fighting worth of a unit and of each individual soldier will be judged by the outward behaviour. The terrorist himself, our most cowardly enemy, thinks so too. He will sooner attack a slack, unmanly soldier than one who strides along erect and confident and gives the impression by his soldierly bearing or his correct salute.

(5) Let yourselves be irritated by nothing, especially not by stupid chattering, pessimistic rumours and idle talk which the enemy seeks to bring to you. Take immediate steps against all such panic mongers. The enemy has lost battles for four years. He has for the first time won a battle against us. He has not won it because he is cleverer and better and braver. He is not a magician. He is not everywhere. If one added together all the tanks which rumour mongers reported they had seen, the enemy would have a hundred thousand. In fact they were

often only very small spearheads. They can be increasingly halted by defensive obstacles of all kinds. Often the rumours have done us more harm than these tanks. With courage and presence of mind make an extra effort; stop important positions being given up needlessly, necessary weapons, equipment and fortifications being over-hastily blown up. For every hand grenade, every rifle, every gallon of petrol is now needed to arm the new line to receive our troops. They are more important than suitcases or useless plunder.

(6) Take thought then that at this moment everything adds up to the necessity to gain the time which the Führer needs to bring into operation new troops and new weapons. They will come.

Soldiers, we must gain this time for the Führer!

(Signed) *Model*
Field Marshal

Document 1/3[5]

The Siegfried Line

Wartime Intelligence Officer's Comments

The order which is translated below has often been referred to by PW[6] as the order from the Führer which cannot be countermanded under any circumstances.

Local Defence Training Battalion I/6   HQ 15 September 1944

Telephone Message

1. The Siegfried Line is of decisive importance in the battle for Germany.
2. I order:

The Siegfried Line and each of its defence positions will be held to the last round and until completely destroyed.

---

5. ISUM 101, 11 October 1944, from *Second Army Intelligence Summary 120*, 2 October 1944.
6. The British PW or Prisoner of War is the equivalent of the American POW. In this book it can be either singular or plural depending on context.

This order will be communicated forthwith to all HQs, military formations, battle commanders and troops.

C-in-C West

Time of origin: 3.45 hours
Communicated by: Signal Reporting Centre (Private Quack)
Time of receipt: 3.45 hours
Accepted by: Private Ebertowski

Document 1/4[7]

Orders to Hold the Scheldt Estuary

C-in-C 15 Army   Army Headquarters, 7 October 1944

ORDERS

The defence of the approaches to Antwerp represents a task which is decisive for the further conduct of the war. Therefore, every last man in the fortifications is to know why he must devote himself to this task with the utmost strength. I have confirmed that so-called 'experts' among the local population are attempting to confuse the German soldiers in this battle task ordered by the Führer.

Whether know-it-alls in some HQs are participating in such nonsense, which then quickly reaches the troops, I do not know. This, I have reason, however, to fear. Therefore, I order commanders as well as the National Socialist indoctrination officers (NSFO)[8] to instruct the troops in the clearest and most factual manner on the following points: Next to Hamburg, Antwerp is the largest port in Europe. Even in the First World War, Churchill in person travelled to Antwerp in order himself to organize the defence of the harbour because he appreciated it as of vital importance to the struggle on the continent. At that time,

---

7. ISUM 122, 30 October 1944.
8. NSFO or *Nationalsozialistische Führungsoffiziere* were created in the last years of the war to ensure that soldiers were thoroughly indoctrinated in Nazi ideology. Largely despised by professional officers, they became more powerful after the abortive assassination attempt of July 1944.

Churchill's plan was completely shattered; the same must happen again.

After overrunning the Schelde[9] fortifications, the English would finally be in a position to land great masses of material in a large and completely protected harbour. With this material they might deliver a death blow at the north German plateau and at Berlin before the onset of winter.

In order to pretend that the battle of Antwerp is unimportant and to shake the morale of its defenders, enemy propaganda maintains that the Anglo-American forces already possess sufficient ports which are intact with the result that they are not at all dependent on Antwerp. That is a known lie. In particular, the post of Ostend, of which the enemy radio speaks frequently, is completely destroyed. Current delays in the enemy's conduct of the war are attributable in great measure to the fact that he still must bring all his supplies through the improvised facilities of Cherbourg. As a result, he has even had to lay a temporary oil pipeline from there to the interior of France.

The so-called 'experts in the civilian population' maintain, as does the enemy radio, that in the last four years the west Schelde has completely filled in and that Antwerp is now out of the question as a harbour for deep-sea vessels. In reply to this, it may be said: The Schelde channel is so deep (in the outer Schelde up to 27 metres) that should a ship be grounded, it can still continue on the flood tide. The entrance to the harbour is obviously possible. The enemy has at his disposal, moreover, a large fleet of medium and small freighters which, in view of the extent of the Antwerp harbour, can be unloaded at the same time. Finally, the English have already prepared dredgers to clear the channel completely.

The Schelde has been mined by every means. Mining will undoubtedly delay use of the port but in the long run it will not render it impossible. It will cost the enemy casualties. But, in view of the importance of the harbour, he will accept these casualties.

In his last speech, Churchill said again 'before the storms of winter we must bring in the harvest in Europe'. The enemy knows that he must assault the European fortress as speedily as possible before its inner lines of resistance are fully built up and occupied by new divisions. For this reason, he needs the Antwerp harbour. And for this reason, we must hold the Schelde fortifications to the end. The German people are watching us. In this hour, the fortifications along the Schelde occupy a role which is decisive for the future of our people. Each additional day it will be vital

---

9. The German spelling of Scheldt.

that you deny the port of Antwerp to the enemy and the resources he has at his disposal.

(Signed) Von Zangen[10]
General der Infanterie

Document 1/5[11]

October 1944: Field Marshal Model Exhorts

Wartime Intelligence Officer's Comments

The following is a translation of an order issued by Field Marshal Model, Commander of Army Group 'B'.

TO THE SOLDIERS OF THE WEST

EXHORTATION OF FIELD MARSHAL MODEL

The enemy is on our native soil. Villages and towns to the west have become battle zones. The last battle has commenced. It depends on every individual soldier whether this battle will turn in our favour.

Comrades: No longer do the hostile population of France and Belgium stand behind you, but German citizens now support your struggle. They would rather see their houses and fields laid waste than surrender. Today the enemy promises us humanitarian treatment, but when we are once defenceless he will keep none of his promises.

Will you abandon German women and children to violation by undisciplined Negro travesties of soldiers?

Soldiers fighting in the east, have themselves set an example and brought the Bolshevist mass assault to a halt before the frontiers of the Reich.

It is your duty to protect their property, their wives and families.

---

10. *General der Infanterie* Gustav-Adolf von Zangen (1892–1964) commanded the Fifteenth Army and stubbornly defended the Scheldt Estuary until November 1944, delaying the opening of the port of Antwerp.
11. ISUM 95, 5 October, 1944, from *Second Army Intelligence Summary* 110, 1 October 1944.

What value is your life if you have to stand ashamed before them and before the garrisons of the fortresses on the French coast, which have been cut off for weeks from home.

The hour is coming when you will have to face them. They will ask you whether you have done your utmost to protect the Fatherland.

Every wall is protection from behind which the enemy can be effectively engaged. How often have a few gallant men with light weapons destroyed complete armoured thrusts?

In the ruins of Cassino, a handful of German paratroops on foreign soil stopped a whole Army. Would you be a lesser man in the eyes of your wife and children?

The enemy is not brave. When he finds stiff resistance he withdraws. Enemy paratroops and airborne troops fight without support, cut off from their base. You can destroy them if you only have the will.

Every village must become a strongpoint. Every block of houses a fortress. Who has a weapon and does not use it does not deserve to live and will be annihilated on the spot by his comrades.

Whoever leaves you in the lurch shall suffer a death of shame, for only the brave have the right to live.

The battle in the west is being waged for time. The enemy needs a speedy victory. It is for you to smash his hopes and pave the way for a German counterblow.

ONLY HE HAS LOST WHO SURRENDERS.

Signed Model
Generalfeldmarschall

Document 1/6[12]

Creation of the *Volkssturm*, October 1944

Wartime Intelligence Officer's Comments

The following summary has been compiled from British, German and Swiss broadcasts between 2100 and 2200 hours, 18 October 1944. It is believed to be correct in general outline, but the accuracy of details cannot be guaranteed.

A *levée en masse* of the German people has been ordered by Hitler and a speech has been broadcast by Himmler.

The order for the *levée en masse* directs that military training will be given to all males between the ages of 16 and 60. This order has been issued on the 131st anniversary of the Battle of the Nations near Leipzig, when Prussians took part in the defeat of Napoleon. It states that after five years of war the Allies are close to, and in some cases have reached, the German frontier. 'Now we are determined to rally our people on a mass scale. We must and will succeed in breaking our enemies' determination and in throwing them back again.'

The order states:

(i)   The '*Deutscher Volkssturm*'[13] will be formed in every *Gau*[14] by men between the ages of 16 and 60 who are capable of bearing arms and they will defend the soil of the homeland with all such means and weapons as will be appropriate.

(ii)   The direction of the '*Deutscher Volkssturm*' will be undertaken in each *Gau* by the *Gauleiter*, who will use the proved and trusted organizations of the Party such as the SA,[15] NSKK,[16] the *Hitler Jugend*,[17] etc.

---

12. ISUM 113. 21 Oct. 1944, from *Second Army Intelligence Summary* 136, 18 Oct. 1944.
13. The *Volkssturm* ('People's Storm') were home defence troops, modelled after the *Landsturm* of the Liberation War in 1813.
14. Nazi Germany was divided into a number of *Gaue* or districts, each governed by a *Gauleiter*, who had quite broad powers, including some military ones.
15. The SA or *Sturmabteilung* was the paramilitary arm of the Nazi Party.
16. The NSKK or *Nationalsozialistisches Kraftfahrkorps* or motor corps was the party organization that provided driver training both for the Nazi party and the army, and roadside assistance to civilian drivers in peacetime.
17. The *Hitler Jugend* or Hitler Youth was the Nazi youth organization for boys roughly equivalent to the Boy Scouts but which, gradually, as the war progressed, took over secondary military duties on the home front.

(iii)   I nominate the Chief of Staff of the SA Schepmann[18] as inspector of training in the use of weapons and the head of the NSKK Krauss[19] as inspector of training in mechanical technique.

(iv)   The members of the *'Deutscher Volkssturm'* are soldiers during their service within the meaning of the Acts relating to the Armed Forces.

(v)   The members of the *'Deutscher Volkssturm'* may remain members of other organizations, but their service in the *'Volkssturm'* takes precedence over their obligations to all other organizations.

(vi)   The *Reichsführer* SS[20] as Chief of the Replacement Army (*Ersatzheer*[21]) is responsible for the training, arming and equipment of the *'Deutscher Volkssturm'*.

(vii) The *'Volkssturm'* will be directed on my orders by the *Reichsführer* SS.

(viii) The military orders will be issued by *Reichsführer* SS Himmler, whilst the political orders will be given by *Reichsleiter* Bormann.[22]

(ix)   The members of the *'Deutscher Volkssturm'* are enlisted as the chief protagonists in this struggle.

The announcer also states that members of the levées will not wear uniform, but would have an armlet bearing the German emblem and the words *'Deutscher Volkssturm'*.

Himmler delivered his speech in a strained, almost hysterical voice. He went over the whole story of Germany's disasters since Stalingrad onwards and put all the blame on treacherous allies. He then referred to the formation of new divisions and also to the creation of new squadrons of the Luftwaffe. He called for a fanatical defence of every inch of German soil. 'Every mile that our enemies advance into Germany' he said, 'will cost them rivers of blood. Every house, every farm, every ditch, every tree and every bush will be defended by men, women and children.' The enemies of Germany would have to realise that a penetration into Germany would involve sacrifices equivalent to national suicide. Even in areas which they believed they had conquered they would still be attacked.

---

18. Wilhelm Schepmann (1894–1970) was the *Stabschef* or chief of staff of the SA in 1943–5. The head of the SA was Hitler.
19. *Korpsführer* Erwin Krauss (1894–1966) was the head of the NSKK from 1942 to 1945.
20. Heinrich Himmler (1900–45) was the *Reichsführer* SS and head of the police including the Gestapo, the SD, SS and the *Ersatzheer*.
21. The *Ersatzheer* or Home or Replacement Army provided support for front line formations. Each combat division had a 'shadow' formation or unit in the *Ersatzheer*, which recruited and trained replacements for it.
22. *Reichsleiter* Martin Bormann (1900–45) was head of Hitler's Chancellery and had tremendous power as he controlled access to the dictator.

Never and nowhere must a man of the 'People's Levées' capitulate. If at any time a responsible leader believed himself in such a position that he must give up the struggle, then he must yield his position to one of his subordinates, even though he might be one of the youngest.

Referring at the conclusion of his speech to east Prussia, the soil on which he was standing, Himmler declared: 'Here there will be no more retreating'. Germany would win the last round against her bestial opponent. 'We believe in Germany, in Hitler and in National Socialism!'

Document 1/7[23]

Goebbels Sums Up the General Situation, 27 October 1944

Wartime Intelligence Officer's Comments

The following is a précis of a speech broadcast by Goebbels on 27 October 1944 setting out Germany's present position.

He opened by saying that some three months had passed by since he had given a review of the position over the radio. That in this comparatively short space of time events of decisive military importance had taken place, of which a great many to their disadvantage, but the enemy's hopes that they would collapse had not been fulfilled. On the contrary, they had stemmed the advances both in the east and west.

He would tell the unvarnished truth and hide nothing. It was a battle which would decide their fate. Struggle would not be given up until they had achieved a peace which would guarantee their life and national independence. They had made enormous sacrifices and must be prepared for more. The enemy's successes had, however, been bought at such cost in men and materials that an early end of the war had become a necessity for them. It was now a race for time and they (the Germans) had, according to the present position, a good chance of winning. Contrary to the Allies, who had only world-imperialistic aims, the Germans were fighting for

---

23. ISUM 122, 30 October 1944, from *Second Army Intelligence Summary*, 28 October 1944.

their very life. They knew what to expect if conquered – hell on earth! This was evidenced by the mass terror in the east. Not a single worker, not a single peasant, thinker, woman or mother desired capitulation, all were united in a desire to fight till a successful end was reached. This the German government would bring about.

The liberated countries, after greeting their deliverers with flowers and garlands, were now paying a high price for that liberation. Many a Frenchman must now be thinking back with regret to the German occupation which was heaven on earth compared with present conditions. They now had before their very eyes the difference between Germany's New Order and the disintegration and destruction following in the wake of the Allies. What the Germans wanted was clear: an understanding between European countries for the defence of the Continent. They (the Germans) knew that this would call for the greatest efforts. There was no point in committing suicide in fear of death, as Bulgaria and Rumania had done, but anyway these two countries deserved no better fate.

The Germans were a young and brave people, whose mission it was to save Europe from Bolshevism. For nearly five years they had fought almost the whole world and yet the enemies' armies had not succeeded in beating them. Therefore they had no intention of laying down their arms, for they knew what the results of such action would be.

Because of the treachery of Bulgaria and Rumania they had had to withdraw their troops, though with reluctance, in the southeast. Hungary had pulled itself together at the very last moment, thrown off its traitors and under new leaders was now prepared to fight side by side with Germany until victory was achieved.

He [Goebbels] would not in any way refuse to admit that the heavy reverses and losses in the west had caused them much sorrow and pain nor what these losses meant. They were now back more or less on the 1939 line, but now Germany's Lines of Communication were shortened, whereas those of the Allies were getting even longer, and the occupation of Russia had taught the Germans what this meant.

Goebbels then paid tribute to the coastal troops, whose bravery and endurance, he said, had denied the Allies the use of the ports on the Atlantic and Channel coasts which were so necessary to them. Those troops had re-asserted by radio their loyalty to the Führer and had donated their pay to the Red Cross and/or to the Winter Help.[24]

---

24. *Winterhilfe* or 'Winter Help' was the Nazi charitable organization that collected money and clothing for distribution of winter clothing for soldiers and civilians.

Turning for a few moments to Italy, Goebbels said that they could only view with amazement and gratitude what the German soldiers were achieving there. Not without reason did the enemy dub them 'Green Devils'.[25] They had literally made the battlefield a hell for their enemies.

Next came some words of commiseration for the home front. The people at home had suffered severely from the inhuman terror attacks from the air, but as these attacks were directed mainly against civilians, production had not been greatly affected. In fact, in view of the measures taken by the government, the output curves in the coal and production industries showed an upward trend. The originators of the terror from the air were on the list of war criminals being compiled by Germany. He had himself recently visited his home in the Rhineland, and had seen with his own eyes that this terror was not getting the people down. Every man, woman and even child was united in a determination that the Rhine should remain German.

There followed a few words of admiration for Japan, by whose side Germany would fight in close brotherhood of arms until victory was won.

Next Goebbels said he would say a few words on the future outlook. Total mobilization of the German people had been in force for three months and had brought about wonderful results. Barracks were full of new divisions and there were more workers than the labour market could assimilate. The German leaders were busy with the construction of the newest type of weapons and were building squadrons of mighty fighters and bombers, but he would warn the people not to expect wonders from the new weapons. The German people had now recovered from the shocks administered to them in the west and were firmly on their feet again, showing a calm and confident front to the enemy.

At last there came a reference to the Führer. He, Goebbels, had recently been to the Führer's HQ and realized more strongly than ever how much the German people owed to that man, standing 'firm as a rock amidst the surging seas.'

Goebbels ended by quoting a letter written by Frederick II in 1759 during the Seven Years' War, in which he said that he loved peace just as much as anyone else did, but that it must be a good, endurable and honorable peace, and that was what they (the Germans) were now fighting for.

---

25. 'Green Devils' was supposedly the Allied nickname for the German airborne troops and this is a reference to their stubborn defence of the monastery at Monte Cassino in Italy.

Document 1/8[26]

Order of the Day by Field Marshal Walter Model, 9 November 1944

Soldiers of the Army Group!
Fighters in the West!

In the midst of stern struggles on the frontiers of the Great German Reich the Front joins with the Homeland in remembrance of 9 November.

The dead of the Feldherrnhalle[27] were an example of a small community of soldiers and young idealists, founded on the National Socialist Ideal, which was born in the midst of the artillery fire of the First World War and now embraces our whole nation. The dead of the 9th of November threw a revolutionary spark into a time of weakness, error and aimlessness. The National Socialist revolution inside the Reich was accomplished through the bitterest tests and hardest trials; because the community of idealists did not lose faith in the face of a preponderance of hatred and indifference. In the same way we too will now wrest the victory, if we now fight with the same fanaticism and the same confidence in victory against the enemy's material superiority and agitation.

In the bitter struggle we have succeeded after retreat in halting the enemy's armies on the western frontier of the Reich and in establishing a firm defence front through the steadfastness of emergency units, young volunteers and determined battle groups of all parts of the army and Waffen SS. The enemy's attempts to break through our front with strong forces at Arnhem, west of Venlo, at Aachen and south of Trier collapsed against the firm resistance of [Infantry] Divisions, *Volksgrenadier* Divisions, Mobile and Panzer formations and Luftwaffe units with the well-proved support of numerous Army artillery units and troops of the GAF. In a glorious battle the struggle for time was won on the lower Scheldt and the Maas. The fight of the fortresses on the coast in co-operation with the Navy remains exemplary. The enemy, therefore, who already believed that victory was

---

26. ISUM 142, 28 November 1944.
27. The Feldherrnhalle was the square in Munich where the police opened fire on the Nazi marchers who were attempting to overthrow the government of Bavaria, crushing their attempt at a putsch. The incident took place on 9 November 1923 and the sixteen men killed were venerated as martyrs by the Nazis. Model makes reference to it as his order is dated on the 21st anniversary of the incident.

firmly in his hands, has so far been shattered against our tough defensive determination.

Steadfastness, energy and faith must and will allow us, strengthened by total mobilization, to win further gains in the struggle for time. The day will come, when a strong German air force will again deal the enemy decisive blows.

For us the German worker in bombed factories untiringly and with a defiant determination is making new weapons, which in the hands of the best soldiers will gain the decision. Women and mothers stand at the assembly line or guide the plough. German youth helps everywhere with the enthusiasm of young hearts to bear the burdens of the war.

This determination to work and fight has found its most profound expression in the call-up of the *Volkssturm*. Its enrolment today is a sign of the unbroken German will to fight.

The bomb terror, which at the moment has reached its peak, could not, in spite of losses suffered, destroy the untiring manufacturing power of the home front. The power of resistance of the Rhineland became tougher as blow fell upon blow, not discord, not cowardice, but a burning hatred will give the answer to the murderers of German women and children. We want to be the avengers of our sorely-tried homeland.

In this great struggle the greatest source of power for the front and the homeland is our beloved Führer. He was called by fate to show Germany the way from poverty to freedom. He created the marvel of German unity. He will lead us through all changes in the fortunes of war up the road to victory. We wish as his soldiers to be the toughest of fighters who ever bore arms for the defence of the German homeland. No soldier in the world shall be better than the soldiers of our Führer!

Just as the Führer could say of the martyrdom of the 16 victims of the Feldherrnhalle in spite of threats and terrorism 'and yet you have won the victory', so is the watchword of our fateful struggle.

We shall win, because we believe in Adolf Hitler and our great German Reich.

MODEL
Generalfeldmarschall

Document 1/9[28]

The Goebbels Grenadiers

Wartime Intelligence Officer's Comments

Few men share Dr. Goebbels's facility for making sensational statements. Fewer still, Germans included, believe these statements. The following passage is an extract from one of the good Doctor's most recent public utterances. In it he announces the formation of more than one hundred new divisions in three months, divisions which are now rolling frontwards in an uninterrupted stream fortified with the best in equipment and training. This imaginative statement maintains Dr. Goebbels' usual high standard of exaggeration, and attributes a hitherto unsuspected excellence to the new Volksgrenadier Divisions.

Over to the Doctor:

13 November 1944

Three months ago I received from the Führer the task, I may surely say the proudest task of my life, to form more than one hundred new divisions within three months. Today I can declare before the world that they are formed and will now roll to the fronts in an uninterrupted stream; Divisions with the best in equipment and training; *Volksgrenadier* divisions destined to defend the freedom and future of our people. Hereby we have regained the old fighting strength. In the next three months, countless further divisions will pass through camp gates marching towards the front. Out there at the Channel ports, German men are proving at seemingly forlorn posts, that they know what it means in war to wait the hour, to gain time, in order to mobilize anew the national fighting force of a nation. This the enemy did not expect. They believed they saw leaders at the head of the Reich, who for their own salvation would sell the salvation of their people. That has been a miscalculation. We are neither morally nor materially worn down.

---

28. ISUM 133, 19 November 1944.

Document 1/10[29]

The High Command Discusses Surrender

Wartime Intelligence Officer's Comments

The following is a translation of a Special Issue of 'Notes for the Officer Corps,' dated August 1944. This issue was marked Top Secret and its distribution was only down to Divisions. It deals in some detail with the circumstances in which surrender is permissible.

I   The Morale of the Troops must be raised

In view of the unforeseen changes in the war situation, maintenance of the morale of the troops has become the most important duty of the Officer Corps.

It has become more and more difficult to supply our air force, armour and artillery. The strategic limit to retreat and elastic manoeuvres of disengagement has been reached.

The High Command of the Wehrmacht is therefore more and more often compelled to give the order: 'Position must be held to the last man and to the last cartridge.'

At present cases are increasing in which commanders' orders are not being carried out to the letter. In Italy troops have frequently given up territory not only after inadequate defence, but even without fighting. The present crisis on the Eastern Front is attributable in great measure to all too frequent surrender without a fight contrary to orders.

In France it is therefore the most important duty of the Officer Corps to ensure that every order by a commander is obeyed to the letter. It is not a question of whether the officer understands the object of the order or not. The officer must ensure the obedience of the troops either by iron severity or by a friendly word of explanation.

II   False Interpretation of the word 'Surrender'

The military interpretation of the word 'surrender' has been mis-understood, particularly in recent times. This false interpretation has probably arisen from the celebrated, but misunderstood, quotation from

---

29. ISUM 87, 25 September 1944.

Ludendorff on this question. This quotation has carried particular weight in the Wehrmacht because it appeared as an introduction to his book 'The Power of Germany' (*Deutschlands Macht*) with the following message from the Führer:

> General Ludendorff, my friend and master in strategy, is the most gifted and admirable example of a true German soldier and officer.'
>
> *Adolf Hitler*

General Ludendorff's conception of the word 'surrender' in the soldier's vocabulary is as follows:

> It is a complete, I might almost say a criminal, misunderstanding of the sacred duty of a good soldier if, when faced by an enemy whose superiority leaves no ground for hope, and by a lack of timely reserves and adequate weapons, he does not surrender, merely because he persuades himself that it is a dishonour to be taken prisoner.
>
> Naturally a soldier breaks his oath if he deserts for the sole reason that he is too cowardly to go on fighting. Suppose, however, that his responsible officers leave him in the lurch amid the utmost danger, either because they are incompetent, or because they have irresponsibly erred to a high degree, then a brave soldier who is willing to fight, commits a senseless crime, not only against his loved ones at home, but also against his Fatherland, if, having nothing to look forward to but certain death, he does not do all in his power to save himself and his comrades by surrender.
>
> Why then have we allowed this way of escape into captivity?
>
> Only because we do not wish to send the individual man to his death, when his superiors have failed him. Indeed, as an old soldier I myself declare, that every patriotic man has the inescapable duty of saving himself from hopeless predicaments of this sort through flight and surrender. He has the duty of preserving his life for the future reconstruction of his country and all the other tasks of peace.
>
> And I believe that I have the right to make this statement: during the shameful November days of 1914–18, I myself provided proof, through my retirement to Sweden, that a man of my experience can achieve great things for his country if he understands how to reach safety in good time instead of allowing himself to be driven in an entirely senseless and stupid manner to a misconceived 'Hero's death.

It is urgently necessary to make clear to the troops the exact sense of this conception on the part of the general.

There is not a syllable in his words which authorizes the individual man, or even a unit of some size, to decide the time of surrender. This decision is obviously a matter for the High Command of the Wehrmacht alone, and for no other.

There is not a syllable in his words which authorizes a company, which has received the order to resist, to do other than obey blindly. Elements which have been cut off may see no other way out of their predicament than surrender; they may be convinced that all resistance is hopeless; the decision as to whether they should surrender or hold out to the last man as ordered is one for the High Command of the Wehrmacht alone. That is also General Ludendorff's opinion in the celebrated quotation. If anyone presumes to put any other interpretation on it, he is greatly mistaken.

The troops are to be instructed in this sense on every suitable occasion concerning the sole authoritative interpretation of these words.

Even the surrender of Cherbourg has given rise to dangerously false views on the conduct of the Wehrmacht in a crisis.

We learn that a rumour has been circulating in army circles concerning the alleged cowardly behaviour of General von Schlieben[30] and his staff. The whispering purveyors of subversive enemy radio propaganda state that they have heard the following:

> From their bomb-proof shelter, 15 metres below ground, General von Schlieben and Rear Admiral Hennecke,[31] together with their staffs, once again issued to the troops fighting above, the Führer's orders: 'Fight to the last man'. Then these gentlemen came out of their shelter to give themselves up to the Americans and allow themselves to be taken prisoner. The American General Collins then offered the high ranking officers an armistice so as to save from certain death the men who were still holding out; General von Schlieben replied, however: 'My troops have to hold out to the last man. I am not prepared to cancel this order'.

Precise explanation will repeatedly be given to the troops in special training periods as to why the high ranking officers acted perfectly correctly in a military sense.

---

30. *Generalleutnant* Karl-Heinz von Schlieben (1894–1964), the commandant of Fortress Cherbourg, who surrendered to American troops on 26 June 1944.
31. *Konteradmiral* Walter Hennecke (1898–1984) commanded the port of Cherbourg and surrendered with *Generalleutnant* von Schlieben on 26 June 1944.

III For Company Officers

Company Officers are responsible for the strict observance of orders for defence.

In many cases the word of the Führer alone can be given in explanation of the apparently senseless sacrifice involved in fighting to the last man. In such cases the company commander must ensure obedience with all the means at his disposal. Usually he will himself ensure that he reaches safety in good time.

IV When and why Officers must Save Themselves

Every officer has the duty of saving himself in an emergency. The view of many junior officers that they must never leave their men alone in the hour of danger is in need of correction.

Every member of the Wehrmacht must realize that it is of paramount importance to save the Officer Corps for the reconstruction of the Fatherland. The German officer is too valuable to be sacrificed, especially in hopeless situations. That he should save himself by withdrawing is in the interest of the country.

It was the German Officer Corps that almost achieved world dominance for Germany in the first assault of 1914–1918. It was this same Officer Corps that rebuilt Germany for this second attempt at world leadership. That this second attempt might also fail, was foreseen. The present trend of the war compels us to exercise the utmost economy of officer material.

Our complete final victory seemed until recently so assured that we can prepare again with high spirits and in good heart for a further struggle. In order to prepare from a technical point of view for this third unavoidable trial of strength for the leadership of the world we have need of our officers. Manpower we have been able to find in quantities at all times.

For this reason care must constantly be taken to maintain the Officer Corps at its present strength. Nevertheless certain company commanders must at the same time be detailed to stay with their troops and in case of necessity to sacrifice themselves as well. Examples of this sort are necessary for the maintenance of the troops' morale. Divisional commanders will nominate junior officers to die the hero's death.

V For NCOs: Instructions for the Handling of 'Soldiers' Groups'

Special attention will be paid to all secret organizations among the troops, such as the so-called 'Solders' Groups', 'Soldiers' Committees', 'Soldiers' Councils', etc. Such associations have been formed with the sole object of inducing the troops to refuse obedience.

It is quite obvious that secret leagues of this kind arise as soon as a war seems to be approaching an unsuccessful conclusion.

Leaders of small groups first very cautiously incite those elements of the troops who are not quite reliable and confident by means of slogans.

By their whispered propaganda these phrase merchants constantly seek to influence more of their comrades and to win their support. They use propaganda slogans, such as: 'All orders to resist to the last man without regard to the superiority of the enemy are issued exclusively by the High Command of the Wehrmacht because the leaders can think of nothing sensible in their predicament.'

The Soldiers' Groups seek to incite the troops individually and in compact units to give up the fight and surrender by means of alluring phrases: 'It is high time that we soldiers looked after ourselves' or 'Comrades, form Groups which can represent you'.

The great danger of subversion created by the formation of such Solders' Groups was already fully realized in 1918. Then, however, it was already too late.

In this war the same mistake must not be repeated. NCOs must therefore be instructed repeatedly and in the most energetic manner to hunt down these groups and report them. They will inspect men's belongings if this appears necessary. In doing this special attention will be paid to leaflets, which are customarily distributed within these groups.

NCOs will be instructed not to proceed openly against the leaders of groups of this kind when they have been brought to light. It is more to the point to detail a man for certain duties in the front line from which experience shows that he will not return. These special details, however, must not afford the culprits any opportunity to desert.

Another method of getting rid of these dangerous subversive elements and of rendering them harmless is to take the following action. The man who has been found out is informed that his family has been bombed out. He is therefore immediately sent on leave. Officers will inform the Gestapo and/or SS. The man is then arrested on his homeward journey.

NCOs will be instructed to submit every man going on leave to a snap body search before starting on his journey home. The danger exists that members of these Soldiers' Groups will take certain documents or leaflets home with them. They do this, in order to plant these papers on workers known to them in the home country. It is known that the workers are also frequently organized in secret leagues with similar objects.

VI Conclusions

In conclusion it must again be insisted with the fullest emphasis that the changed war situation makes it essential for the Officer Corps to enforce the strict observance of these instructions.

The High Command of the Wehrmacht will henceforth often be no longer able to meet demands, however urgent and justifiable, for air, armour and artillery support, even when enemy superiority is overwhelming. Any shortage of weapons must therefore be made good by strengthening the morale of the troops.

The war must be carried through to a victorious conclusion.

Document 1/11[32]

Major Eberhard Furst von Urach[33]

Wartime Intelligence Officer's Comments

The interrogation of Major Eberhard Furst von Urach, Commander of 505 Mobile Battalion, provides some insight as to the reaction of the Officer Corps to the present dominant trend of German fortresses. Being a regular officer and a member of the nobility, von Urach is in sympathy with the Nazi Party only insofar as he has to be, in order to remain an officer.

(i)   Current Operations

Garrisons of Boulogne, Calais and Dunkirk

It was believed that all these ports had ample stocks of food and ammunition, that there were plenty of troops available and that the defences, especially at Dunkirk, were very strong. These garrisons should be able to hold out for a long time, and von Urach was surprised to hear that Le Havre had fallen so soon. He did not know any of the commanders of these garrisons, but had heard a story that, after a colonel (name unknown) had taken

---

32. ISUM 77, 13 September 1944.
33. Major *Fürst* Eberhard von Urach, Graf von Württemburg (1907–69) commanded the reconnaissance battalion of 50th Infantry Division and was captured near Bruges on 9 September 1944.

over command at Dunkirk and had taken the special oath necessary to commanders of beleaguered garrisons, a certain division commander (not known) arrived there, whose commander as the Senior Officer wished to take over the duties of Garrison Commander. The colonel was unwilling to give way and the Divisional Commander eventually left Dunkirk with part of his staff, leaving his division behind.

Bridgehead on south bank of Scheldt Estuary

It was not originally intended to hold a position here, but events forced the Germans' hand. It is now intended to hold out here until the maximum possible number of troops have been shipped away. In view of the flooding programme carried out in this area, it will be largely impassable for tanks. This fact, together with the fortifications already existing, should make it possible to hold out until a large number of troops have been evacuated. What would happen to these troops thereafter PW did not know.

Siegfried Line

The only course left to Germany was to try to hold the West Wall. For this there were few troops left and it was unlikely that the line would hold up our advance for long. The concrete works were well built, but they were now to some extent out of date, and bombardment from the air should easily force a passage.

New Divisions

New divisions were divided into two groups – the 'leave-party' divisions, e.g. 59 and 64 Divisions which were fighting now, and the Himmler Divisions which had been hurriedly formed after Himmler took over the command of the *Ersatzheer*. Although both groups contained a high proportion of seasoned soldiers from Russia, it was improbable that they would be able to achieve much, partly through lack of equipment, especially weapons, and partly because they had been so hurriedly put together that there had been no time to develop any sense of unity. The experienced element would be thoroughly disillusioned at finding themselves so situated and would have little desire or urge to continue fighting for long.

(ii)   New Weapons: V.2[34]

Von Urach was sure that V.2 existed but because of the thick veil of secrecy surrounding it he knew no facts. Although troops had been urged frequently to 'hold on for 14 days more' (or for longer periods) this was not a mere propaganda trick because he had recently had private letters from persons in close touch with the highest circles which, in spite of everything, had an air of optimism not, in his opinion, to be attributed to an official policy of cheerfulness. However, he did not consider that V.2, when it did appear, would produce any catastrophic changes in Germany's fortunes, but would merely add to the general hatred of Germany.

Poison Gas

PW was completely confident that no use would be made by the Germans of gas, for the reason that under present circumstances the inevitable sufferers would be the German civil population.

(iii)   Higher Command

Ever since the invasion there had been an uncertainty about the higher command which was something new in the German Army. For this there were two reasons. First, the relative positions of Rundstedt and Rommel had never been made clear and they had opposed theories about defending the coast. Rundstedt appreciated that, owing to aerial bombardment and naval gunfire, it would be impossible to prevent a landing and that therefore the coast should be thinly held with reserves lying back ready for a counter thrust. Rommel, on the other hand, thought that the landing must be stopped on the beaches and therefore put the bulk of his troops forward. This difference of opinion was never properly solved.

Second, even Field Marshals are now no more than the interpreters of the Führer's intuitions. It is quite definite that Hitler still controls events personally, laying down the general plan to be carried out. It is quite common for a unit to receive a special 'Führer Order' demanding that a certain village be held at all costs, even though a second order cancels the first inside 24 hours. Hitler is also especially interested in anti-tank positions and at his HQ a portfolio is kept containing maps of all divisional sectors marking all anti-tank gun positions. These maps are kept constantly up to date – except in periods of particularly elastic defence as at present.

---

34. The V-2 or *Vergeltungswaffe* (Vengeance Weapon) 2 was the world's first long-range ballistic missile. It could carry a 2,200lb explosive warhead a distance of 200 miles. Commencing in September 1944, nearly 3,000 V-2 missiles were launched against targets in Europe and Britain, killing an estimated 9,000 military personnel and civilians.

(iv) Morale   In Germany

The war cannot last longer than two more months. The most important thing is that the front should hold in the east as the fear of Bolshevism is the strongest factor helping the Germans in the war. The industrial workers and the civil population are completely war weary and, but for fear of Bolshevism, would make an end to the war despite the Gestapo.

Amongst Officers

The hanging of von Witzleben[35] was a very grave blow to the Army and a very large number of officers were disgusted with the whole affair. Even more serious, however, was Ley's speech soon after the attempted assassination, accusing the 'blue-blooded swine' of complicity.[36] Von Urach, with others, was ready at that time to hand in his papers but the highest authority banned any mention of the speech in newspapers or on the wireless. PW was personally acquainted with von Stauffenberg,[37] the actual assassin, and observed sardonically 'He should have got a proper sapper to do the job for him.'

---

35. *Generalfeldmarschall* Erwin von Witzleben (1881–1944) was a leading member of the July 1944 plot to kill Hitler. He was tried by a 'People's Court' and executed on 7 August 1944.
36. A reference to an infamous radio speech made by Robert Ley, head of the *Deutsche Arbeitsfront*, in the days immediately following the 20 July assassination attempt, which viciously criticized the aristocracy and the officer corps.
37. *Oberstleutnant* Claus Schenk von Stauffenberg (1907–44) was a leading member of the conspiracy to kill Hitler and the man who planted a bomb in the dictator's headquarters. He was executed within hours of the failure of the plot.

Chapter 2

Practical and Impractical Measures for Improving Morale on the Western Front

Editor's Comments

A variety of measures – some practical and some not – are instituted to improve morale and stiffen resolve. They include listening to the Führer's words and singing patriotic songs (Document 2/1); signing pledges to fight to the death (Document 2/2); improving behaviour in public (Document 2/3); holding morale-boosting talks (Document 2/4); and issuing 'Battle Creeds' (Document 2/5). Despite these efforts, German morale along the Western Front and at home seems to be sagging in the face of the Western Allies' materiel superiority (Documents 2/7 and 2/8). It is doubtful that an order to reduce rations even further at the besieged fortress of Dunkirk (Document 2/9) improved morale. As it was, Dunkirk's German garrison of about 10,000 men constituted one of the larger self-sustaining and self-guarded Allied prison camps in Europe as did the other German Atlantic fortresses such as Lorient, La Rochelle and the Channel Islands.

Document 2/1[1]

'Führer Words' and Battle Songs

Wartime Intelligence Officer's Comments

The following document on how to sing for the Party is an illustration of what the Wehrmacht does to keep the troops beating their chests in a vigorous manner.

DER POLITISCHE SOLDAT (The Political Soldier)
Political Information Bulletin for Unit Commanders
No. 10, September 1944

New Political Instructions Should be Directed

The Commander of National Socialist Propaganda for the Army has issued the following directive for the entire Army designed to give political lectures the military spirit and soldierly form they deserve!

HQ Army High Command
8 August 1944

Unit Political Instruction periods must be introduced with a quotation of the Führer's words (*Führerwörter*) and concluded with a song of our Movement.

Commanders will give their subordinate officers appropriate instructions. If they are not in possession of a copy of '*Mein Kampf*' or compilation of the Führer's speeches, NSF officers must supply suitable quotations for the use of unit commanders. In any event, however, junior officers must endeavour to compile these quotations themselves. Particular emphasis must be placed on the great songs of our Movement.

I trust that political instructions will be conducted with the dignity and elan necessary for the proper emphasis of our Faith, particularly in rear areas and among units at home.

---

1. ISUM 172, 20 December 1944, from *Fifth U.S. Army G-2 Report.*

Führer words and battle songs give a military form to political lectures which force the unit as a whole to give evidence by their songs of their allegiance to the National Socialist Revolution.

By Order of the Führer
v. Hengl[2]
General der Gebirgstruppe

With orders of this type a new and fresher wind blows through our National Socialist instructions. Lectures which are opened by a Führer quotation remain a source of reflection for all men in the unit. There are many soldiers who still know little of the Führer's speeches, and who must be exposed to his words. Needless to say, all men will rise from their seats when the Führer's words are spoken. It is unnecessary – in fact, not even advisable – for the unit commander to read these quotations himself. It is much more effective to circulate this duty among various men and NCOs in the unit.

It is very important, however, to restore the soldier's battle song to its proper place in military life, the place which it justly deserves. For too long we have neglected the educational force of our battle songs. Consequently the singing in some of our units has disintegrated to a pot-pourri of trite, superficial and sentimental songs produced by smart tune fabricants, or of American-type military hits. No one should come up and say that after all it does not really matter what we sing. Soldiers who sing:

Wir ballen die Fäuste and werden es wagen,
Es gibt kein Zurück mehr und keiner darf zagen.

(We clench our fists, resolved to stake our all,
We cannot now go back and none may hesitate).

are certainly differently inspired from men chanting Marie Helen[3] and the horseman who, as everyone knows, could not continue on his way when he beheld her. Far be it from us to repudiate all our exuberant soldiers' songs of love and farewell and of beautiful girls. But still the 'rotten bones of the world' must 'tremble' and we must still go out 'into the fields, on to

---

2. *General der Gebirgstruppe* Georg Ritter von Hengl (1897–1952).
3. Possibly a reference to the song 'Marie Elena', a song first recorded in 1932, which became a hit for the Jimmy Dorsey band in 1941. German personnel liked to listen to *Soldatensender* Calais (later *Soldatensender* West), a British propaganda radio broadcast, which disguised itself as a German military programme. *Soldatensender* Calais played the latest American and British hits, provided sports news of interest to Germans and occasionally interspersed these attractive items with clever propaganda.

freedom', where the 'man is still worth his own', because 'his heart is still weighed' with the proper coin. And along with 'Rhenish girls and Rhenish wine', those songs must accompany our men which say:

> Hitler treu ergeben, treu bis in den Tod
> Hitler wird uns führen einst aus dieser Not.

> (Faithful to the Führer, loyal to the death,
> He will lead us one day out of this distress.)

The term 'Song of the Movement' need not be taken too literally. All songs filled with fighting spirit and enthusiasm for our patriotic heritage are acceptable if they were sung by the Movement, regardless of whether they were born in this or any other country.

Document 2/2[4]

To the Last – Well Almost

The following document was found in the bunker occupied by Lieutenant-General Heim,[5] Commander of the garrison of Boulogne. This pledge to defend Boulogne to the death was signed by the officers of 1408 Fortress Battalion and 27th Machine Gun Battalion, and since these particular units were given no more vital sector to hold than other formations in the port, it is likely that all officers in Boulogne were asked to sign a similar undertaking. Among the 9,500 prisoners that were taken from the city, there were over 200 officers, who if they did at one time decide to fight to the last, soon changed their minds.

Of the 14 names that appear on the document reproduced here, ten of them, including Heim himself, also appear on the PW Cage roll of those who entered its portals hale, and relatively hearty. The other four probably were lost in the administrative shuffle that usually accompanies the taking of so

---

4. ISUM 96, 6 October 2014.
5. *Generalleutnant* Ferdinand Heim (1895–1971). Heim had commanded a panzer corps in Russia which failed to stop the massive Soviet offensive that encircled the Sixth Army at Stalingrad. He was placed under arrest and dismissed from the army but was restored in the summer of 1944 and placed in command of Fortress Boulogne. He surrendered the port after a five-day siege by First Canadian Army.

many prisoners at one time. It is extremely likely that they also are safely in our hands. The ease with which these officers decided that life was sweet after all, probably explains the need for including the words 'to the end of my life' twice in a two-paragraph pledge.

PLEDGE

HQ Boulogne
2 September 1944

On 2 September 1944 I undertook in the presence of Lieutenant General Heim, Commander of the fortress of Boulogne, to hold and defend the strong point or sector under my command to the end of my life and that of the last man under me.

I am conscious of the great responsibility of my talk and of my commitment and I swear to hold and defend the strong point or sector under my command to the end of my life and that of the last man under me.

1408 Fortress Grenadier Battalion

Bn Comd	Capt Gerhard Rieger
Bn Adj	Lt Karl von Thümen
OC 1 Coy	Lt Hans Behrend
OC 2 Coy	2/Lt Helmut Engelhardt
OC 3 Coy	Lt Alfred Pudelko
OC 4 Coy	Lt Martin Schottstadt

27th Machine Gun Battalion

Bn Comd	Capt Max Schmitz
Bn Adj	2/Lt Edward Forster
OC HQ Coy	2/Lt Tyroller
OC 1 Coy	2/Lt Josef Hartmann
OC 2 Coy	2/Lt Gröbel
OC 3 Coy	2/Lt Martlindl
OC 4 Coy	Capt Braun

in the presence of the Fortress Commander
Heim
Generalleutnant

Document 2/3[6]

Behaviour of Officers

Wartime Intelligence Officer's Comments

The following captured document presents an interesting picture of the enemy's present state of morale.

This Document Must Not Fall Into Enemy Hands!

246 Volksgrenadier Division
Division HQ, 2 October 1944
National Socialist Indoctrination Officer

The following order of the Seventh Army Commander is to be distributed for information and guidance of all officers of the Division:

For the Division Commander: GSO 1
Commanding General Seventh Army   Army HQ, 10 September 1944

To the Officers of the Seventh Army

The war now has also come to Germany's western border. Thus begins the hardest and most difficult part of this struggle determining our existence or annihilation.

We are fighting directly under the eyes of our people who are fulfilling their duties in a flawless form and fashion. They expect, and have a right to expect, the same from us.

Now, more than ever, the officer has to set a shining example. This includes above all:

Exemplary behaviour towards the civilian population, especially towards the women.

Each family has members at the front, about whom they are worrying. Many families mourn the dead and the missing. The bomb terror has torn the families themselves apart, and has forced them to live under the simplest of conditions. The worker toils 60 hours per week.

The people look upon the officer with full confidence.

---

6. ISUM 144, 23 November 1944, from *Ninth US Army G-2 Periodic Report*.

For that reason, no officer may ever reiterate rumours, let alone defeatist or even doubtful remarks. Wherever he encounters such trends of thought, he will oppose them energetically.

He is the bearer of the nation's faith and will and he knows of victory!

Exemplary relations with our party and its affiliates!

The party has drafted everyone, from the oldest political leader and SA man to the Hitler Youth boy, yes, even women and girls, to work on defences.

Here we have to help wherever we can. Wherever difficulties and questions arise, they must be solved and answered immediately in the most tactful manner. There will be no requisitioning of vehicles, nor will interference with the work of the party be tolerated. Requisitioning of motor vehicles will be done by the Army and by officers authorized by the Army.

Exemplary Personal Conduct

All habits which may have been understandable in enemy territory must now disappear. The population at home cannot have any understanding for club parties, intoxicated or flirting officers, or for food 'obtained' over and above the regular rations. Food of that kind is simply stolen from women and children.

Consequently, there are no special privileges which had never been granted in the first place. Exemplary fulfillment of duty and exemplary diligence are the real privileges now!

Everybody will live in quarters. Where bunkers are available, they will be used. I forbid categorically any and all social gatherings in houses and evening parties. There is no time for that now; neither is there time for hunting. If any hunting has to be done in order to supplement rations or for any other reason, it will be done on my orders only.

Now there is only time for the fulfillment of duties. It is impossible for an officer to have more spare time than is required to write a letter to his relatives.

He who devotes even one hour to things other than his duty violates his honour.

Be An Example More Than Ever!

> signed Brandenberger[7]
> *General der Panzertruppe*

---

7. *General der Panzertruppe* Erich Brandenburger (1892–1955), commander Seventh Army.

Document 2/4[8]

Festung Walcheren

Wartime Intelligence Officer's Comments

Two weeks ago, PW reported, Walcheren Island was declared a Fortress to be held to the last man. Following are extracts from notes for a pep-talk to troops on the 'Festung Walcheren' theme. They were prepared by an officer of 1018 Grenadier Regiment (70th Infantry Division) which moved recently from Walcheren to the Antwerp sector.

Walcheren has been declared a fortress! Just what does that imply?

(a) The purpose and task of a fortress: To draw off enemy troops and force the enemy to divert ever increasing quantities of manpower and material! In this way the enemy is weakened and any other plans he may have are delayed or cancelled. Our own command gets time and opportunity to adopt its own measures for changing the battle situation and bringing relief to the fortress.

(b) Where are fortresses set up to carry out their task of engaging and diverting enemy forces? At every point the enemy must reach to carry out his intention. Most important are road and railway junctions, river crossings, mountain passes, tactically important ground – and harbours! (Ask for examples – each man should be able to give some from his home province.)

(c) Why and for what purpose, then, was Walcheren declared a fortress?

The English must get Antwerp in order to relieve their supply difficulties (quote English statements) which prevent them from acting as they would very much like to. Because he did not possess Antwerp, the enemy had to use airborne troops in Holland. Pretty risky! His entry into Antwerp would mean direct supplies from England. What would that mean to him and to us? (Elaborate!) In order to get Antwerp, he must have the Scheldt Estuary. That happens to be just where we are. We must make it tricky for him to drive us out. Those forces which he must keep here to deal with us are forces which he cannot launch across the German border. In this way we

---

8. ISUM 100, 10 October 1944, from *2 Canadian Corps Intelligence Summary* 68, 7 October 1944.

BLOOD AND STEEL 2

gain time for the *Vaterland* to prepare for the big counter-blow. The enemy knows this blow is coming and is afraid of it.

(d) What vital support the morale of the whole nation can draw from the determined resistance of a fortress is shown by the stories of Kolberg, Verdun, Cherbourg, St. Malo and Brest. Every man must keep these examples before him. We must not be outdone by those who went before. We must fight now as our comrades fought in St. Nazaire, Boulogne and Calais. And we will be fighting under far more difficult conditions. All forces which the enemy must employ here are forces he would like to commit on the German frontier. The enemy is war weary and fears our counter-blow. His alternatives are either to win quickly or contend with war weariness at home.

Document 2/5[9]

Battle Creed of 2nd Parachute Division

Wartime Intelligence Officer's Comments

When the enemy bridgehead near Boxmer E7740 was eliminated [in early October 1944], one of the youthful members of 2nd Parachute Regiment was found carrying the following soul-stirring document . . . The intensity of this resolve shows the efforts now being adopted to instill in these newly-reorganized formations the fanatical, even if slightly jaded, Nazi spirit so badly mauled during the fateful days of 1944.

Battle Creed of 2nd Parachute Division

I dedicate myself – in consideration of my oath to the colours; to the battle communion of my Division.

I am resolved – to offer my life and blood and my entire strength in the present decisive battle for the life and liberty of my people

Never – will I forsake my comrades nor abandon the weapons and equipment which my country has forged for me, at the greatest sacrifice.

---
9. ISUM 212, 30 January 1944.

I believe in the German people united through National Socialism and in our rightful cause.

I will do everything to maintain and to strengthen, by the written or spoken word, the power of spiritual resistance of the German people, at the Front and at home

I believe – as a National Socialist soldier – in my leader Adolf Hitler.

Document 2/6[10]

Special Awards for Snipers

Wartime Intelligence Officer's Comments

Strangely reminiscent of orders published by Neumann of 712th Infantry Division, 88 Corps and Fifteenth Army and published while the ground south of the Maas and west of s'Hertogenbosch was being cleared, is the following extract from the daily orders of Stellungs Bataillon VII/1 dated 4 November 1944.

In order to stress the importance of snipers, to appreciate their achievements and to stimulate the efforts of beginners to fulfil the conditions for the award of the Sniper's Medal, the following decorations and privileges are established:

After 10 Kills:	7 days' special leave, Iron Cross 2nd Class and citation in Divisional Daily Orders
After 20 Kills:	Sniper's Medal 3rd Class
After 30 Kills:	14 days' special leave and citation in Corps Daily Orders
After 40 Kills:	Sniper's Medal 2nd Class
After 50 Kills:	20 days' special leave, Iron Cross 1st Class and citation in Army Daily Orders
After 60 Kills:	Sniper's Medal 1st Class
After 75 Kills:	German Cross in Gold

---

10. ISUM 154, 3 December 1944.

Document 2/7[11]

Analysis of Mail

Wartime Intelligence Officer's Comments

The following is a translation of part of a captured document:

Army High Command 1   Army HQ 5 November 1944

G-2/AO No 1424/44 secret   Commanding General LXXXIX Korps
Received on 8 November 1944

Intelligence Special Report

Extracts from mail-censorship report for October 1944 (only for information of Chief of Staff, Acting Chief of Staff, Intelligence Branch and NSFO).

Mail from the front to the rear and from front to front

In spite of the fact that there are now more letters showing a rather weak belief in the final victory, the whole of the mail still proves a strong confidence. They still trust the Führer as much as ever, and some even think that the destiny of the German people depends on him alone. Of course nobody knows how things will look, but there is a general hope that there will be a sudden alteration of the situation favourable for us. Only a few speak of revenge, but during the last days of the month there was an increasing number of letters believing in a long war. Those who write about military events mostly mention the fighting around Aachen and in East Prussia, whereas the Russian break-through in Hungary is never being considered. Regrets about the fact that there actually is a war going on, on German soil are numerous, and everybody pities the population in the areas occupied by the enemy.

Many a letter mentions that V-1s flew over the front line. The commitment of new weapons was a favourable theme in early October – but during the last days there were more and more doubts about them. The general belief can be expressed in the following manner: All our efforts are useless if the new weapons will not be committed very soon.

---

11. ISUM 173, 31 December 1944, from *SHAEF Intelligence Summary*, 17 December 1944.

Himmler's speech and the creation of the *Volkssturm* found only a few commentators; there are doubts about the effectiveness of this *Volkssturm* against the enemy. Though there is a general disgust for the way our Allies left us, and though the majority wishes them the strongest oppression from the Soviets, there is also a certain percentage who are afraid of the increasing number of our enemies. Our own propaganda is never mentioned, neither are the activities of the NSFO. A great deal is being written about the terror attacks on Germany. The sorrows about relatives and the wishes for new weapons to stop these attacks are continuously increasing. Often we find complaints about the growing number of enemy planes and about the lack of our own. The belief in the small combat activity of enemy infantry remains a fact. A fact also is the unbelievable enemy superiority as far as material is concerned. Besides the complaints about the lack of heavy weapons and planes, there are also complaints about bad Special Service activities, bad mail service and the cancellation of all leave. Some also complain about the lack of warm clothes which, lost during the retreat, have not yet been replaced.

Only rear echelon troops moan about the food; it seems as if the front line outfits find what they need in evacuated localities.

During the month of October there was an increased number of letters showing low morale and a lack of confidence – but there are still many letters full of faith and belief in victory.

Sometimes doubts about the happy ending of the war are expressed in a more or less covert manner, and expressions such as 'Let's hope that this mess will soon have an ending' or 'Ach, if only this misery could end – it has lasted long enough' show a certain fatigue of war.

We also have to mention letters from front soldiers asking their relatives in border countries not to leave their homes too early, as the enemy will soon be stopped.

Mail from the rear to the front
Military events are also less mentioned in these letters than in letters from the front to the rear. Farmer-women write a lot about the gathering of the harvest, about the digging of root vegetables. But though there are a few 'doubting' elements the Fatherland still entirely trusts the Führer and believes in a happy future. They hope and wait for new weapons to free us from the enemy's pressure. But sometimes we find thoughts like: 'All these promises will never be kept, and all we can rely upon is the courage of our soldiers.' The major part of the mail is concerned with the bomb terror; it cannot go on that way – something must be found to stop it. Low-

flying, man-hunting planes depress terribly. Border people write about the defence works, about the proximity of the front and about the possibility of being forced to leave their homes – which nobody likes. Consequent to the terrorizing behaviour of the enemy on German soil, there is a general fall-down of spirit and confidence to be reported in border regions. Women writing to the front use a depressed tone; but in almost every letter a 'spark' of hope can be found.

The creation of the *Volkssturm* is scarcely mentioned. It seemed as if the writers meant to withhold their opinion. Some think it is our last effort, some are enthusiastic about it.

The rear equally complains about the bad functioning of the post system. As far as leave is concerned, all hope there will be a release for Christmas. No complaints about food, but several about the lack of heating fuel.

Document 2/8[12]

A Propaganda Company Officer
Reports on Morale on the Western Front

CONFIDENTIAL
Lt Frank Freckmann (War Reporter)   *November 1944*

For the most part our troops are very much fatigued owing to their continuous front line employment since D-Day. Already a motley crew through the constant addition of replacements, the soldiers are to a large extent physically unable to cope with the difficulties of mountain warfare. Wherever, after his strong attacks, the enemy became less active, such as in the 159th Infantry Division sector on both sides of the Lure/Belfort road, or in the 198th Infantry Division sector in the vicinity of Gerardmer, our troops recovered and displayed more inner fortitude. Generally speaking our troops suffer under the impression that we will not be able to compete with the strong enemy superiority. It is often necessary for company commanders and particularly for battalion commanders to

---

12. ISUM 197, 14 January 1945.

muster all their patience and their untiring determination in order to get their obstinately indifferent men to go to work at the front or to undertake any activity whatsoever. Patrols often lack the courage necessary for the accomplishment of their mission. They approach enemy lines, lie low for ten minutes, and then return to their units. On the other hand the superiority of the German soldier is demonstrated again and again in cases where such patrols happen to meet up with the enemy. It has happened often that two of our men brought back three, four or even more prisoners.

The enemy disposes of a clear superiority of men and material. In addition to Americans we encounter increasing numbers of French troops, the replacement units of which have only mediocre training, while their Moroccan mountain and police troops are excellent. A new element is a Japanese unit, probably of regimental strength, under American command. It is composed of naturalized Japanese who display all the dreaded attributes of their race. Prisoners claim that they would fight against Japan without hesitation. American prisoners display disappointment about the long duration of the war, in individual cases marked battle fatigue, but generally a calm confidence due to their knowledge of their superiority in material. One prisoner asked whether the German Luftwaffe still existed at all. It is remarkable that the majority claims that no hatred against Germany exists while Japan and the Japanese are considered the real enemy. About Bolshevism the average American has no opinion. He could probably be influenced to a much greater degree if the anti-Bolshevist propaganda would greatly increase its emphasis of the Asiatic elements, in which he senses much greater danger.

Our own position is such that the thinly strung out Main Line of Resistance, with only one man every 30 to 80 metres, presents constant possibilities of danger. For example on the morning of 31 October a colonel commanding a regiment in an armoured division sat in front of his map and said 'At this point some American company or even more marched through our Main Line of Resistance, creating a gap of 500 metres. I have nothing with which to close it. Be interesting to see where they'll wind up.'

Another example was a Corps Order to occupy a hill by means of combat patrols. The regimental commander had to reply that, if he sent out any patrols at all, it would mean opening a gap in the front line. One regimental commander told the writer 'We still make the impossible possible. It is a good thing for us that our enemy is so cautious.' Individual enemy thrusts, such as the ones at Belfort, Remiremont, Cornimont, and later at Bruyeres and Baccarat, always give us the possibility to patch our lines. Experienced officers on our side are of the opinion that the enemy could easily and completely break through our lines if he would boldly concentrate his forces in the manner of a strong point.

Document 2/9[13]

Hunger at Dunkirk

Wartime Intelligence Officer's Comments

The following document discovered by the Czechoslovak Independent Armoured Brigade shows that the prospect of starvation now looms large in the thoughts of the garrison of beleaguered Dunkirk. This appeal by Vice Admiral Frisius, commander of the port, apparently failed to convince the most recent deserters who came over to us simply because they were hungry.

Present rations consist of a half can of black bread per man together with two packages of hard tack. Horsemeat is served twice a week and hot soup about every third day at the evening meal. Other types of meat provided amount to only one third of the normal ration. Four cigarettes are issued daily and coffee still seems plentiful. This monotonous fare is believed to be sufficient for another month or two of present conditions. If Frisius hopes to keep his men in the line, he will have to provide a more adequate substitute for a solid meal than the fancy words cited here.

Officer Commanding Dunkirk Fortress   *17 November 1944*

TO THE SOLDIERS OF DUNKIRK FORTRESS

You have learned by now that the enemy has not enough manpower available to attack us in full strength. Therefore I informed you recently that we must expect an attempt to starve us out. If we are reasonable, the enemy will not succeed.

A reasonable man provides for the future. Therefore I shall cut rations even more.

During my long career as a soldier, I have had opportunities to prove the truth of the old saying that the best way to a soldier's heart is through

---

13. ISUM 164, 12 December 1944.

his stomach. During a poll conducted by an important newspaper in regard to the problem of what a wife has to do to keep her husband's love, the answer 'feed the beast' was awarded a prize.

It is therefore quite obvious that I shall try continually to let you and, above all, those of my comrades who are manning the front lines, have whatever is necessary. God willing, this will be the last cut in the rations that I will be compelled to order. I hope confidently that later on it will become better again, at the latest when we know that our troops from the outside are on their way to relieve us.

Put yourself in my place. What would you say if we would just eat as we liked so that our supplies would have been spent by Christmas – leaving only the choice between starvation and surrender? You would say, and quite rightly so: why do we have an OC Fortress? He simply must have known a long time ago that this could not be done. Even a blind horse could have calculated that we ought to have started to save a long time ago. Every lance-corporal would have done better in his place.

So you see, you yourselves share my opinion and you would not act differently in my place.

It is much better to tighten the belt for some time and be able to carry the head erect as a free German soldier, of whom everybody can be proud, than to capitulate facing the smallest difficulties.

Think of your families. They certainly do not get more food now and yet they have to work twice as hard as before. Even if they still have their beds, they often cannot use them as they have to sit in the cellars.

We must not take second place to our brave women and men who are working hard in Germany under the most trying conditions.

Nobody will starve with the rations I have fixed. Show that in this regard too, you are true Germans.

Signed: Frisius[14]
Vizeadmiral

---

14. *Vizeadmiral* Friedrich Frisius (1895–1970), commandant *Festung* Dunkirk.

Chapter 3

The Individual Soldier's Experience

Diaries, Letters, Reports and Memoirs

Editor's Comments

An officer records his experience as a prisoner of the French resistance (Document 3/1), while a sergeant ponders what the future will bring (Document 3/6). Members of the garrison of Calais, which surrendered on 1 October, write home expressing a variety of views (Document 3/3). A private soldier chronicles the last days of the defenders of Walcheren (Document 3/5). Other Germans are more aggressive after the defeat in France, rebuilding their formations (Document 3/2) and fighting hard at Arnhem (Document 3/4). A young fighter pilot expresses confidence despite the losses in his unit (Document 3/7).

Document 3/1[1]

Extracts from Diary of a German Officer captured by Belgian Partisans. This diary is called 'My time as a Prisoner'.

3 September 1944

We withdraw to the north and intend to make the Flemish ports to get back to the Reich. Already flags are out in all the villages and posters are up

---

1. ISUM 91, 1 October 1944, from *8 Corps Intelligence Summary 62*.

to welcome the Allies. The nearer they are to the main roads the greater the excitement. There is much activity amongst the civilian military groups. OPs, cyclists, etc. All the men disappear from the streets when we pass. We reach the main road. There are columns of tanks and motorized infantry so that we cannot get through. We turn east but there again everything is blocked so we prepare for surrender and burn our maps etc. There is no possibility of escape since the partisans have already surrounded us. A fight, we press on towards the main road. Taken prisoner, we are disarmed. Armed civilians with F.F.I.[2] brassards make a good impression and behave correctly. They hold back the mob that is threatening us. There is cheering in every street, girls kiss passing soldiers and the people wear the colours of the Allies. The howling of the mob is only natural. All the same one can understand the joy of a people whom the Germans have failed to befriend and who are now celebrating their independence. A lot is grotesque; children with rifles, hand grenades under civilian belts (probably not even primed and none may be able to use them). We feel rather depressed. What are we to do, what is going to happen to the Reich? When shall we get to our houses, when will our families get news?

5 September 1944

Conversation is beginning gradually. We sound each other for our experiences and opinions. Quite a few accusations are brought up about the incompetence of staffs, the general indecision, and the suspicion of sabotage. There is also some criticism of internal matters. We have an interesting chat in the afternoon with a doctor who is a Sudeten German, and experienced in dealing with people of foreign nationality. Interesting remarks on the German and Austrian ways of treating foreigners. Opinions held by them about us and the expression of 'Prussian' which has not changed for a century.

What will the situation in Germany be after a lost war? Will there be again a period of political disinterestedness, a new bourgeousie; shall we with the flight from the political sphere become again a nation of poets, philosophers and musicians? In the afternoon talks with two Belgian Reserve Officers. Quite a few complaints about treatment by the Gestapo. It really does seem that things were not always handled correctly. We have a rare gift of putting our foot into it in our dealings with foreigners and with our cultural propaganda.

---

2. 'F.F.I.' is *Forces Francaises de l'Intérieur*, the French resistance.

9 September 1944

A visit to the OR [enlisted] prisoners. The first impression, a superficial one, they appear bored. The outer coat of military discipline seems to have worn off quickly. In one room someone attempts to call them to attention as I enter but it requires the 'debut' of the Belgian gendarme accompanying me.

Document 3/2[3]

Experience of an Officer of the 17th SS Panzer Grenadier Division Götz von Berlichingen, June–November 1944

Wartime Intelligence Officer's Comments

This is in substance a translation of an account written by a staff officer of 17th SS Panzer Grenadier Division in the presence of one of his interrogators. PW officer had lost his diary at the time of his capture, and inaccuracies in the report should be considered mistakes of memory.

On 7 June 1944 17th SS Panzer Grenadier Division received orders to leave the marshalling area in Thouars and to move to the invasion front in Normandy. Everyone was in a good mood and eager to see action again, – happy that the pre-invasion spell of uncertainty and waiting had snapped at last. In some minds there was a gnawing doubt that perhaps this was only a repetition of the Dieppe raid in which the Allies would withdraw after a German show of force. Perhaps the Götz von Berlichingen would even be too late to get into the scrap.

Our motorized columns were coiling along the roads towards the invasion beaches. Amidst this rumbling of motors and grinding of vehicle tracks the Panzer Grenadier was in his element again. Then something happened that left us in a daze. Spouts of fire flicked along the column and splashes of dust staccatoed the road. Everyone was piling out of the vehicles and scuttling for the neighbouring fields. Several vehicles were

---

3. ISUM 152, 1 December 1944.

already in flames. This attack ceased as suddenly as it had crashed upon us 15 minutes before. The men started drifting back to the column again, pale and shaky and wondering that they had survived this fiery rain of bullets. Had that been a sign of the things to come?? This had been our first experience with the 'Jabos' (fighter bombers). The march column was now completely disrupted and every man was on his own, to pull out of this blazing column the best he could. And it was none too soon, because an hour later the whole thing started all over again, only much worse this time. When this attack was over, the length of the road was strewn with splintered anti-tank guns (the pride of our division), flaming motors and charred implements of war.

It dawned on us that this opponent that had come to the beaches of Normandy was of a somewhat different format. The march was called off, and all the vehicles that were left were hidden in the dense bushes or in barns. No one dared show himself out in the open any more. Now the men started looking at each other. The first words passed. This was different from what we thought it would be like. If things like this happened here, what would it be like up there at the front? No, this did not look like a feint attack upon our continent. It had been our first experience with our new foe – the American.

During the next few days we found out how seriously he was going about his business. Although now we only travelled at night and along secondary roads rimmed with hedges and bushes, we encountered innumerable wrecks giving toothless testimony that some motorist had not benefitted from the bitter experience we had had. After about five days we moved into our assigned sector east of Periers. The divisional staff, to which I belonged, crawled into a small village, obviously intent to have as many trees, sunken roads and as much other cover about as possible. But now the 'Jabo' plague became even more serious. No hour passed during the daytime without that nerve-frazzling thunder of the strafing fighters overhead. And whenever we cared to look we could see that smoke billowed from some vehicle, fuel depot or ammunition dump mushrooming into the sky. The common soldier began to think. What would all this lead to, and what was being done about it? Where was the 'Luftwaffe' and why had it not been committed during the past few days? If he asked his superiors about it, they shrugged their shoulders and remarked that German planes would make their appearance at the opportune moment. But that moment never came. Instead, bad tidings reached us from the front, and all around us ambulances were carrying away the victims of the strafings. And when the soldiers became more insistent in their queries, they were finally told that the 'Luftwaffe' was operating in adjoining sectors where the situation was even more serious than in ours. This excuse calmed them for a while until contact had been made with those adjoining sectors and the soldiers found out that the absence of air cover there was just as conspicuous. And there the men had been told that the German planes were operating in our sector. And to make things even worse, the American artillery became stronger by the day, and the naval guns tore into our lines while it was impossible for us to get back at them. Complaints became more frequent that artillery ammunition stores were running low, that weapons needed replacements, that communications were out. The hope of driving the Americans back into the Channel had already given way to a hope of being able to hold our own against the invaders. And then came the great American breakthrough in the direction of Coutances. The way of the cross for the German soldier had begun.

At first the retreat of our sector was orderly. We started leapfrogging back. The divisional staff was able to hold for eight days in Lozon. But our regiments had been depleted to such an extent that we could not count upon any effective resistance. Under heroic efforts and with terrible losses we were able to hold a small sector NW of Marigny for eight days. The divisional staff was separated during the ensuing flight and cut off from its trains. Even though some dispersed fragments of the unit were reclaimed on the road back, only a few bedraggled remnants arrived in the Merzig reforming area. No human account could ever describe the hardship, the sacrifice, the misery the men of this division alone experienced. No one who finished this retreat still alive will ever forget this Gethsemane, because each village, each road, even each bush has seared into his brain the memories of terrible hours, insufferable misery, of cowardice, despair and destruction. All those towns of Cerisy-La-Salle, St Denis, Domfront, La Ferte Mace, Carrouges, Alençon, Mortagne, Laigle, Verneuil, Nonancourt, Dreux, St. Germain-en-Laye, Montmorency (where for the first time German planes were sighted on the occasion of a propaganda flight), Chateau Thierry, Espernay, Chalons-sur-Marne, St Menehould, Verdun, Etain, Conflans, Gravelotte and many others, are moments of a massacre which no other division could have ever experienced before.

Still the old fighting spirit glowed here and there a little, as in Mortain, where *Kampfgruppe* Fick,[4] attached to 2nd SS Panzer Division Das

---

4. Probably *Obersturmbannführer* Jacob Fick (1912–2004), commander of 37th SS *Panzergrenadier* Regiment of 17 SS *Panzergrenadier* Division.

Reich for the purpose of a counter-attack, succeeded in penetrating the town, or in St Menehould where the following incident took place. 17th SS Division was to hold a sector 20 km wide. This was to be done with remnants of 49th and 51st SS Panzer Grenadier Brigades which were put under control of the division. The divisional staff scouted around for a while without being able to locate these elements (it had not been known at that time that these brigades had already fled across the Moselle). When Major Konrad of the staff called up Seventh Army HQ and apprised it of this fact, the Army commander replied: 'If you have no other troops to employ in the sector, then hold it with your divisional staff!' The divisional staff obediently deployed over the 20 km sector, but withdrew when the American spearheads were within 5 km distance.

But this was just the wind in the dying embers. Higher HQ soon saw this, and, in order to keep the name of the division alive, it went into the reforming area Merzig. Here all means were employed to get the division back up on its feet. Every available officer of the divisional staff, including the (then) divisional commander *Standartenführer* Deisenhofer,[5] went out cruising in the Metz area with instructions to gather troops. The officers would stand at road crossings and shanghai every passing soldier who did not have a ready answer to the inquiry after his destination. In one instance I was directing traffic in the divisional area. The army men, not quite satisfied that they were being impressed into an SS unit, circled the area until they hit another road, only to run into me at the road junction again, and I re-directed the men into the division area, rather amused at the merry-go-round. When anti-tank guns were needed, an officer with a few prime movers at hand would set up shop at a road crossing and wait for passing guns, the crews of which were not quite certain about their destination or attachment. The horses would be unhitched, the crews piled into the waiting prime movers, and the caravan proceeded into the reforming area.

And that is the history of 17th SS Division Götz von Berlichingen up to my capture on 1 November 1944.

---

5. *Standartenführer* Eduard Deisenhofer (1909–45), commander of 17th SS *Panzer-grenadier* Division.

Document 3/3[6]

Calais Calling

Wartime Intelligence Officer's Comments

A bag of captured mail from the beleaguered garrison at Calais, captured on its way to Germany, reveals the state of mind of the defenders called upon to hold out until the last.

Obergefreiter Josef Koller writes home   4 September 1944

I am still alive, perhaps this is my last letter to all of you. We are in the port of Calais and expect to be encircled very soon. The ring will soon be getting smaller. How we shall all end I don't know, death or imprisonment. Our strong points have been left in a panic, hence no ink. Demolitions are going on day and night and the town looks like Stalingrad. A pity because [of] all the huge wealth which is being destroyed. Yes! the Atlantic Wall is no more. The average soldier is not to blame for this mess. I never thought that things would turn out this way. I would not like to see all those who have been killed. I have seen scenes which can hardly be described. The Flak units will be better than the others since they are not so disorganized ... At the moment the front line runs north of Arras, not far from us (look up the map). Food is good, we still have enough but only 'strong point' rations ... The French cannot be trusted any more. They hang around all the street corners with their hands deep in their pockets. Yes, when will the end come? Not a sign any more of the V.1 in our sector. Our pill box keeps shaking from all the demolitions and big pieces of concrete keep on flying past when one happens to be on guard duty outside.

Pte F. Gerber to his parents   5 September 1944

We have just been informed that there will be vehicles going to Belgium, enabling the mail to be despatched. However, I will not be able to get any more mail from you. The OKW report will give you an idea of how critical the situation has become. I do not intend to keep silent any more about our situation. We arrived in Calais on Saturday. You will find it on the map. It is on the Channel coast. The picture is as follows. The Tommy has left Paris far behind. In the north he is right in Belgium. We are completely

---

6. ISUM 74, 6 September 1944, from *SHAEF Intelligence Notes* 26.

encircled. We cannot retreat any further. We shall most likely have to face a Dunkirk. I hope God will not leave me. Without His will nothing happens.

Our task is to defend Calais. How we shall do it remains to be seen. Our only fate is to be taken prisoner. Now my dear ones I send you my last greetings from the west, and should we not see one another in this world, our only hope is a reunion above.

Pte Gerald to his sweetheart   6 September 1944

My beloved beautiful child,

We disembarked at Calais on 2 September. Other units which were there were leaving the post. In Calais we do only sentries and patrols and we have hardly any time for sleep. It seems that things have slightly improved. The French behaviour is fairly correct. Only at night are we being shot at and this is unpleasant as one cannot see anything.

Provost Willi Roeder to his wife   7 September 1944

A few lines whilst standing on guard in the rain. We are all encircled and our only hope of remaining alive is to be taken prisoner. The battle will be very, very bitter. It is hard for us but nothing can be changed. The Tommy is shooting pretty hard into our positions. Let's hope I shall remain alive.

Korvettenkapitän[7] Plate to his wife   7 September 1944

I am not clear how these letters will get through. The battle begins. No news apart from OKW reports. No mail for ages. The enemy is apparently in Holland and further south he is on German soil. Where are the wonder weapons?

A sailor to his parents   6 September 1944

As to the future, we face a sad lot. It is obvious that the higher ups have betrayed us. The Army left us in the lurch. For days they are on the run towards the east. We are sad and nobody believes in Victory any more.

A soldier to his family   6 September 1944

My dears,

All is well. In a few hours we shall be taken prisoner. The enemy is not here yet. Thus you will know that so far I am alright.

---

7. A German naval rank equivalent to lieutenant-commander in the Royal Navy and United States Navy.

Lieutenant Fritz Ranker   *7 September 1944*

Everything is done for the victory. The weapons ordered by the Führer will liberate us. We will hold out until relieved. Whatever may come, however, I shall be with you one day. My optimism, my faith in our Führer are so great that it is generally noticed, but you know that I always believed in final victory, in a thousand years Reich and a peaceful Europe.

Document 3/4[8]

A German Account of the Arnhem Battle, September 1944

Wartime Intelligence Officer's Comments

The document translated below is a German war reporter's account of the battle of Arnhem. It is taken from a German army newspaper, Der Westkurier, *dated 8 October 1944.*

The Fight of the Elite

This is the story of how the First British Airborne Division was destroyed. (From a *Propagandakompanie* special report for *Der Westkurier* by the War Reporter Erwin Kirchhof.)

Finally the assignment that we have been waiting for has been given to us. It is an airborne landing on the greatest scale with the purpose of clearing the way for the Second British Army through Holland to Northern Germany. Each and every soldier must know the importance of these bridges. These under all circumstances must be kept intact for the army that is to follow. This may possibly be our last job. Let us all make the best use of this opportunity.

Extracted from the Order of the Day of the British Divisional Commander[9]

---

8. ISUM 162, 10 December 1944, from First Allied Airborne Army.
9. The commander of the 1st Airborne Division was Major-General Roy Urquhart.

On the morning of 17 September only minor activities were reported along the Albert and Maas Schelde Canal. But this resulted in the greatest activity at Field Marshal Model's Headquarters. During the last 14 days of uninterrupted offensives the British Second Army had tried with the concentrated striking power of more than 12 divisions to break through the German positions stretched behind the barricades of the streams and canals of southern Holland, in order to push through Holland and reach northern Germany.

The very heavy air attacks on airports and traffic installations in the plain of the Lower Rhine and other indications pointed to Eisenhower's intention to break the stalemate and continue his push. For that he would use all the forces he had assembled in England since the beginning of the invasion.

Where Would the Enemy Try to Surprise Us?

It was an early Sunday afternoon. The cinemas in the small Dutch towns were slowly filling up, and the streets and highways along the canals and small streams were crowded with young people on bicycles. And then out of the blue sky roared several hundred enemy fighter bombers. Their aim was to attack the German defensive positions and locate the flak positions. Barely had they disappeared beyond the horizon when, coming from the west, across the flooded coastal areas, appeared the planes and gliders carrying regiments and brigades of the enemy's Airborne Army. They were flying low. They were headed by the four-motored transport planes, loaded with parachute battalions. Following them came the two-motored tow-planes of the large cargo gliders. Our flak batteries, which had refrained from firing at the fighter bombers, now opened up with all they had at the close flying formations. Each and every soldier of the line and even the headquarters personnel and the cooks helped. Split into two fleets, the enemy's formations turned before Eindhoven and Arnhem in a large circle towards each other. The first parachute landings were made on a front of about 70 kilometres and approximately 100 kilometres behind our lines. The troops bailed out from a very low altitude, sometimes as low as 60 metres. Immediately after that the several hundred gliders started to land. In those first few minutes it looked as if the descending masses would suffocate every single life on the ground. Coinciding with these mass landings behind our lines the enemy started to attack with increased ferocity on the whole line along the Albert and Maas Schelde Canal and on both sides of Aachen. His armoured columns, the backbone of his strategy, were ordered to start to push again.

They Call Themselves 'Red Devils'

Shortly after the landings of the British and American divisions, our recce troops went into action. By searching the countless forests and large parks in that area, cut by numerous small streams, they had to ascertain where the enemy intended to concentrate his forces: only then could a basis for our counter-attacks be established. The telephone lines were cut. The recce cars could move forward only slowly. Some of the enemy dug themselves in near their landing places and brought weapons into position. Others moved up to the houses and barricaded themselves, using the furniture inside the buildings. From there they tried to dominate the bridges and beat back our counter-attacks. Elements of the Dutch population assisted the enemy in their task. An SS *Obersturmführer* and bearer of the *'Ritterkreuz'* was on reconnaissance near Arnhem, when he collided on a forest road with one of the enemy jeeps. Before the British lieutenant and his 3-man team recovered from their surprise, they were captured. From their personal papers it was clear that they belonged to the First British Airborne Division and had taken part in the campaigns in Africa, Sicily and Italy. They wore red berets and called themselves 'Red Devils'. Now they blamed themselves for not being more careful and doing their job better. *SS Obersturmführer* 'G',[10] after a drive of several hours in his reconnaissance car, reached the Arnhem bridge and crossed it to the southern bank. His reconnaissance had constantly been interrupted by air attacks. The German guards on both sides of the bridge had hardly suffered any casualties. There was no trace of the several hundred men who had landed nearby. All of a sudden a steady stream of machine gun bullets hit the centre of the bridge, coming from the direction of the southern bank. The bearer of the *'Ritterkreuz'* was hit. An SS *Unterscharführer* took over. In the late hours of the same evening he was able to report to the SS *Obersturmbannführer*, now the *Kampfgruppe* commander: 'The strength of the enemy that landed is approximately 3000 men supported by heavy weapons which include 7.65 cm Anti-tank guns and 15 cm infantry howitzers and light armoured vehicles. They landed in the area west of Arnhem between the railroad tracks and the Rhine River, reaching the line Wolfheze, south of the Rhine and on both sides of the highway from Arnhem-Ede, 6 km northwest of Arnhem. The enemy intends to hold the Rhine bridge until he can establish contact with Montgomery's army.'

---

10. This was *Hauptsturmführer* Viktor Gräbner (1914–44), commanding the reconnaissance battalion of the 8th SS Panzer Division. He was actually killed in the ambush.

The area in which the landing of the First Airborne Division occurred had a width of 10 km and a depth of 12 km. SS *Obersturmbannführer* 'H',[11] a giant-like officer who has never lost his wits, even in the most hopeless situation of a battle, acted as general staff officer and dynamic commander. Together with the commander of an SS Panzer Corps[12] who is also an energetic personality, he forged the steel pocket of Arnhem. In the cold and rainy night the town was entirely cut off, particularly from the northwest. On the morning of 18 September the SS units arrived from the north to reinforce the northwestern part of the pocket. In line, northwest of Arnhem near Ede, the *Alarmeinheiten* (Alarm or Emergency Units) attacked. These units consisted of soldiers from every part of the earth. The attack was towards the east. The British at this time were receiving two parachute battalions and numerous airborne units, including more heavy weapons, as reinforcements, but they realized that encirclement threatened them. They dug in even deeper, they used every bush and every tree for cover, they converted every building into a strongpoint bristling with weapons. They were all volunteers and members of British regiments with a long and victorious tradition. The majority of them were officers and NCOs. The German troops who beat those first-rate British troops back, metre for metre, inflicting heavy casualties on them in close hand to hand fighting, were men of every branch of the service. Only 24 hours before they had not known each other: the aeroplane technicians still worked on their planes; the soldiers of the Waffen SS were refitting their unit in a small Dutch village; the *Landesschützen*[13] units were still employed as guards on military objectives; the naval coast artillery men had just returned from their strongpoints; the boys of the RAD[14] were still constructing field positions. Only a few of them were familiar with the principles of fighting in forest and hedgerow or street fighting. But they fought. In one infantry battalion members of as many as 28 different units fought side by side. Their battalion commander was a *Ritterkreuzertrager*[15] and also the bearer

---

11. *Obersturmbannführer* Walter Harzer (1912–82), commander of the 9th SS Panzer Division, which fought at Arnhem.
12. Probably *Obergruppenführer* Wilhelm Bittrich (1894–1979), commander II SS Panzer Corps.
13. Reserve troops, composed of older men, primarily used for security and guard duties.
14. *Reichsarbeitsdienst*, the German labour organization. All young German males were required to complete six months' national labour service prior to their compulsory military service.
15. Holder of the Knight's Cross.

of the golden *Verwundetenabzeichen*.[16] He was a Captain with a wooden leg. Yet this particular battalion fought as one of the best and the most fanatical. The thought of their Fatherland drove them forward, lending them miraculous strength.

On the German left flank the attacks came to a halt about midday. The enemy had set up a well camouflaged Anti-tank position in the forest, flanked and surrounded by numerous MGs and snipers. Even the assault guns could not break through. Several times they tried to roll up from behind the positions of the 7.65 cm long-barrelled Anti-tank guns, but the British recognised the danger every time and established the Anti-tank guns on the threatened flanks, using their fast-moving vehicles. All the German attacks were unsuccessful. Then an SS *Unterscharführer* together with a handful of men, armed only with a few hand grenades, worked themselves up to the front of their positions, up to the Anti-tank gun positions. They overpowered the crews and the German attack rolled on.

On the right flank, between the railroad tracks and the Rhine, in the residential suburbs of Oosterbeek, the struggle for each building continued for hours. In the narrow streets, hand grenades were thrown from one side of the street to the other. Further down the northern bank of the Rhine the fight for buildings from which the enemy dominated the bridge with his guns, had continued since dawn. Hand to hand fighting raged on each floor of the houses. In the power station on the Oost Straat men of the Luftwaffe mounted to the first floor and exchanged hand grenades with the British on the floor above.

In the evening a British radio message was intercepted in which a battalion commander, barricaded with four hundred of his paratroopers in the buildings along the Rhine bridge, asked for the dropping of masonry tools and cement. He intended to build a defensive wall around his positions.

The battles raged deep into the rainy night.

The Encirclement Must Be Broken

19 September. SS *Obersturmbannführer* 'H', day and night at the front with his men, now himself led the sharp thrust to the left of the right wing, covering the northwestern edge of Arnhem. The same day he made contact with the left flank, arriving from the west. The British Airborne Division was now encircled in an area of only a few square kilometres, between the

---

16. The *Verwundetenabzeichen* or Wound Badge was promulgated in 1918 and came in three orders – Black, Silver and Gold – depending on the number of wounds suffered.

railroad line and the Rhine. While under heavy enemy fire, the light flak guns broke up an enemy thrust. Only a few minutes later, the same guns shot down seven fighter-bombers. The enemy received reinforcements of two para battalions, one of them Polish, and several glider units. German fighters and flak inflicted heavy losses on the escaping enemy planes. Even Radio London admitted that the German Luftwaffe in the whole Dutch area was as active on that day as in their days of glory. Artillery and mortar batteries hammered the pocket. Around noon, two British envoys asked for a one-hour armistice to take more than six hundred casualties into German hospitals. Their proposal was accepted. A doctor of the Waffen SS and a British doctor supervised the transport. Afterwards there were further heavy attacks by the enemy. The number of prisoners rose to 904. Among them was the divisional commander. Several hundred automatic weapons, 50 trucks and light tanks and numerous heavy weapons were captured.

20 September

The period of bad weather kept up. Between the railroad track and the Rhine heavy house to house fighting continued. The enemy received reinforcements of 1000 parachutists and numerous glider units. Our flak shot down 10 supply planes. The major part of the weapons and food containers fell into our hands. This was caused by concentrated defensive fire. Fierce dog fights took place over the battle area. Our own fighters attacked the enemy on the ground. The enemy bombing attacks did not hit our mortar batteries. The enemy fired on Oosterbeek, directed by the infantry. It generally took four minutes from the call for fire support until the first shells landed. Again the enemy handed over more than 800 wounded in a period of armistice. The number of prisoners was now well over 2,000.

21 September

The British Division again received several hundred reinforcements and attempted in desperation to break the ring of iron; but despite this, we compressed the pocket still further. The size of the pocket was now an area of 1,200 metres by 750 metres. Mortars, artillery and flak fired into the forests and into the positions in the streets. Again 700 wounded were handed over to us. The number of dead was by now extremely high. Our light and medium flak was forced to destroy every single building on the southern bank of the Rhine. Opposite the power station, where a strong force of enemy paratroops were holding out, the officer directing the fire of a medium flak battery established his position. Even though he realised that the first shells might hit him, he called for fire on the power station. The first salvo seriously wounded him. The next brought down the large building. After the enemy charged three times at point blank range from Oost Straat, he was mowed down. An SS *Unterscharführer* escaped from the enemy and reported that 180 Germans were being held prisoner in the Tennis Court at Arnhem; ten metres in front of an Anti-tank and mortar position of a Battalion HQ! For days they had not received any food, and fed themselves with beets, potatoes and ersatz coffee. Many were deprived of their valuables. The *Unterscharführer* had useful information for the mortars. The enemy again suffered many casualties.

The Last Hours

In the following days Eisenhower continued to send new parachute battalions and glider units to the encircled remnants of the British Division. On the south side of the lower Rhine, between Nijmegen and Arnhem, a Polish parachute brigade landed with the task of breaking open the ring. Their attack failed. Then the American General Dempsey was again ordered to break through to Arnhem from the south with his armoured columns and to contact the British. Only a few of his tanks managed to break into the German encirclement. They were soon destroyed by our medium flak guns. The enemy's air force was over the battle area at all times with light and heavy bomber squadrons, but strong German fighter formations and massed flak batteries prevented the enemy from attaining any real success. From inside the ring the hard-hit enemy attacked desperately day and night. By 23 September they had already sustained several thousand casualties. In addition, about 2,000 wounded had already been transferred to German hospitals.

In London they spoke of the crisis of the Lower Rhine, but it was hoped that Dempsey would succeed in saving the remnants of the division. During the night of 25-26 September, the First British Airborne Division, now only about 400 men strong, attempted to break through from Oosterbeek under American covering fire, and cross the Rhine. The British wrapped rags around their feet and crept over the asphalt roads to the Rhine bank. Suddenly German mortars caught them. Three, perhaps four, assault boats succeeded in reaching the opposite bank.

The OKW report of 27 September claimed that this elite British division lost 6,450 PW, thousands dead, 30 Anti-tank guns, additional guns and weapons, and 250 trucks. In addition, 1,000 gliders were destroyed or captured and more than 100 planes shot down.

Document 3/5[17]

Life on Walcheren in the Autumn of 1944

Wartime Intelligence Officer's Comments

The following diary extracts contain the impressions of one Hans Specht, who helped to garrison Walcheren Island from his bunker on the coastline. Taken prisoner during the latter stages of the operation which cleared the Zeeland Islands, he kept a fairly careful record of the developments leading up to the capture on 8 November of himself and his bunker mates. The diary also contains an account of the circumstances of his surrender and of his reactions to the initial stages of life as a PW.

Tues. 17 October 1944:

Alert at about 2000 hours last night. Guard duty until 2400 hours. Lots of mail yesterday, but nothing for me.

Wed. 18 October 1944:

Night quiet. Bad weather. Several flights of enemy aircraft over our position. Watched the crash of a four-engined bomber. In the afternoon a bath in Domburg, the first one in weeks.

Thurs. 19 October 1944:

1500 hours heavy seas during high tide. They say that between 17 and 19 October spring-tide will set in.

Sat. 21 October 1944:

Heavy thunder of guns from the direction of Flushing all night long and still going on (1000 hrs). Since yesterday the water has risen quite a lot. The meadows in front of our position are all under water. Cattle from the surrounding country have been brought together into a small area, they appear very hungry and thirsty. Wrote home yesterday but it is doubtful whether any mail will leave here anymore. At noon bomber attack on Breskens.

---

17. ISUM 140, 16 November 1944.

Sun. 22 October 1944:

Heavy artillery fire in direction of Breskens. According to the radio, Breskens has been partly occupied by the Tommy.

Mon. 23 October 1944:

Stand-to during the night but nothing happened. No more artillery fire can be heard from Breskens. Bomber attacks during the afternoon. Two four-engined bombers brought down, one at 1605 hrs the other one at 1622 hrs, both of them near us. One of them fell into the sea, none of the crew were saved, but the Navy brought back a rubber boat.

Fri. 27 October 1944:

Nothing special to report during the last few days. Tonight we received notice that we will move tomorrow.

Sat. 28 October 1944:

Clear weather, night quiet. At 1130 hrs attack by bombers on our *Stützpunkt*.[18] Bomb crater only about 5 m from us. No casualties. Our company marches off in the morning.

Sun. 29 October 1944:

We were supposed to move with the rest of the company to our new location. From 1030 to 1330 bomber attack. This time we stayed in our bunker. The bunker was badly shaken but nobody was hurt! 1630 hrs we started marching to the new *Stützpunkt*, where we arrived at 1830 hrs.

Tue. 31 October 1944:

Yesterday morning I went with Sgt Kempe and Rotmeier to our old *Stützpunkt* to get the rest of our things. Shortly after we left there the time-bomb in the entrance to the dump exploded. At Domburg new attacks of strong bomber formations, could not observe the hits. In the afternoon returned to new location. After arrival we moved into a different bunker. At 1900 I went with S. to get the rations. Very dirty! The ration ship did not arrive.

Wed. 1 November 1944:

During the night heavy fire of our battery from Domburg towards Flushing? During the morning heavy naval gun fire on West Kapelle and Domburg. Also strong bomber attacks. Towards 1300 hrs only spasmodic fire. The enemy is said to be in West Kapelle.

---

18. Strongpoint.

Thur. 2 November 1944:

Night quiet and rainy. In the morning more artillery fire. Domburg to Flushing in the hands of the enemy. Weather clears and fighter-bombers come over again. During the day the small weakly garrisoned isle across from Walcheren was occupied. Our retreat is cut off now.

Fri. 3 November 1944:

Night was quiet except for some artillery fire, and the day until now – 1600 hrs – was also comparatively quiet. Is it the hour before the storm? A small cat strayed into our bunker and I am looking after it.

Sat. 4 November 1944:

Contrary to expectations the night was quiet. Building a raft in the hope that we will still be able to get out of here. In the morning it cleared and the fighter-bombers were getting active again. In the early hours of the afternoon an air attack on our position.

Mon. 6 November 1944:

Artillery fire, in the afternoon fighter-bomber attacks. S. is sick and is to be sent back to Hildesheim. He is taking some letters to his wife and family along.

Tue. 7 November 1944:

Half past five in the morning we left for *Stützpunkt* Heidelberg. Artillery fire and three fighter-bomber attacks. All day on sentry duty. Miserable weather, miserable quarters, not much sleep.

Wed. 8 November 1944:

1000 hrs: Enemy is said to have broken through. No connection left or right. With me in the bunker are six comrades. Looking forward to being captured if everything goes well. At about 1330 we surrendered after the bunker of the Sergeant-Major was found to be empty. We were searched right away, watch and money taken away. Then to Domburg, where were put into a school. We met most of our comrades here, we were the last ones to be taken prisoner.

Thur. 9 November 1944:

0800 hrs: Start of march in direction Frouwenpolder. Should have been transported to Flushing. On account of the stormy weather had to turn back and were put into barracks of the former *Stützpunkt* Johannmichel. 40 men in the barracks.

Fri. 10 November 1944:

Very stormy and cold. The officers among us were taken away by boat yesterday. We are supposed to start at 0900 hrs. Our guards are very decent.

(Concerning the surrender of our company)

During the night about 3 o'clock heavy mortar fire, and again at 6 o'clock in the morning. Under the protection of this fire the Tommy came up. Our men had taken cover. At 9 o'clock the whole company were PW except the men in our bunker who didn't surrender until 1330 hrs. Great superiority of the enemy in material, especially tanks. We had no heavy weapons. Morale of our men in spite of everything, good. The oppressive feeling of inferiority and useless fighting is over with. Don't know the casualties of our company.

Document 3/6[19]

The Thinking Sergeant

Wartime Intelligence Officer's Comments

The following extracts were translated from the diary of Sgt Heinz Frick, who appeared in the 1st US Infantry Division cage on 26 November. In some ways the prisoner is typical of what has happened to the small free-thinking segment of the German population. It is apparent that he approaches everything (including his own propaganda) with an open mind, yet he is unable, or unwilling, to act upon what he believes. In Germany there is no such thing as a conscientious objector. On the contrary, the Sergeant fought skillfully and hard and only his diary revealed that he was anything other than a hard-boiled and determined Landser.[20]

---

19. ISUM 155, 4 December 1944, from *1st U.S. Infantry Division G-2 Report.*
20. *Landser,* a slang term for a soldier in the German army, particularly a combat soldier, equivalent to the British 'Tommy' or the American 'GI'.

December 1943 – Russia:

The soldier from my platoon was badly wounded and I tried to get him back to the aid station. A Major's car drove up and I stopped it, but the bastard refused to take the soldier because he might get the upholstery bloody . . . I spoke to the regimental CO about it and he will investigate the case, but will he have the courage? There must be justice some place.

February 1944 – Norway:

This world is really going to pieces. Here I am in a little Norwegian cafe talking to a Norwegian volunteer in the German forces. He openly calls Quisling a traitor to his country, yet he himself wants to fight to preserve the Aryan race from Bolshevism. Now I ask myself, how can a traitor represent Germany and the German cause? Is Quisling unworthy of Germany or could it be that Germany has become low enough to be worthy of a Quisling???

June 1944 – Norway:

Since the war of 1812 the people of Germany have been fighting for their liberty and the goal has never been reached. Even after 'the victory of 1870' we were not satisfied and we had another war in 1914. Is it we who are bringing all this misery to the world or could it be the English? . . . I am trying not to fall for our propaganda, which also has its necessary part in warfare, but I will try to judge apart from the politics. Does the world still recognize German Nationalism as separate from Hitlerism? I am beginning to doubt it, but for myself German Nationalism is the equivalent of British Imperialism and for the Americans it must be the 'United' part of their United States. I think America has enormous possibilities; it has proven it during the last decades. Come to think of it, Roosevelt can't be so very bad. For Mr. Goebbels naturally, he is a Jew. How silly! But Germany believes it all. Why don't we wake up?

September 1944 – Norway:

I pray day and night that God will let me see the day when I can do my share of constructive work for this world I have been helping to destroy since 1938. I have been destroying Russians mostly and I don't like them – neither do they like us! Funny, I like Marx and I could read his books when we were still able to buy them and understand the Russians' problems. I didn't have to like it. Today we kill each other and settle it that way.

October 1944 – Denmark:

I feel like an old man, today, not in years, but in spirit. I should not have seen all the things I have seen; they are blinding for young people. I should be madly in love right now with the most beautiful girl I know, and here I am trying to kill some other girl's beloved or some innocent children's father. That is civilization! Hurrah, the 20th Century is here, it needn't hurry! There was nothing we missed.

En route to Aachen sector, October 1944:

I am going to the front. The train continues its monotonous rhythm. I am going towards the front. I will meet my fate. Will I get away alive? What have I to look forward to? Is it worthwhile?

Document 3/7 [21]

Morale of Pilots

Wartime Intelligence Officer's Comments

Until recently, the scarcity of Luftwaffe prisoners falling into Allied hands has made any assessment of morale virtually impossible. On 3 December however, an unusually large number of pilots, all from the same unit, were shot down over our lines. The resulting assessment made by the interrogation officer is therefore of considerable interest.

Though most of the pilots of Jagdgeschwader 4 are comparatively new, they appear to face their dangerous and difficult task without flinching. The morale of prisoners of war examined was, if not exuberantly high, at least determined and unyielding. All were security-conscious, and while most yielded information eventually, several were very resolute in their refusal to talk. Recent briefing in security was very evident. There was little of the arrogance noted among Luftwaffe pilots in the early years of the war, but there was a determination bordering on desperation.

An unmailed letter written by one of these pilots (6th Staffel, Jagdgeschwader 4 based near Rheine) throws a strong light on the unit's

---

21. ISUM 173, 21 December 1944, from *SHAEF Intelligence Summary*, 17 December 1944.

operations and on a rather typical fighter pilot's reaction to the personal problems involved.

1 December 1944

Dear parents, especially dear Dad,

I almost forgot your birthday. We are very busy here. They nearly got me on my last operational flight. You must realize that we are now the first unit in the west to meet the enemy. As you know 800 fighters accompany the bombers as escort. Our unit is praised again and again. All heavy fighters ask for us as high altitude cover. So you can imagine how busy we are with only 30 planes. Losses are high. Two of my best comrades did not return last Sunday, and never will. In our *Staffel* with ten pilots you feel that sort of thing. But now I am finding just how useful experience is. Aachen is our sector for ground-strafing missions. That is a terrific sight. When one sees the front for the first time, you hear nothing, but below you see clouds of smoke, and guns flashing. The flak fires like mad. In this mad house you force yourself to be calm, seek your target, and shoot. I have four operational flights now, among them two against enemy bombers over Reich territory. Operational flights are those in which air combat takes place.

Chapter 4

The Home Front

Editor's Comments

Aachen was the first major German city captured by Allied troops and the attitude of German civilians toward their occupiers became a matter of great interest to American intelligence officers (Document 4/4). It quickly became clear that many younger Germans, inculcated with Nazi philosophy since they were toddlers, did not accept that the Reich was going to lose the war. The diary of a German teenage girl (Document 4/2) and the rather confused world view of another female teenager (Document 4/3) testify to the strength of that philosophy. An officer in the 90th Panzer Grenadier Division hears from his fiancée, sister, father and grandmother who relate experiences of life on the home front (Document 4/1) with constant fear of Allied air attacks and continuous belt-tightening.

Document 4/1[1]

War Comes to a German Family

Wartime Intelligence Officer's Comments

The following letters addressed to a German officer of 361st Panzergrenadier Regiment of the 90th Panzergrenadier Division on the Italian front depict the thoughts of a German family during those fateful days in early September

---

1. ISUM 145, 22 November 1944, from *Eighth Army Intelligence Summary* 832.

when the threat of an Allied penetration of the Reich was so very close. Although a trifle dated at this time, the letters nevertheless show the difference in views held by the old and the young in Germany. The grandmother is definitely antagonistic to the Nazis, the father is non-committal, the young sister is frightened but trusting, while the fiancee is ironical and bitter.

From his Grandmother   Forchheim, 26 August 1944

In the larger places such as Emendingen, Freiburg, all members of the old Centre, Social Democrat and Communist parties who held any sort of office before 1933, even if only that of a local representative, have been taken into protective custody ... I hear that all of them have been sent to Dachau, nobody knows why. You can just imagine how uneasy all of us feel. It will soon reach the stage when we fear what the next day will bring. It would be dreadful if, after 25 years of work and worry and saving to make a good home for your children, it should all be lost in one day. When I think of all this I am grateful to God that your dear mother is no longer alive to see it. She at least has peace and quiet. She could never have endured these times.

From his Fiancée   Taun, 28 August 1944

Yes, Sepp, I expect you will have heard that things are 'getting hot' here. And what can one do about it!!! Can you give me any advice? In a fortnight's time I shall be working in a munitions factory, like so many others. The colleges and schools are being closed. All school-mistresses etc. are to work on munitions. Isn't it marvellous? I don't think! My studies are finished too. The Academy in Mulhausen has been levelled to the ground (music school too). Marvellous situation isn't it, Sepp? Mulhausen looked perfectly awful after the second raid.

From his Fiancée   Taun, 2 September 1944

We have started to 'get our shoulder to the wheel' here, too. 60 hrs a week and all that. In a few days I shall also be working in the factory. All the girl students and schoolmistresses are already on munitions. I've already had a talk with several of them. And what a mood they're in! We must just let everything go over us, we certainly can't alter anything. It's simply a question of 'orders' and 'obeying'. I can't send you any more papers because the Post Office won't accept them.

From his young Sister   *Forchheim, 4 September 1944*
Who knows, Josef, how things will be here by the time you receive this
letter? I can only tell you that there are dark days ahead. If you should get
no mail from us for some time you will know why. We are just hoping and
trusting in the Retaliation, for in a way our home would be spared. I can
only tell you that none of us have any more interest to dig fortifications,
it was said. Just imagine – Walter Z. Erwin H. etc etc – such big strong
boys. I'm sure the British will run away the minute they see them. In two
days all the girls between 14 and 15 years old have got to go away to dig
fortifications. They say it's to dig a big Anti Tank ditch at Wyhl. Soldiers
have already arrived at Endingen, Kenzingen, Riegel. I must tell you quite
honestly, Josef, that I'm really glad mother is not alive, for she would never
have been able to endure all the hardships that lie ahead. We are all of us
so afraid, even if only one aircraft comes over.

From his Grandmother   *Forchheim, 14 September 1944*
For some days now there has been no mail, no telephone, no newspaper,
scarcely a train. Since your last letter things have changed here considerably
and, unfortunately, not for the good. You will have read in the official
communiques how far the enemy has advanced, and I can tell you that we
are already suffering from it. Aircraft are overhead the whole day, shooting
up the railway and the villages, and have already caused several deaths.
On Tuesday they attacked our village and set many of the houses on fire.
You can imagine the misery of it – and winter so near! Richard Zoller
was on his way home on his cart across the fields when he was struck
down by a machine gun bullet. He died later in great pain. The funeral
is at 7 o'clock tomorrow morning. It has to be early because of enemy
aircraft. Dear Josef, that's how things are now in your home. The boys of
14–17 have been away a fortnight now in the Vosges digging fortifications.
All prisoners of war have been made to dig defences at Wessweil for the
past 10 days, and with them one person from each house, whether man
or woman makes no difference, as long as they are under 65. Work in
the fields has stopped completely. Dear Josef, I have been thinking of you
all day. It's your birthday. What can I wish you? Up till now you have
achieved whatever aim you set yourself – what the future holds we must
leave to fate, in these uncertain times. I can only wish you will one day
come home safely and find us still alive and your home untouched.

From his Father   *Forchheim, 15 September 1944*

This business is making itself felt here, too. It is sometimes 2 or 3 days now before the mail van arrives. No trains can run at all by day because enemy aircraft patrol up and down the line and if they see anything they shoot it up until the engine is set on fire. It's getting uncomfortable here. Nobody goes to work any more and all we do is to fetch something to eat and try not to be afraid. It is about time the war ended but it looks as if it may become very serious for us here.

From his Grandmother   *Forchheim, 15 September 1944*

Today is the 15th September and has brought another big surprise for us. As we came home from the funeral this morning we found that 500 soldiers had marched into our village, and they were all Russians in German uniform. They are to dig defences at Wyhl. Some of them are quite good-looking and intelligent, many of them NCOs. I wonder if the world has ever seen a bigger swindle than the one being practiced upon us now?

And I must tell you that Karl Schicher is dead. He fell off the hay cart yesterday and broke his neck. So every day brings news but never the kind we long for, of peace. Richard Zoller was given a grand funeral this morning. I think everybody left in the village was there. Your father was there too, and wept bitterly. He has never known how to accept the inevitable and he worries about you, too, the pair of you . . . Well Josef, at the moment I have nerves of steel and hope to keep them, no matter what happens. The position is very serious here but it will all pass over. At the moment we are all busy packing and hiding things. The mayor told me today that we shall probably have to leave the village. I don't think that I shall go, however. How the people who were once so big are very small indeed and I remember an old saying about rats and a sinking ship.

Goodbye, my dear boy, don't worry too much about us and home – for it will all blow over – even this . . .

Document 4/2²

Diary of a Nazi Girl

Wartime Intelligence Officer's Comments

To all who are still wondering what will be the attitude of the German people toward Allied occupation, the attached diary written by Maria Bierganz of Monschau makes interesting reading. Maria is typical of the fanatic Hitler Youth. She is only seventeen years old but has already been actively associated with Naziism for seven years – four years in the Jungmädchen³ and three years in the Bund Deutscher Mädel.⁴ She attained the rank of Mädelschaarfuhrerin and joined the Nazi Party last April.

After the Americans arrived in Monschau, the older German people acquiesced, fearing American punishment, but not so with Maria and her associates. They had nothing but contempt for the American soldier. Two of her close comrades broke American communications. Seven or eight of these Nazi Youths met with Maria on Monschau street corners to discuss their Nazi problems and to ridicule Americans. Several of their meetings were significantly held near the Military Government Office, beside the bulletin board on which are posted all proclamations issued by General Eisenhower.

After arrest by the Ninth Division Counter Intelligence Detachment, Maria, like most of her gang, insisted, 'Ich habe nichts getan, bestimmt nichts' (I have done nothing, definitely nothing).

This diary (which takes the form of a series of letters written to her SS lover, Peter) has been accurately translated by Agents of this detachment because it gives a glimpse into the future problems facing the Counter Intelligence Corps and other Intelligence Agencies in occupied Germany. It is, however, a key-hole view of the Nazi problem-children thumbing their noses at Allied authority and planning revenge.

Monschau, 7 October 1944

First of all, please excuse me when I write with pencil for the actual circumstances do not permit otherwise. Then I have another request: do not pay

---

2. ISUM 201, 18 January 1945, from *First US Army Intelligence Report.*
3. The *Jungmädchen Bund* or *Jung Mädchen* was the junior component of the Nazi youth organization for girls, which comprised girls from ten to fourteen.
4. The *Bund Deutscher Mädel* or BDM was the senior component of the Nazi youth organization for girls. Its members were aged from fifteen to eighteen.

any attention to the foolish handwriting for my eyes are full of tears. For a few days I have had a severe cold. But really nothing can unbalance me now any more. The last weeks were simply terrifying. It is quite impossible to write about it. If I should ever get out of this witch's cauldron and overcome this affair, maybe I will tell you something.

Now, really something else. Where are you? Yesterday, I heard that the rest of the 27 and part of the 28 had been inducted. Peter, if I only knew where you are, I believe I would feel better. I heard indirectly that on our beloved Cologne there were again some dastardly, mean terror-attacks. Yes, dear Peter, slowly I realize that this is absolutely no honest holy fight for the right to live but a damned war of materials. It is not the fault of us poor Germans that we do not have such a fertile country as America. Also we do not have the quality of character to exploit small helpless countries in such a low way. When one takes a look at the American way of waging war one really needs telephone wires instead of so-called nerves. A little example: when the Americans entered here, all bridges and some streets had been blown up in advance, all blockhouses started firing. Hell broke loose. After approximately one hour the noise died down and it became dead quiet, a German feint. The following morning I was in the garden to get some apples. You know the long wall where we picked up the 'Stealing Fellows' that time. I was sitting majestically on the tree. Christel just went to fetch a basket when the first tankgun shells brushed over my head on our hill. A real shell symphony started. You know how I ever got down from the tree that morning I still do not know. The soldiers came down behind the wall. Little children stood crying on the road. Never did I run as fast as in those seconds. Up to now I still do not know how I got the five children all at once into the cellar, the poor ones were stiff from fright. Besides that also Christel could not keep herself under control. After half an hour we were able to bring the children home and return ourselves to our shaking mothers at double time. At the first shots and also later – the terrifying mix up, I always heard the sound of your 'Good-bye. Stay brave.' Let's go on: You will probably remember where last Sunday the boys had run into the woods, you know at an angle from our house. There, was a machine gun position with a sharp-shooter. Fourteen days a Lieutenant still remained there although the machine gun was already blown up by the Americans a long time ago. How much trouble he gave the Americans is indescribable. Four machine guns hammered all day long with only short interruptions and sent salvo upon salvo into the hill. Armoured vehicles fired shell upon shell into the dark wood, but our Lieutenant replied from time to time with his sharp-shooter's rifle. This unequal fight lasted for fourteen days. Then there were German reinforcements. This heroic Lieutenant deserves the highest reward. Still today, the 'snails' are fighting in Menzerath and Imgenbroich. Menzerath is a locality with only 6 houses. Up to now no American has been there. Slowly this war of snails gets on my nerves. Nowhere is there any advance in spite of the incessant bombardments. There is nothing doing but to shake the head again and again and say again and again, 'There is really nothing better than German soldiers'. The cowardice of the Americans is simply indescribable.

8 October 1944

Today is real Sunday weather. The sun is shining from the blue sky. There is only one thing that is wrong – the continuous detonations of bombs, firing, buzzing explosions of the armoured guns and artillery as well as German shells landing. The Germans defend themselves superhumanly against the attacking mass. But still unfortunately they have to return foot by foot. Dearest Peter, why do we deserve that? Has not the German worked without rest with an honest intention in his heart? Shall everything be in vain? No, Peter, I feel it so clearly that we, the Youth, are a sorely tried but also a steeled Youth and hard as iron, destined to fight on for the idea of our indispensable leader. When everybody deserts the leader he will be able to depend on his real Youth. They will never betray him. O, Peter, if you would only be with me, how much easier would I be able to handle these things. Here I can not talk with anybody about it. Nobody would be able to understand me here. But, Peter, you understand me. The glorious deeds of our Army, the incredible acts of individual heroes, and all those sacrifices of the people, may they not be in vain. Maybe fate will be kind once more to us and will permit us anyway to march through the Arch of Victory. Peter, of this sad end my heart would never have thought. Let us now talk of something else.

Peter, if I did not always remember your last words, 'Stay Brave', I would not know sometimes what to do. But this always incites me again. Then I sing a few times the German 'Wochenschau'[5] and then everything is better again. Believe me we sit here in a real witch's cauldron. The roaring and exploding of the shells, the buzzing and bursting of the bombs, the shaking of the house are things one gets used to; one only shakes with fright when a piece of shrapnel comes through the glassless windows or a shell explodes directly behind the house.

---

5. The *Deutsche Wochenschau* was the weekly newsreel and the source of information on the war. Its opening shot was always a Nazi eagle accompanied by a massed trumpet salute.

Monschau, 9 October 1944

Blue Monday. Really, Peter, today I miss you. Instead of getting better, my cold is getting worse. I believe I could bet that I would be well soon, if only you were here. Now I have to use other unnatural means. Today there is not as much shooting. I will go to the town in a few minutes, to get to know the latest news. A club 'Heimatstreue' (Faithful to the Homeland) where I have to admit being ashamed about my own sex, since I am the only girl. If I only think of it, I get mad. But on the ones who belong to the club one can depend fully. All leaders of the Hitler Youth. Peterle, please don't think anything bad about me. Just think logically, and besides, I have you, even if far away. But believe that I always think of you lovingly. Do you also think at least one minute of the day of a poor creature, who craves to be with you again as soon as possible? You should really feel how my thoughts are continuously with you. No, Peter, I would have never thought it possible that fate would have tried to prophesy this to me – it would have gotten such an ear boxing that it would not have been able to walk home. The poor Germans had always to suffer a cruel fate. We will prove ourselves worthy of our forefathers. I hate the Americans, especially since they are almost all former Germans. Just now the whole house shook again, bomb explosions. The enemy is still fighting for Wahlerscheid, Rohren, Menzerath, Imgenbroich, Konzen, Lammersdorf. Now, my Peterle, I will have to end in order to do something for my bodily well-being, so that I am at least a little on the ball at our conversation today.

Now I send you a very loving kiss and thousands of hearty greetings into unknown distances and say softly, 'Good-bye'.

Monschau, 10 October 1944

After having taken some pills and God knows what else, yesterday, I feel better today. It is still early in the day, 10 o'clock. Today, not a single shot yet. Ghastly. Wait and see what the day will bring. You know Peter the meanness of my dear neighbours and former girl comrades is simply boundless. Yesterday someone of the faithful overheard that in town people say the two German girl club leaders who stayed back in Monschau had danced with Americans. Peter, this is really not a joke any more, it is a limitless baseness. After many a gossip, this really hits the ceiling. Wait and see who laughs last.

In the meantime it is evening 1930 hours. The first evening that we have had light, if you call it that. Not even the radio works, so weak is the current in Monschau. As I said already at the start of this letter, this day was ghastly. At about 1630 hours machine guns rattled from all sides. It looked like a rain of specks in between the sharp whistling of bullets. Really Peter, we are not over the hill yet. In our woods roams the SS in arms. Darling, again bomber fleets go overhead. They fly very low now. If I would only know where you are I would not have to be continuously afraid for you. But as it is?

So tonight we talked in the club among other things also about the speech of Dr Goebbels: Peter I will never pardon him for saying that the people from the territories occupied by the enemy in the west, are no longer Germans, that we had by staying here, gone over to the Americans. Peter, he's made everybody mad in our club, too. Peter, only now I realize completely what a great happiness it is to call oneself a German. Formerly, one used to regard it as natural. Today, to be German means to fight. Now we still had a great disappointment, for our club is melted down to three men (respectively, two fellows and me), Walter J (locality leader), the student of the 'academy' and me.

Now still another shame, our comrades from yesterday have squealed on us so to say. And now they incite against us. All good things are three. If only you would be here then we would be a clover leaf, which might be luckier. I just had to stop, my darling nose started bleeding. Naturally it is still doing so but I hold a plug underneath it now.

This writing is really romantic, so to say, at starlight. Now the bombs start falling. Oh, Susanna, how can life be beautiful? Really we don't have to complain about boredom. Back to the club, however, I heard that the Americans delivered an ultimatum to Aachen to surrender by ten o'clock or to be crushed by 'air eggs' and artillery. Will the SS ever surrender? Tonight, I don't believe so yet. But then the poor people. I know now by experience what it means to live through the newsreels. But Peter, the thought of you always gives me new force. If you ever see Monschau again, your hair will stand on end. War in the country! A terrifying thought about our poor leader. But, sweetheart, that Goebbels wants to take away our being German presses down like a heavy stone on my head. (The artillery is firing again, menacingly near). I will never forgive him that. To ask frankly, where should we have gone to? To the Rhine and expose ourselves to the enemy's bomb terrors, leaving the last belongings behind. The people who went to Morsch were all killed. It is really horrifying that Goebbels throws such a meanness on our heads, like a rotten potato. Are not the sacrifices of German women who give birth to children in woods, without any assistance, more than enough? All this because we want to

German prisoners, August 1944. After the collapse of the German front in Normandy, the Allies captured hundreds of thousands of prisoners, many like the second-line troops seen here.

Dolle Dinsdage (Mad Tuesday) was the Dutch term for 5 September 1944 as the amazed civilians watched the Wehrmacht's panic-stricken flight through their country in a variety of vehicles. Here a farm wagon is used to pull a 37 mm anti-aircraft gun.

Above: Allied airpower. By the autumn of 1944 the Allied air forces ruled the skies over western Europe. These medium tactical bombers are engaging targets in Belgium.

Right: Western Front, September 1944. At this point the war was close to being won but logistical problems and dubious strategic decisions slowed the Allied advance.

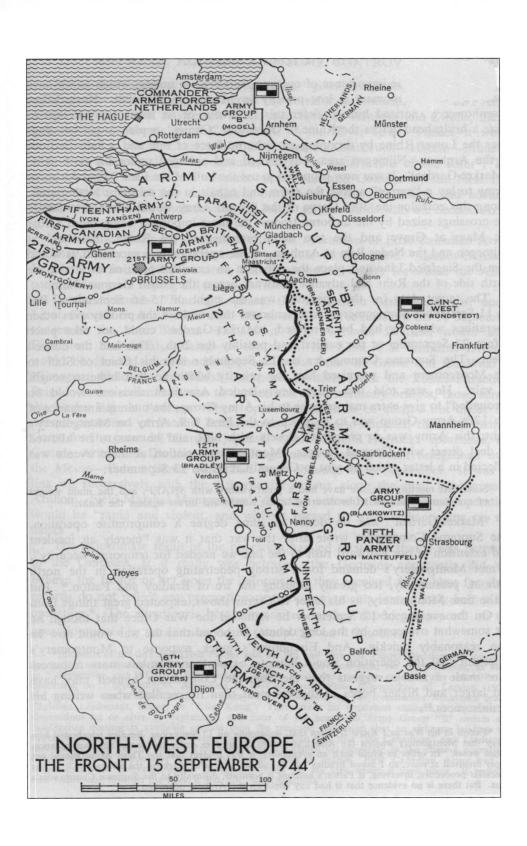

NORTH-WEST EUROPE
THE FRONT 15 SEPTEMBER 1944

Amsterdam

COMMANDER
ARMED FORCES
NETHERLANDS

THE HAGUE

Utrecht

Rotterdam

Rhine

ARMY
GROUP
"B"
(MODEL)

Arnhem

Nijmegen

Münster

Rheine

Hamm

Dortmund

WEST WALL

Wesel

Essen

Bochum

Duisburg

Ruhr

Krefeld

Düsseldorf

Maas

Waal

FIFTEENTH ARMY
(VON ZANGEN)

FIRST PARACHUTE ARMY
(STUDENT)

FIRST CANADIAN ARMY
(CRERAR)

Antwerp

München-
Gladbach

Cologne

Bonn

21ST
ARMY
GROUP
(MONTGOMERY)

Ghent

SECOND BRITISH ARMY
(DEMPSEY)

21ST ARMY GROUP

Sittard

Maastricht

"B"

C.-IN-C.
WEST
(VON RUNDSTEDT)

Louvain

BRUSSELS

Liège

Aachen

SEVENTH ARMY
(BRANDENBERGER)

Coblenz

Lille

Tournai

Mons

Namur

Meuse

FIRST U.S. ARMY
(HODGES)

Frankfurt

Cambrai

Maubeuge

BELGIUM

FRANCE

ARDENNES

Trier

Moselle

Guise

Oise

La Fère

Luxembourg

WEST WALL

Saar

Mannheim

Rheims

Marne

12TH
ARMY
GROUP
(BRADLEY)

Verdun

THIRD U.S. ARMY
(PATTON)

Metz

FIRST ARMY
(VON KNOBELSDORFF)

Saarbrücken

ARMY
GROUP
"G"
(BLASKOWITZ)

Troyes

Seine

Toul

Nancy

"G"

FIFTH
PANZER
ARMY
(VON MANTEUFFEL)

Strasbourg

Yonne

NINETEENTH ARMY
(WIESE)

Rhine

WEST WALL

6TH
ARMY
GROUP
(DEVERS)

SEVENTH U.S. ARMY
(PATCH)
WITH FRENCH ARMY "B"
(DE LATTRE)
TAKING OVER

Belfort

GERMANY

Dijon

Canal de Bourgogne

Dôle

Seine

FRANCE
SWITZERLAND

Basle

NETHERLANDS
GERMANY

Ijssel

0   50   100
MILES

'For Freedom and Life': German poster extolling the *Volkssturm*.

Feldmarschall Walter Model (1891–1945), a difficult adversary on the Western Front.

A *Volkssturm* unit prepares for battle. In civilian clothes and carrying various obsolescent and foreign weapons, they were the bottom of the Third Reich's manpower barrel.

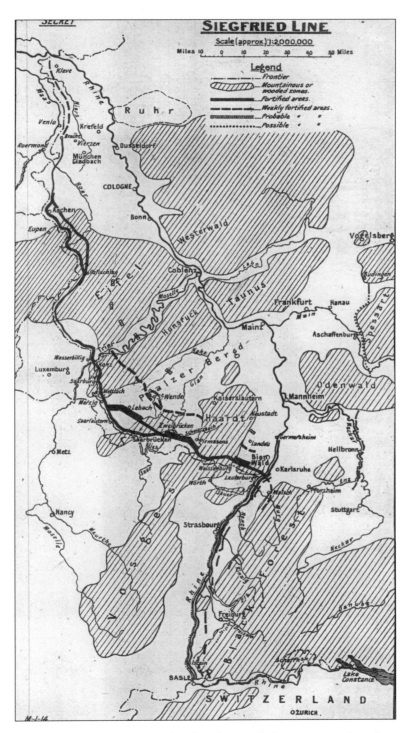

The Siegfried Line, 1944. This fortification belt, constructed in the late 1930s, still posed a difficult defensive work in late 1944.

'Front and Home Front – the Guarantors of Victory'. A German propaganda poster of the late war period. Following major defeats on all fronts, the late summer and autumn of 1944 saw an unprecedented mobilization of the German war effort.

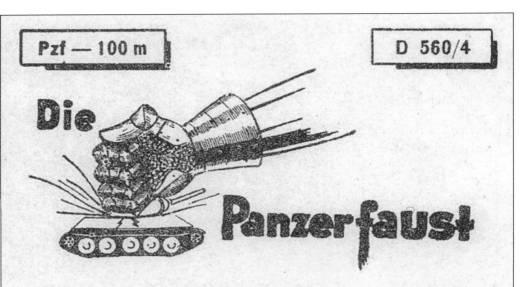

Die Panzerfaust

Die Panzerfaust ist **Deine** Pak! Du kannst mit ihr jeden Panzer bis auf Höchstentfernungen von 150 m abschießen. Je näher Du ihn aber herankommen läßt, um so sicherer erledigst Du ihn. Lies Dir dies Merkblatt richtig durch, dann kann Dir, wenn es darauf ankommt, nichts passieren.

Wie sieht die Panzerfaust - 100 m aus?

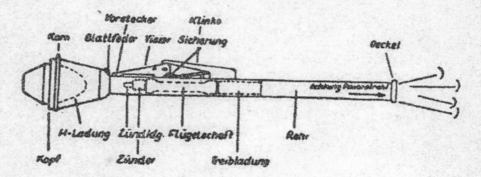

Der Kopf enthält eine H-Ladung, die jeden zur Zeit bekannten Feindpanzer durchschlägt, auch an der dicksten

Page from a manual for the *Panzerfaust*, the hollow-charge weapon that was deadly at close range to Allied armour. 'The *Panzerfaust* is your tank gun!' reads the first line of the text. These disposable weapons were manufactured by the hundreds of thousands in the last year of the war.

German paratrooper, 1944. The Wehrmacht units in Holland included a number of
nominally paratroop units consisting of personnel transferred from the air force
and built around a cadre of veterans like this man.

Above: Destroyed bridge over the Albert Canal, Belgium, 1944. The Germans made skilful use of demolitions to slow the Allied advance.

Right: Generaloberst Kurt Student (1891–1978). The father of the German airborne forces, Student was placed in command of the troops in Holland and proved to be a very wily and obstinate opponent.

Polderland. The polders were land in Holland reclaimed from the sea and the Germans flooded them, restricting the Allied advance routes as seen in this picture of Canadian armour moving along a dyke in October 1944.

Dismissed as C in C West by Hitler in June, *Feldmarschall* Gerd von Rundstedt (1875–1953) was brought back in September to stem the German collapse in the west.

Canadian armour advances east of the Scheldt. This Sherman Firefly of 4th Canadian Armoured Division is moving toward Bergen-op-Zoom in October 1944.

The first ship to enter Antwerp, November 1944. The campaign to clear the Scheldt and the approaches of Antwerp took weeks of brutal fighting and cost 10,000 casualties.

Above: Nijmegen Bridge, 1944. Captured by U.S. airborne forces during Operation MARKET-GARDEN, Field Marshal Montgomery's ill-fated attempt to secure a bridge over the Rhine.

Above left: Canadian armour knocked out in Holland. German resistance was variable but could be determined. These vehicles were destroyed at close range by *Panzerfausts*.

Left: Dead German, Holland 1944. Someone has removed the weapon from this corpse but his arms and hands have stiffened into the position in which it was held.

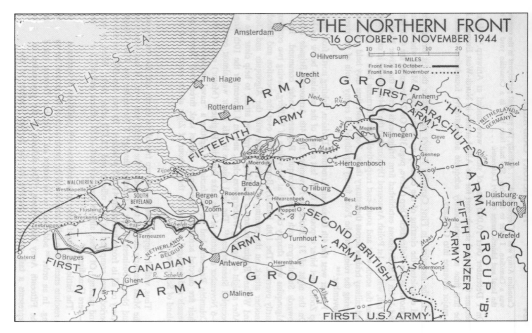

Northern Front, October–November 1944. Operation MARKET-GARDEN resulted in a lengthy salient that led nowhere. After heavy fighting, the Scheldt was cleared and the Germans in Holland pushed back to the line of the Maas.

German assault gun, 1944. Along the Western Front in the autumn of 1944, Allied troops commonly encountered more assault guns than tanks. Well armoured, with a low profile and a powerful gun, they were very good defensive weapons.

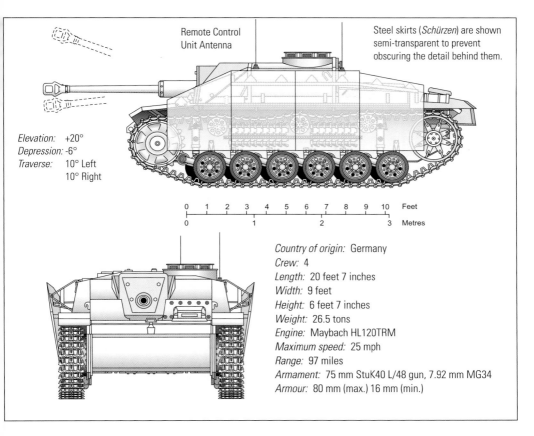

Remote Control
Unit Antenna

Steel skirts (*Schürzen*) are shown
semi-transparent to prevent
obscuring the detail behind them.

Elevation: +20°
Depression: -6°
Traverse: 10° Left
10° Right

0	1	2	3	4	5	6	7	8	9	10	Feet
0			1			2			3		Metres

Country of origin: Germany
Crew: 4
Length: 20 feet 7 inches
Width: 9 feet
Height: 6 feet 7 inches
Weight: 26.5 tons
Engine: Maybach HL120TRM
Maximum speed: 25 mph
Range: 97 miles
Armament: 75 mm StuK40 L/48 gun, 7.92 mm MG34
Armour: 80 mm (max.) 16 mm (min.)

The Sturmgeschütz III Ausf. G was the last in the line of German assault guns based on
the chassis of the PzKpfw III series. Originally developed as an assault gun for infantry
support, the Sturmgeschütz evolved into a dual-purpose assault gun and tank destroyer.
German tank production fell short of operational requirements as the war progressed
and the StuG III was often pressed into service to supplement the tanks in panzer
divisions. In contrast to American self-propelled tank destroyers equipping British and
Canadian units, the StuG III provided overhead protection for the crew, together with
a low silhouette. A shortcoming of the turretless design, though, was restricted traverse
for the main gun. The StuG III illustrated here has an additional antenna indicating
service in a *Funklenk* (remote control) company where it would be the control vehicle
for a *Sprengladungstraeger* demolition charge carrier.

Typhoon fighter-bombers, 1944. Armed with four 20 mm cannon
and eight 5-inch rockets, the Typhoon was perhaps the Allied
aircraft most feared by German ground troops in late 1944.

stay German. And this parasite dares to blow it out over the radios, 'Those are Americans and traitors to the Fatherland'. No, really, Peter, that we have to stand for that besides all the sacrifices, is that not too much? But enough of this.

17 October 1944[6]

To begin with, a sunny kiss on a rainy day. Well, this year you'll hardly have a hangover and thirst for water. Or does one still know what such a thing is. Well, I hardly believe so! At any rate, I've wished the best for you. Since last night hell has broken loose here again. Waffen SS have come in here again.

They're a bit rude, though, for this morning they had already awakened me by six o'clock sharp with machine gun clatter. That was really impolite, right? But, after all, they're Germans. Today I spoke with one who was a prisoner. He was inducted just two weeks ago from Hessen-Nassau. What a happy coincidence it would be if you should stand before me so unexpectedly. You know, if you were to set off a blank cartridge from the wood, the sound might not reach me. Man I would hug you. Then you would come jumping into the air overjoyed. I went to the house again today and got my personal radio set. It's a small French one. Just imagine, I just about rushed into a buried mine. An American saved my life. My dearest Peter, the more young SS men come in here, all the more yearning for you grows within me. Like the News Service reports, Ehenfeld Nippes Bayenthal is completely destroyed. The flames are licking up to the Rhine and escaped oil must be burning in the Rhine itself. Cologne, my Cologne. One's heart twists inside on hearing that. Now there's no point in going to my homeland it was consumed by flames. Our pride of Cologne, the cathedral. Peter, isn't there any justice any more which would make the culprits pay for such a deed. Our hearts cry out for reprisal. Where is it? Oh, Peter, why do I sit here in this battle so alone? Why can't you cheer me up? Couldn't you just whisper into my ear: I love you, and what about you? I would roar out loud, I too. Listen, sweetheart, do you sense my thoughts?

At noon today I had a frightful scene with my brother. Well, it's all past. Of course you could help me. Wouldn't you? Night is creeping on and it's getting dusky. Now I'm going to the conference. Yesterday one of 'our group' learned that Hitler Youth Leaders had to go to France to do debris-clearing work. Let's wait and see. Before I go there, Man I would go AWOL. If I only knew where you were. I would come this very day. But now, my

---

6. The remainder of the Berganz diary is from ISUM 203, 21 January 1945.

love, I've got to part from you and with best wishes and a heartfelt good-night kiss, I remain

19 October 1944

What do you have to say now about the German People's Army? Here they call it a crime and wholesale murder. In any case, this, in my opinion, is a sign that we have no new weapons. Peter, it wrings one's heart just to think that our Youths have, all through these years, brought about these enormous accomplishments and sacrifices in vain. It can't be. What would become of us, the Youth, then. Peter, when will I see you again.

Just imagine, behind our house on the hill are SS Hitler Youth. How easily I could get a sign of life to you through these buddies. If I only knew your location. Writing to Cologne seems to me almost useless. Seven terror raids in five days. These pigs. Please excuse the harsh expression, but it comes from the heart. All week long German reconnaissance patrols were in the streets of Monschau night after night. You can surely picture the crash. Then through the day all the tanks fired aimlessly into the hills. Let's hope our house doesn't get another direct hit. We have enough without that. You know, Peter, I long most of all for you, but also for energetic work again. What I've almost never done before, but am doing now, I'm knitting socks. What one doesn't do to make time go by. The night is also so long. At 6.30 PM, the American curfew starts. That's pretty early, isn't it.

A German heavy machine gun just began to hammer again. You know, it's exactly like it was mentioned in yesterday's 'Mirror of Time', fighting in the Eiffel woods is very tough. The American comes, and then just gets no farther. If our soldiers had the stuff that is at the disposition of these weaklings, they would fly into a high arc to America. They're not soldiers. Jitterbugs (like you, dear, but a thousand times worse) and Tango lovers, but to fight and advance, those are foreign words to those guys. Let's hope they still get a good thrashing.

Peter, when I think of our time together in Monschau, I can't conceive that this wonderful period has to be over so quickly. Where is humanity's consideration. They have no pity for two creatures. But what am I saying. We don't want any pity. To live means to fight. In this sense, my dear and best chum, I believe in our having a 'happy reunion again'. This belief and strength of will besides, will help me to overcome the hours of vacillating and despair. Peter, it's terrible when, in such hard times, you don't have a soul who really understands you. I can't and will not change. I'm not a weather vane. I'm still what I was and will always stay the same. Being German means to be faithful, and I'll remain faithful to my last work and purpose. My children will also be brought up on that principle. I swear it at this very moment. Now I must close, for our conversation conference begins in five minutes. I join fondest greetings to a soft 'Goodbye' and kiss you with all my heart.

Having skipped Saturday, I make use of this rainy Sunday morning to write you, merriest of chums ... Today the announcer of *Soldatensender* said so clearly: 'Keep your ears open'. You surely know my favourite saying. Head high, even if your neck is dirty. Yes, Peter, you and these sayings help me to endure the awful disappointments which I'm obliged to experience. Dearest, why can't we be German any more. Three loyal ones are still in Monschau. Isn't that terrible? The youth demoralized. American cigarettes are put into the hands of 15-year-olds and often still younger boys, and they are taught to smoke. On Sundays all the young people sit in a group and smoke. Moreover, the Americans help them do it. Peter, doesn't your heart just twist inside you? I hope you'll be spared this sight.

Where is our ideal, the customary morale of the German youth? Peter, will all our efforts and striving have been in vain? No, it can't be! We, the faithful ones fight on. Our work gradually serves to show us new tasks. Peter, if you were only here. But I know, you are in the place where they've put you to do your work exactly as we here in the occupied territory. I can't give you a more detailed report of our work because ...

Imagine, yesterday we had permission to go to the house to get food. As I was coming to the hill, there where the road goes down to the Public School, I met our former Squad Leader and a co-worker of the District Administration office with two Americans. They simply took her away from her little child and drove off with her. She was also very loyal, however didn't take part with us on account of her child. They want her to tell where the District Administrative Official and all the others have gone. But she will never do that, nor because of her child either. Perhaps my turn will come then. You know what I'll say: that he's gone to Aachen, that he can be recognized by his two legs that are gone. I lied, but that makes no difference. From Monschau they took away several more, besides. Where to? I've got to come to the end gradually, for it's getting towards twelve o'clock and my 'old lady' might come storming through the door at any moment and then my note pad would doubtless be sacrificed to the flames. That would really be a shame, wouldn't it?

Wishing you a very good appetite, rather a good Sunday dinner, I take leave of you. All the very best and with tenderest greetings and an intimate kiss, I keep hoping to see you again.

Document 4/3[7]

A Race-conscious Nazified Girl

An Aachen school teacher once told us that the young students in his school fell into two categories – *'verkränkelt'* (sickly, infected) and the *'vergiftet'* (poisoned) with Hitlerism. The majority, he said, are merely *'verkränkelt'* and can be redeemed with some effort.

Trude Steinbusch, 17, a Würselen student, belonged in the category of the *'verkränkelt'*. The daughter of a locomotive engineer, she considers herself one degree higher than the working class and displays the symptoms of a petty bourgeois. If Germany had won the war, and if Würselen were not a solid proletarian community, Trude Steinbusch would certainly have grown into a fully-fledged Nazi. As it is, she can probably be deflected into another course.

She joined the BDM when she was 10 and enjoyed the frequent meetings, especially the sports (she likes swimming, track, tennis). Once a week she met with her *Schaar*[8] of 10 girls and they discussed politics. Trude was bored with that. The *Führerin*,[9] she said, talked politics *'bis zur Verasung'* (to the point of asphyxiation). Political lectures were in the form of a catechism. The *Führerin* asked, 'What did the Führer do for Germany?' The girls replied: 'The Führer abolished unemployment. He built roads. He constructed factories. He made cities flourish.' Trude was cynical as she told us about it. 'It's all *quatsch* (nonsense),' she said with a grin.

Trude's friends at school were enthusiastic for the war. She was enthusiastic too. They basked in the glory and in the conquest of the world by the mighty Wehrmacht. The young boys, she said used to boast: 'Wait till we join the Wehrmacht – then it'll be over quickly, we'll show them.'

Her father, the locomotive engineer, served in Russia where he was wounded, and when he came home he cursed the campaign, cursed the war. 'Our soldiers,' he said, 'had to fight against tremendous odds. The war is lost.' Trude did not believe what her embittered father said. Only now does Trude realize that the war is lost and she thinks, quite cheerfully, that she was *'belogen'* (lied to). Asked in what sense she thought herself

---

7. ISUM 233, 18 February 1945, from 12 Army Group.
8. A unit of organization in the BDM equivalent to a section or squad.
9. The *Schaarführerin* or squad leader in the BDM.

'*belogen*,' she said: 'Take, for example, V-1; Goebbels lied about that. He said to us that the enemy will beg us on his knees to give him peace. The V-1 will force the enemy to his knees. And what happened? When we heard of the V-1 we hoped for victory, and in the end nothing came of it. Thus we were lied to.'

Up to 1943, at least three-fourths of the youth of her acquaintance were Nazi. Now most of them have 'melted away.' The realization of defeat undermined their patriotism. 'Losing the war,' Trude said, 'meant losing also our *Vaterlandsliebe*' (love of fatherland).

We asked her to define what in her opinion constituted a young Nazi. She described him as (1) a person who believes everything the government says, (2) believes in victory, (3) says Heil Hitler, (4) is *Gottgläubig*,[10] and (5) goes to party meetings Sunday morning during mass time.

In her disappointment at Germany's losing the war, Trude has turned against everything that is openly Nazi. Asked if she would marry a Nazi, she exclaimed: 'For God's sake, no.' Would she marry a Frenchman or a Russian? Her answer was an equally vehement No. 'Everybody knows that they are so crude.' This led her to discourse on the subject of race, which, it turned out, was her favourite study.

Germans, she explained, must marry only Germans. 'It is not right to marry a non-German'. She might marry an American because 'most Americans are of German race'. When we hinted that the German race is mixed, she denied it indignantly. She could not answer what race Goebbels and Hitler belonged to. All she knew was that the Nordic race, to which the Germans (and she too: she is big and heavy) belonged, was the superior, the most valuable. A Nordic, she defined as if memorizing the whole sentence, is 1.70 meters high, big, has grey-blue eyes, and is earnest. Originally these Nordics, 'the best racial and spiritual type', were members of the SS. The Nordic SS were the ideal males of girls like Trude Steinbusch.

Who were the lower races? Russians, Poles, Italians, French, Jews, she said. The French are inferior because 'they are small, temperamental, excitable (*hitzig*), and changeable'. The Italians are also 'temperamental and changeable'. German soldiers in France and Italy were forbidden to have any contact with the women of those countries, Trude told us with some pride. Of Jews, Trude said that there were 'many intelligent ones among

10. *Gottgläubig* (believer in God) was a rather amorphous term used by the Nazi Party to denote those who had officially left the Christian religions but still believed in a supreme being. Most senior party leaders and many of the rank and file were officially designated as *Gottgläubig*.

them', but that they weren't perhaps good for Germany. Still she thought that since the German race was made up of six (Nordic) racial tribes, she saw no reason why there should not have been a seventh race, the Jewish.

Among Nazi youth, especially between the ages of 16 to 18, Trude told us, about half had close relationships with the opposite sex. This was particularly true of the little *Führers* and *Führerinnen* who 'harmonized together'.

Trude said that she likes to read books, mainly love stories about the gentry. She also claimed to be a student of history and we asked her what she knew of Germany's past. Her knowledge was not extensive. Of the Republic she knew nothing. In this connection she mentioned 'Bismarck, who wanted to solve the German question'. Wilhelm II? 'He was a cowardly fighter; he ran away.'

We wanted to know how the present war came about and Trude explained that it began with Poland. 'The Poles mistreated Germans. The German government would not stand for it and sent in German soldiers. This was the right thing to do, but Hitler should have made an end with the war after he took the corridor.' Then Germany had to fight France because the latter had an alliance with Poland. 'As for Russia, we had to go to war with the Soviets because they began to transport troops and munitions, so we went there first.'

How did Germany get involved in war with America? Trude said she heard Hitler's declaration of war on the US and she told a friend: 'This is stupid (*'blödsinn'*). America is too big and produces too much.' But her friend laughed at her.

Trude expects Germany to be divided up among the powers, the left bank of the Rhine to go to France and England, and the right bank to be taken over by Italy, Poland, Czechoslovakia and Austria. Then she said, 'everything will be over with race and fatherland, and their heroes' – and Trude's too – 'will be Charlemagne, Frederick the Great, and Bismarck.' Did she not count Hitler among the heroes? No, she said. 'If Hitler were really a great man, he would make an end of this war.'

Maybe, Trude thought, Communism would come to Germany. What is Communism? 'It is against Nazism. Communists say that wherever you're well off, there is your fatherland.' I think that's true. This was said by Jew Marx. He incited the workers, which wasn't so good. Am I a communist? Now everybody wants to be a communist. I personally would like to see a government like we had before 1918, a government with a Kaiser at the head of it, and not an ordinary man of the people (like Hitler).'

Trude's mind is thus a portrait of monumental confusion – at the same time a Nazi, and anti-Nazi, an anti-Semite, a Communist, a monarchist, and a snob.

She is also a good ping-pong player.

Document 4/4[11]

Roetgen – Six Weeks after US Occupation

Roetgen, Germany, 15 miles south of Aachen, was occupied by troops of the First US Army on 10 September 1944. The normal population of 2400 has been slightly increased in recent weeks by the influx of refugees from Aachen. Although Roetgen is partly agricultural, many of the town's inhabitants work in nearby weaving establishments. The town is predominantly Catholic. The following survey made on 24–26 October describes the attitude of the people of Roetgen after six weeks of American occupation. Although the interrogators talked with scores of people, 30 men and women of all age and income groups were the main source of information. This included the Evangelical and Catholic clergymen, a store keeper, the director of the local branch of the district savings bank and a school teacher.

(a) Attitude Towards American Occupation

The people are unanimous in expressing their admiration for the correct behaviour of our troops. No one, not even former party members, looks upon us as an enemy. Many call us 'liberators' from Hitler tyranny. There have been no incidents between the inhabitants and American troops. Our administration and the regulations promulgated are praised for their correctness and justice.

The people have one fear: that some day we will move on and that Belgian or French troops would occupy the land.

---

11. ISUM 122, 30 October 1944, from *First US Army G-2 Report*, 29 October 1944.

(b)   Attitude Towards German Government and Continued Resistance

The people are unanimous in their condemnation of Hitler and his policy of continuing a 'lost war'. Former members of the Party cry loudest in their accusations against the 'Führer'. All former Party members always claim that they had been forced to join the Party, that they would have lost their job or would have got into grave difficulties if they had not joined up.

Hitler is generally held responsible for the war. A majority of people do not condemn Hitler for starting the war as such, but only for starting something which he apparently cannot bring to a successful conclusion.

Chapter 5

Formation and Unit
Organization and History

Editor's Comments

The near-collapse of the Wehrmacht in France and the frantic German efforts to build and rebuild, organize and re-organize formations and units caused much head-scratching among Allied intelligence officers who were forced to deal with a bewildering variety of organizations. They quickly amassed information on the new 'panzer brigades', which were largely the remnants of German armoured divisions destroyed on the Russian front (Document 5/1) and catalogued information on the state of the elite parachute divisions (Document 5/2), the Hermann Goering Training Regiment (Document 5/3) and the Flying Bomb Regiment (Document 5/4). Intelligence officers were dismissive of such units as the 279th Magen (Stomach) Battalion (Document 5/5) and confidently wrote off the 3rd Parachute Division (Document 5/6). As it turned out, the Wehrmacht displayed a remarkable resilience and the 3rd Parachute Division was resurrected in time to cause much trouble during the Ardennes offensive.

Document 5/1[1]

Organization of the 107th Panzer Brigade, September 1944

Wartime Intelligence Officer's Comments

The detailed interrogation of twenty PW from 107th Panzer Brigade corrects and expands the information previously given and published in Summary Number 88. PW who were all captured on 24–25 September were described as being above average in physique and intelligence.

General organisation of the brigade was given as:

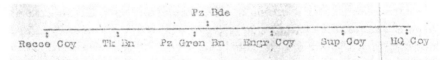

The Supply Company is under Brigade control and not part of the Panzer Grenadier Battalion. There is no Signals Company but a Signals Platoon in HQ Company. There is no Medical Company as such, as previously reported. Each company in the brigade has one SPW ambulance and there is a Medical Section in HQ Company. The Reconnaissance Company which did not appear in the last organisation given us is not an integral part of the brigade but consists of the remnants of Battle Group Heinke.

2017 Panzer Battalion

The organization is as shown previously except that 4 Coy is equipped NOT with Pz Kw IV with long 7.5 cm, but with 7.5 cm long assault guns on Pz Kw IV chassis. In each company HQ there are two AFVs, NOT one. Total strength is therefore 33 Panthers and 11 Assault Guns.

2017 Panzer Grenadier Battalion

The amended organisation is as follows:

---

1. ISUM 94, 5 October 1944, from *Second Army Intelligence Summary* 118, 30 September 1944.

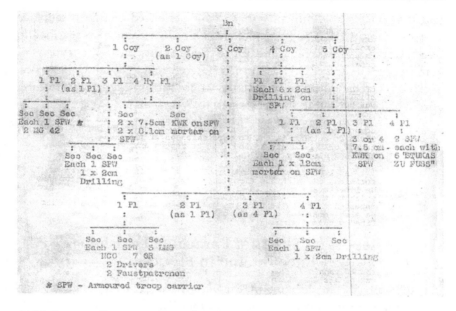

2107 Panzer Engineer Battalion

This consisted of Company Headquarters and three platoons. Each platoon had three sections, each with an NCO and 8 men. 2 SPW and 1 reserve SPW, two MG 42 per vehicle, 1 magnetic charge per vehicle, 3 Tellermines per vehicle and about 6 S-Mines on the reserve vehicle. There was no proper bridging equipment but sufficient timber was carried in each platoon to build a light auxiliary bridge (9 tons).

Recce Company

As stated above this was not an integral part of the brigade and not part of the original organisation. It consisted of the remnants of Battle Group Heinke (10 SS Pz Division personnel) and had two platoons of three sections, equipped with bicycles and one LMG per section. On 24 September the company strength was reduced to approximately 30 and all the bicycles had been destroyed or stolen. They were then employed as ordinary infantry.

Further details of the formation of the brigade were that it started 17 July at Mochove near Mielau in southern East Prussia. The brigade was to be ready for action by 15 September and on that date the training programme was completed and it left Mochove. PW stated that training was less complete than had been intended owing to the late arrival of equipment and the considerable difficulty that was experienced owing to sabotage of equipment, particularly the adulteration of lubricants, was ascribed to Czech workers. Personnel of the brigade were almost entirely survivors of 25th Panzer Grenadier Division which suffered heavy casualties in Russia.

The replacement unit was given as 215th Panzer Grenadier Training and Replacement Battalion, Reutlingen in *Wehrkreis* V.[2]

Document 5/2[3]

Report on Status of Parachute Divisions Encountered in France

The following is an account of the Parachute divisions engaged this summer in France. Only fragments of the four Parachute divisions actually identified, now remain.

2nd Parachute Division

2nd Parachute Division was of course mostly destroyed at Brest, but some detached elements are still to be found, the chief being 6th Parachute Regiment. 6th Parachute Regiment had long been detached from the division and fought independently throughout the French campaign. It was largely destroyed in Normandy but has reappeared in action in Holland, sometimes under the name of its original commander, von der Heydte,[4] sometimes as Parachute Regiment Hoffman.

Other units of 2nd Parachute Division avoided being caught in Brest, because they were still forming in eastern France and never went to Brittany. Thus 2nd Parachute Artillery Regiment, having been completely destroyed on the Russian front, was reformed entirely afresh at Luneville at the beginning of July. By the middle of the month 1st and 2nd Battalions were complete, and a PW states that they were sent back to the eastern

---

2. Military District V. The German army was raised on a regional basis, each district providing replacement, reinforcement and training for distinct formations and units. *Wehrkreis* V encompassed Württemberg, part of Baden and Alsace, and had its headquarters in Stuttgart.
3. ISUM 101, 11 October 1944, from *21 Army Group Intelligence Summary*.
4. *Oberstleutnant* Friedrich *Freiherr* von der Heydte (1907–94), commander of the 6th Parachute Regiment.

front. 3rd Battalion and the headquarters troops were not ready until later, and they joined 6th Parachute Division in Paris early in August.

2nd Parachute Anti-tank Battalion is also said to have been formed in August and has appeared with 6th Parachute Division. It has apparently from the first had some intimate connection with 6th Parachute Anti-tank Battalion; and a PW says, though the story sounds unlikely, that both 2nd and 6th Parachute Anti-tank Battalions were formed only to train parachutists in the handling of close combat and anti-tank weapons, after which they were to return to their units. He further says that a 2nd Parachute Anti-tank Battalion had guns, the others being armed with bazookas. The whole story sounds like a false rationalisation of something that happened in the confusion of August.

3rd Parachute Division

3rd Parachute Division has not been identified anywhere in the present phase of operations. After being continuously in the line from early in June until the final collapse of Seventh Army in Normandy it had been reduced to almost nothing; and though its tradition would certainly warrant its being reformed, there is no evidence that it ever has been so.

5th Parachute Division

5th Parachute Division has preserved more continuity than the others. It made a shaky start in Normandy, being committed piecemeal in the vain attempt to stem First US Army's breakthrough from St Lo to Avranches; but somehow preserved its identity during the retreat, and has been holding a sector on the left of Seventh Army north of Trier, where it is still engaged. This is surprising, for at one time it looked as though remnants were far more likely to be incorporated in 3rd Parachute Division.

6th Parachute Division

6th Parachute Division is the ugly duckling of General Student's[5] command. While the battle was going on in Normandy it was still forming on the Somme, and the first of its three rifle regiments (Parachute Regiment 16) was taken from it in the June crisis on the northern Russian front to be consumed at Bialystok. The rest of the division was moved down in August to cover the western approaches to Paris; and from there retreated to

---

5. *Generalleutnant* Kurt Student (1890–1978) was the father of the German parachute corps. He planned and commanded the airborne landings in Holland and Belgium in 1940 and on Crete in 1941. In the autumn of 1944 he was appointed commander of the First Parachute Army, composed of various Luftwaffe and paratroop units and assigned the defence of Holland.

Belgium and was one of the formations caught by the Americans at Mons. Its headquarters was identified from a document found behind the Albert Canal about 7 September; and some other units have been identified: e.g. 6th Parachute Anti-tank Battalion (see 2nd Parachute Division above), and 2nd Company of 6th Parachute Engineer Battalion, formed at Joigny in June 1944 with four companies each initially 200 strong. Two PW captured south of Mons on 3 September stated that the division comprised an Anti-tank Battalion, an Engineer Battalion, a Signals Battalion, 6th Parachute Artillery Regiment, a Projector Battalion attached from First Parachute Army, a *Feldersatz* Battalion and an *Einheit* Reiter, consisting of stragglers from other parachute units. It seems that the Field Replacement Battalion absorbed the output of a training school for NCO candidates at Nancy in May. 95 per cent of them are jumpers, and it should be a better unit than the name suggests. Reiter's Battalion was formed at Melun in mid-June from remnants at that time to hand, of 3rd, 5th and perhaps other parachute divisions, and consisted of four companies each of 100 men without heavy weapons. The whole of first company and Reiter himself are believed to have been captured. *Feldjagerregimente* 17 and 18 have never materialised at the front; instead the division had for infantry, besides the Field Ersatz Battalion and Battalion Reiter, Parachute Lehr Regiment attached from First Parachute Army. As for artillery, one PW says that all three battalions of 4th Parachute Artillery Regiment, also formed at Luneville in June 1944, were attached to 6th Parachute Division. It is not plain whether this is the same as 6th Parachute Artillery Regiment or not.

Its main infantry constituent would seem therefore to be the Hermann Parachute Lehr Regiment, which includes Battalion Lorenz. Prisoners state that this regiment started forming in Italy in March 1944, was sent to Nevers and then on 12 June to the mouth of the Somme and finally to Abbeville, where it was incorporated in 65 Parachute Division. About half the men have had jumping training. Hermann had a battalion in Crete which afterwards became a Lehr or experimental battalion. It fought in Cyrenaica late in 1941 and again in the summer of 1942, and was later employed as an instructional unit and made films of parachute jumps. In the winter of 1942-1943 it was at Döberitz, and in the spring of 1943 transferred to Orange. It was one of the units that took part in the rescue of Mussolini from the Gran Sasso. A second battalion of the Parachute Lehr Regiment distinguished itself, according to a newspaper cutting, at Nettuno at the beginning of April. At Nevers the regiment received assorted drafts of lower grade men, clerks, etc., who had 'volunteered' for combat duty. Hermann, now Lieut-Colonel, has been the commander throughout.

The present location of 6th Parachute Division is obscure. It is evidently not the same as Parachute Division Erdmann, on the Second Army front; and as a division is nowhere identified on the front. Hermann's regiment was identified on 3 October at Groesbeek, on the front controlled by 84th Division, and it seems likely therefore that 6th Parachute Division has been withdrawn, leaving Hermann to provide much needed strength for 84th Division, otherwise a skeleton.

Other Parachute Divisions

The *fin de siècle* character of 6th Parachute Division, which obviously has never taken proper shape at all, blunts the edge of any stories of a 7th and 8th Parachute Division; and when PW state the 7th and 8th are forming in Germany, and should be complete in the near future, they need not cause alarm. If we are to believe all we are told, General Student envisages an ultimate empire of no less than twenty parachute divisions. The intention to form 7th and 8th Divisions is probably genuine enough. The numbering system adopted for ancillary units or Corps and Army seems to be a pledge that the Luftwaffe at least does not look beyond.

Document 5/3[6]

Hermann Goering Reserve and Training Regiment

This regiment, originally intended to supply replacements for the Hermann Goering Panzer Division, has long been located in various parts of Holland and is now participating in the general withdrawal towards the Maas River. It was last identified between Roosendaal and Bergen Op Zoom on 28 October, when the order of the day was '*sauve qui peut*', which four PW, recently interrogated, complied with by giving themselves up to Canadian troops.

---

6. ISUM 124, 1 November 1944.

History

Designed to maintain Hermann Goering units in the field, the regiment's history shows a slow expansion proportionate to and coincidental with that of the Flak Regiment 'Hermann Goering'. This unit, originally the elite Flak Regiment in Berlin in 1938, became a brigade in 1942 and later expanded to divisional size, after being badly mauled in an anti-tank role in Africa. It fought as a division in Italy until early 1944 when it was sent to the Warsaw area.

During its training phase, the reinforcement regiment appears to have adhered to the normal organization of depot, convalescent and *marsch* companies. Coastal defence duties occupied its three battalions until mid-September, when the threatening Allied advance forced front-line employment upon every *ersatz* unit the Wehrmacht could lay its hands on. In the early part of September, elements of all three battalions were despatched to Ruppin, West Prussia, to form part of the new Hermann Goering Parachute Reserve and Training brigade. The elevation of this reinforcement unit to brigade status is accounted for, according to PW, by the redesignation as a Parachute Panzer Corps of the Hermann Goering Parachute Panzer Division.

As for the title 'para' which Hermann Goering units both active and reinforcement have assimilated along the way, PW are inclined to regard it as a propaganda device to induce enthusiasm of young recruits. Personnel have not received training for function with paratroops, or in weapons suitable for air-landing attack. The only tangible reason for the use of the term 'para' appears to be the fact that the former commander of the Hermann Goering Division. Lieutenant-General Conrath,[7] has been made Inspector of Parachute Troops, while one unit officer is alleged to have stated that the newly formed Corps has been placed under command of the German Parachute Army.

When first committed, the regiment was intended to remain in the west only until 27 September, on which date it was to be withdrawn, regrouped and sent to West Prussia to join the new reinforcement unit. The September fashion being, however, to retain every man and his dog in the west, the unit remained in western Holland, moving to the Bergen Op Zoom-Roosendaal sector at the end of September.

---

7. *General der Fallschirmtruppe* Paul Conrath (1896–1979), commander of the Hermann Goering Panzer Division in Italy.

Personnel

The unit consists entirely of young recruits and young servicemen transferred in 1942-43 from Luftwaffe ground personnel. All are between 17-21 years of age, and all men transferred as above from the Luftwaffe have signed a document certifying that they have done so voluntarily. One PW has had the choice of retraining as infantry for the Russian front or volunteering for the Hermann Goering Division. At the time of its formation in 1938, the Flak Regiment required a high standard of physique and athletic prowess. These conditions of entry have long since been relaxed, but nevertheless PW from this unit are of a better type than those encountered in regular army units. About 10-20% of II Battalion were Austrians, largely former Luftwaffe personnel, the rest all pure Germans. Morale, particularly among the Austrians, was only fair, as a result of the rough handling the regiment had received.

Training

Probably less than half the officers and NCOs have previous experience at the front, and the rest are all experienced instructors. The latest recruits were called up in July 1944 and have received only basic training for four or five weeks. PW were unanimous that no personnel of the unit had received parachute training.

Organization

The regiment got its baptism of fire about 14 September in the Turnhout-Riel sector in Belgium. At the time it was committed, it contained four battalions, organized as follows:

I Battalion

HQ Company and four rifle companies, each of four or five platoons, each of three sections. Last platoon in each company is a heavy platoon with 2 x SMG (34 & 42) and 2 x 8 cm mortars. Light platoons were equipped with 2 x LMG (34, 15 or 42) per section and rifles (98 K) with 2–3 Panzerfausts per company.

II Battalion

HQ Company, four rifle companies organized as in I Battalion and four special companies. 8 and 9 Companies were of tank personnel, 10 Company (Assault guns), 11 Company (anti-tank) and 12 Company (armoured reconnaissance). There were no Panthers or Tigers in 8 and 9 Companies, probably only Mark IVs. Nothing is known of 12 Company.

III Battalion
Contains 12, 14 and 15 (possibly 16) Troops. 13 Troop has 8.8 cm and 2 cm flak guns. 14 Troop is equipped with 2 x 10.5 cm LFH (18) and 2 x 15 cm SFH (18). All guns are mobile and tractor drawn. 15 Troop is a heavy troop, believed to contain only 15 cm SFH (18).

IV Battalion
Motor Transport Battalion – located in Berlin and responsible for training all types of drivers for the Hermann Goering Panzer Corps.

20th Signals Reinforcement and Training Company
A separate company training signals personnel for all arms represented in Hermann Goering Corps.

The present allotment finds I and III Battalions under command of Battle Group Dreier. A percentage of II Battalion was sent back to Germany, the remainder being committed under Battle Group Ohler. All personnel except those of III Battalion have been committed as infantry and losses have been heavy, both in weapons and personnel.

Document 5/4[8]

Organization and History of the Flying Bomb Regiment

The organization and history of *Flakgruppe* Creil (attached 65th Corps), said to be the only V-1 regiment in the German armed forces, have been given in some detail by a reliable Polish deserter.

(i) History and Personnel
Formation of the regiment commenced near Königsburg in November 1943. For periods varying from one to three months, drafts of men drawn exclusively from the Luftwaffe (flak, air signals, or flying personnel) received preliminary training prior to being sent to France. The chief prerequisite for service was some previous experience in metal work. State of health was apparently of little or no importance as several men accepted

---

8. ISUM 87, 25 September 1944.

into the regiment were capable, for medical reasons, of only limited service. Strangely enough, no exception was taken to the employment of foreigners, approximately 250 being included in the original draft of personnel. Of this number, however, the Alsatians and Italians were later withdrawn. The unit was known as Flak Regiment 155W until January 1944, at which time it became *Flakgruppe* Creil (after Colonel Creil,[9] who commands the regiment).

(ii) Organization

The regiment contains five battalions, each 150-160 strong. Four of these function as firing battalions and the fifth as a signals battalion. Four V-1 batteries and two supply batteries comprise a firing battalion. The firing element of the regiment is thus 16 batteries. These are maintained by 8 supply batteries, each with a strength of 200 men and numbered from 17-24, 17 and 18 serving I Battalion, 19 and 20 II Battalion, and so on. Originally the personnel of each firing battery was so organized that four flying bombs could be launched simultaneously. At present, however, only two crews are available for each battery, and consequently, although four catapults (*Schleuder*) are still carried, no more than two bombs can be despatched at the same time. The signals battalion is split up and its sections sub-allotted to the firing battalion. The code names *Zylinder*, *Werwolf*, *Zwiebach*, *Zeghine* and *Ballette* were used by the five battalions respectively, while the firing batteries used the code name of their parent battalion, adding their battery number. Supply batteries added Number 5 or Number 6.

(iii) Locations

Moves from the training area near Königsburg took place between December 1943 and February 1944, I Battalion going to the Calais-St Omer area, II Battalion to Amiens-Abbeville, III Battalion to Neufchatel-Rouen, and IV Battalion first to the Valognes area in the Cotentin Peninsula and subsequently to the Buchy area, north of Rouen. In these areas, they remained, according to PW, until the Allied advance made their positions untenable. In the withdrawal, firing battery 15 (IV Battalion) blew up its equipment on being overtaken in Maastricht by US armoured columns. In addition, 23 and 24 (supply) batteries are believed to have been at least partially intercepted, but the majority of the regiment presumably made a successful getaway. Their destination is by no means clearly established

---

9. More likely, the name comes from the town of Creil in France, which the unit was stationed near.

but PW thought it likely to be either northern Holland where 65 Corps is believed to be located and where V-1 sites are said to have been prepared, or, possibly, Germany. In this connection, PW, who belonged to 23 (Supply) battery, had been told by his company commander that new V-1 positions had been prepared in the area from Antwerp to Bochum and that the supply batteries would follow the firing batteries to the new locations.

(iv)   General Notes

(a) Experimental firing of V-1 took place near Warnemunde.

(b) The main bomb supply depots were in underground caves at St Leu near Creil, north of Paris, and at Nonancourt, northwest of Paris. In the last month of operation the supply of bombs, originally drawn from the caves mentioned above, had been brought in by rail.

(c) Maximum range of the flying bomb was stated to be 350 km or 225 miles. The bomb is launched now from collapsible catapults which take only a few days to mount in any convenient location. To 'ready' the flying bomb for firing is a process requiring 45 minutes. The catapults, which use compressed air when in operation, consist of 6 (or perhaps 8) parts, two of which require one railroad car for transportation.

The 'Argus Rohr' pipe,[10] said to be a French invention, is used to operate V-1 by the employment of alcohol (or gasoline) as a propellant.

(d) One supply battery is supposed to have 24 Hanomag prime movers and 48 trailers. Each trailer can carry two flying bombs, but losses in both prime movers and trailers have been high recently as a result of Allied bombing.

(e) The last V-1 to be fired in France was launched by 2 Battery in the vicinity of St Omer on 30 August. Orders were then received to blow up ammunition and withdraw. The suggestion that flying bombs were purposely directed on Paris was emphatically denied by PW, who insisted that any such change of direction was purely unintentional.

(f) Apart from having been told that V-2 would be an enlarged version of V-1 and that personnel would be drawn from army rather than Luftwaffe channels, PW had little to offer on the potentialities of Hitler's second forlorn hope.

---

10. Actually a pulse jet engine.

Document 5/5[11]

History of the 279 *Magen* (Stomach) Battalion

The extent to which low category troops are being used to reinforce the enemy divisions in the west is well illustrated by the story of two Polish deserters from 857th Grenadier Regiment of 346th Infantry Division. The main significance lies in the fact that drafts of troops with stomach ailments are being hurriedly rushed from training and convalescent areas in an attempt to contain Allied progress on the western front. A number of these units consisting mainly of '*Magen*' personnel, have been identified on the First Canadian Army front during the past week, over and above those hailing from the 'Whitebread' ranks of 70th Infantry Division.

The original unit of these two PW was 279th *(Magen) Ersatz und Ausbildungs Bataillon* which was stationed at Eschwege. This unit was composed of the three companies (Depot, Training and Convalescent), which generally comprise a battalion of this kind. Company strengths on 1 October were as follows:

Depot Company:	500 men of which 250 (all '*Magen*' personnel) left on 1 October
Training Company:	500 men (75% '*Magen*' personnel) all aged over 35
Convalescent Company:	Approximately 150 men

During the preceding few months, personnel of these companies underwent a fairly thorough training course in field manoeuvres, weapons and (particularly since August 1944), gas. According to the PW, it has been stated by the instructional cadre that use of gas by the Allies was a possibility. No new methods were introduced, or new type of equipment employed, but gas training was taken much more seriously than before and the instruction given was more detailed and rigid.

On 1 October a draft of 250 men, all of them suffering from some kind of stomach ailment, were formed into a *marsch* company and herded into six freight cars for the move to the front. Like so many reinforcement drafts, they had no inkling of their destination, and even now it is by no means easy to establish their route. The journey appears, however, to have carried them from Eschwege through Dortmund, Bochum, Essen, Duisberg,

11. ISUM 115, 23 October 1944.

Zutphen, Apeldoorn, Utrecht and Zundert. Most of this was achieved by train, although PW had a hazy recollection of a lorry journey somewhere in Holland, and of some distance travelled on foot. It was ten days, from the time of leaving Eschwege, before they reached Zundert, where they rested for two days prior to going to their unit in the line. During the journey, several detours had to be made to circumvent damaged rail centres, and no attempt was made to travel by day due to the threat of our air attacks. According to one PW, the men hid out in wooded areas during the daytime, and occasionally obtained food from local resources. As a result of one of these foraging expeditions, forty men missed the train, and in the course of the trip about fifty more fell ill and had to be left behind. A Regimental Sergeant Major and three men were killed in a bombing attack at Rheine and of the original 250, only 160 finally reached the dispersal area.

On 12 October, after two days' rest at Zundert, the company marched to a village near Calmpthout. There they were split up into groups. PW finding themselves surprisingly quickly in the front line (as part of 7 Company, 857th Grenadier Regiment) where they stayed for about a week before gratefully accepting an opportunity to desert.

Document 5/6[12]

In Memoriam: 3rd Parachute Division

Somewhere in American PW camps, and even to a greater extent, under the fertile French soil, rests one of the best, if not *the* best German division so far encountered on the western front – the 3rd Parachute Division.

The 3rd Parachute Division was organized in February 1944 on the Brittany peninsula. Its cadre came from the 1st and 4th Parachute Divisions which saw action in Italy and Russia. Among its high officers and NCOs one could find veterans of the German airborne invasion of Holland and Crete; the remnants of the suicidal defenders of Monte Cassino as well as elements of the daring parachute detachment which successfully undertook the rescue of Mussolini. The bulk of the division comprised well trained replacements ranging in age from 17 to 21, the majority of

---

12. ISUM 167, 15 December 1944, from *First US Army G-2 Periodic Report* 186, 13 November 1944.

whom were volunteers. The division moved from the Brest area two days after the invasion and, after a hectic 10-day journey, the division arrived in Normandy on 18 June and was immediately committed to battle. It was especially in the Ferriers-St Lô-Berigny triangle where the men of the 3rd Parachute Division proved themselves masters whose motto was '*Ein Fallschirmjäger – der stirbt im Loch*' (a paratrooper – he dies in his foxhole). The paratroopers fought for every inch of ground and did not yield their positions in spite of heavy casualties. The prisoners taken from the division were almost invariably fanatical Nazis; proud, arrogant and security-minded. Their morale could be best exemplified by a statement of an officer PW who said: 'As much as I formerly believed in the gospel and in Almighty God, so do I now believe in a German victory within three months. This opinion is shared by all of us.' It must be said to their credit that even after our breakthrough near St Lô on 25 July, when almost all PW arrived at the cages bewildered and shaken from the effect of our 'carpet' air bombardment, the majority of the PW from the 3rd Parachute Division still maintained their composure and were the only PW in the cage who behaved like soldiers. Though some of their illusions were shattered, their firm belief in German victory remained with them.

Unlike many other German units, in which PW complained that their officers deserted their men, in the 3rd Parachute Division PW talked about their officers with awe and admiration. General Schimpf[13] was their idol and to many a man in the 3rd Parachute Regiment the name of Major Stephani[14] (CO of the 9th Parachute Regiment) was a legend. When later in the campaign a group of PW from the 9th Parachute Regiment was told that Major Stephani had been killed, they burst into tears. The reputation of Major Becker,[15] CO of 5th Parachute Regiment, was equally famous. His name was often mentioned in Wehrmacht reports and even after the 5th Parachute Regiment was badly depleted the *Kampfgruppe* Becker won many laurels and Becker received the *Ritterkreuz* for his achievements. Colonel Liebach,[16] CO of 8th Parachute Regiment, was wounded early in the campaign and returned to Germany.

The 3rd Parachute Division was also caught in the Falaise–Argentan gap and when it tried to break through near Chambois, the number of

---

13. *Generalleutnant* Richard Schimpf (1897–1972), commander of 3rd Parachute Division in Normandy. Schimpf also served as general officer in the post-war *Bundeswehr*.
14. Major Kurt Stephani (1904–44), commander of the 9th Parachute Regiment of the 3rd Parachute Division.
15. Major Karl-Heinz Becker (1914–2000) later commanded the 3rd Parachute Division.
16. *Oberstleutnant* Egon Liebach (1905–45), commander of 6th Parachute Regiment.

dead was exceeded only by those of the notorious 1st SS Panzer Division. When a group of officers, who had broken out of the encirclement, learned that General Schimpf was wounded and still in the pocket, they formed an expedition to rescue their beloved general. Their mission was not successful and various reports had it that General Schimpf was dead or seriously wounded, and back in Germany; others said he was unharmed and had taken command of the 2nd Parachute Corps.

The division, after having suffered heavy casualties until 20 August, was supposed to return to Germany to reform, but each time a hole developed in the German lines, the remnants of the division were called upon to make one last stand. This continued until the battle of Mons, where the rest of the division was practically destroyed. The last time elements of the division were in contact with our forces was approximately 10 September.

It was more than one division that we destroyed by eliminating the 3rd Parachute Division. Having been the special pride of General Meindl[17] (CO of 2nd Parachute Corps), the 3rd Parachute Division had first call on replacements and they poured in from the Parachute jumping schools of Lyon and Dreux as well as from the Parachute training centres in Melun and Gardelegen. The division also received high praise from General Choltitz[18] (then CO of 84th Corps). In contrast to this, when one regiment from the 5th Parachute Division arrived from Brittany, General Choltitz let loose with one of his famous remarks: 'Da schicken sie mir tausend Männer mit einem Spazierstock' (Now they are sending me 1000 men with canes).

The new 3rd Parachute Division which recently emerged from its reforming area in Enschede, Holland, is far from being a carbon copy of the original division.

Aside from a small cadre of officers, NCOs and men who were with the division during the fighting in France and Belgium, most of its personnel are 17-18-year-old draftees of August 1944, with inadequate training and correspondingly inferior combat efficiency. There is no doubt that these youngsters try hard to live up to the tradition of the unit, but youth and devotion to duty cannot make up for hard-won experience and schooling. Besides, many of the men now fighting as common infantry soldiers, had hoped at the time of their induction to follow the careers of pilots, mechanics, and other specialized personnel in the Air Force. To many of them it came as a sobering, if not a shocking blow, when they were

---

17. *General der Fallschirmtruppe* Eugen Meindl (1892–1951).
18. *General der Infanterie* Dietrich von Choltitz (1894–1966), later the last German military governor of Paris.

transferred to a parachute unit, however great a contribution this unit was known to have made in the past.

The replacements of officers and NCOs encountered so far, likewise have been of a proportionally poorer quality. The bulk of them also have been transferred from other air force units and it is not unusual to see a former observer in a fighter squadron doing duty as a Battalion CO. It can be assured that the relative incompetence of such officers as infantry commanders has an adverse effect upon the combat efficiency and morale of the troops they command.

Another manner in which the new division differs from its predecessor is the type and number of weapons with which it is equipped. Whereas the original unit was amply supplied with the best equipment available, the new unit uses, in part, antiquated models and foreign-made substitutes. Moreover, many of these weapons are not properly maintained or used, for the training period of the men in Holland was too short.

The typical PW from this division in no way resembles his arrogant, tough predecessor of the Battle of France. Rather, he is an under-sized, self-conscious, disillusioned youth with little self-confidence and not at all security minded. He still believes in a German victory but only with this qualification: that Germany can bring new and devastating weapons into action. That these weapons will be forthcoming he does not seriously doubt, for they have been promised by the all-mighty Führer himself.

So far, the three infantry regiments (5th, 8th, 9th) the Anti-tank battalion and the Engineer battalion of the new division have been identified. All these were haphazardly committed, along with Army units, in the area NW of Dueren. It is already evident that the division, now commanded by Major-General Wadehn,[19] has suffered heavy losses. Nevertheless, its men cling tenaciously to their positions, surrendering only when their individual fate becomes hopeless. In this respect only can they be compared with their non-vanquished comrades who fought with such uncompromising fanaticism a few months before.

---

19. *Generalmajor* Walter Wadehn (1896–1949).

Chapter 6

Tank and Anti-Tank Weapons and Tactics

Editor's Comments

The heavy tank losses suffered on both the Eastern and Western Fronts during the summer of 1944 and the need to rebuild many of the veteran panzer divisions meant that the assault gun brigades (battalions in terms of their strength) became very important on the Western Front. This was particularly true in Holland as almost all panzer units were deployed farther south in the Moselle area. Although many panzer divisions possessed assault guns, the independent brigades were controlled by the artillery arm not the armour arm of the Wehrmacht. They were primarily intended and used for infantry support and their tactics were simple and straightforward (Documents 6/1 and 6/2). The Tiger tanks of the heavy tank battalions, on the other hand, were the cream of the armoured arm and their presence on the battlefield could be crucial. An intelligent prisoner recounts their tactics in detail (Document 6/3). Some weapons, from which much was expected, such as the 88mm anti-tank gun, had drawbacks (Document 6/5) while others, such as the humble Panzerfaust, were adapted in ingenious ways (Document 6/6).

Document 6/1[1]

Tactics of German Assault Gun Brigades

From a variety of captured documents and PW interrogations it has been possible to put together a fairly complete appreciation of German assault gun tactics, particularly their employment as a battalion or brigade, as they are now designated.

It has become obvious that for the true assault gun units (and to a slight extent the Panzer division anti-tank/assault gun units) the Germans have been trying hard to get a proportion of both 7.5 cm long guns and 10.5 cm assault howitzers in the troops. The following discussion assumes the presence of both equipments, generally in the proportion of 3 to 4 respectively.

General Principles

(i)   Manuals say, and PWs confirm, that assault guns are for use at the point of main effort and are not to be frittered away on unimportant sectors.

(ii) The 7.5 cm gun fires only direct fire, but the 10.5 cm assault howitzer should normally be used for indirect fire – both from a stationary position.

Note: Documents differ on the employment of the 10.5 cm assault howitzers to engage targets with direct fire from an open position.

(iii) Assault guns should be protected as much as possible for they are vulnerable and profitable targets. Specific measures for this include covering fire for assault guns moving to new positions, careful camouflage against air and artillery observation, use of masked firing positions for the 7.5 cm gun and concealed firing positions for the 10.5 cm howitzer and holding back of all assault guns not immediately needed in the attack.

(iv) The battalion is to be committed as a battalion and kept together as a battalion if its capabilities are to be fully realised. The smallest unit is the troop, which should never be broken up.

(v)   To get the most out of assault guns they should not be subordinated but should work in co-operation with supported units.

1. ISUM 101, 8 October 1944.

Don'ts for Assault Gun Units

(i)   Don't use assault guns at night (except assault howitzers in indirect fire).

(ii) After a battle don't use assault guns in a security role, particularly at night. They should be withdrawn for maintenance.

(iii) Don't dig in or hold assault guns in the main line of resistance, they must be in reserve for counter-attack at critical points.

(iv) Don't use assault guns in delaying actions without local protection.

Special Conditions

(i)   Assault guns support infantry approaching or entering a forest but do not fight in the forest themselves, since fields of fire are not available, manoeuvre is denied, and premature bursts will endanger friendly infantry

(ii) If the defence is primarily the responsibility of the artillery, the 10.5 cm assault howitzers can supplement the normal artillery with their indirect fire.

(iii) Armoured ammunition carriers must follow within 300 metres of the assault gun, since the assault equipments themselves carry such a relatively small allotment. Also, restocking of ammunition must take place in such a manner that at least half the assault guns remain ready to engage the enemy.

Document 6/2[2]

Assault Gun Tactics

The interrogation of an NCO instructor from 394th Assault Gun Brigade by Second British Army has provided excellent material on the latest employment of German Assault Guns.

While the bulk of the information given confirms the current doctrine on the employment of this equipment (see First Canadian Army Intelligence Summary Number 101 of 9 October 1944), actual practice in

---

2. ISUM 131, 8 November 1944.

the field varies on items such as employment of the Assault Gun at night or dug in, in an anti-tank role as will be seen below.

(i) Characteristics of assault gun employment

The role of the Assault gun is quite different from that of similar weapons.

The tank is capable of operating independently of any immediate supporting arm. It is charged with the tasks of breaking deeply into enemy defences, where possible into his gun area, and of pursuit.

The Self Propelled artillery retains all the characteristics of pure artillery, with enhanced mobility.

The close support Infantry SP Gun is the nearest weapon to the Assault Gun, differing only in that it forms an integral part of the parent infantry unit.

The Assault Gun, as distinct from SP Artillery of the 'Wespe' (Wasp) and 'Hummel' (Bumble Bee) types, is purely an infantry supporting weapon. It does not operate independently, but is used to help the infantry forward both morally (in that it provides an armed rallying point for assaulting infantry, impervious to Small Arms fire), and physically by engaging and neutralising heavy defence weapons, centres of resistance, etc. Conversely, the Assault Gun requires the support of infantry, or, occasionally, engineers used in an infantry role, for its own local protection.

(ii) Tactical Unit

The Assault Gun is not used in less than platoon strength (3 guns); normally at least one Coy of 9 guns should be employed. The size of the infantry unit supported and the type and degree of opposition expected determine the size of the assault gun sub-unit committed for any particular op, but the support of one infantry company by one platoon of assault guns is abnormal.

(iii) Employment in attack

Assault guns are employed only at the *Schwerpunkt*.[3] They go forward with the infantry, engaging centres of resistance, built-in MG positions, pillboxes, anti-tank guns or enemy close-support infantry weapons, either as these targets are picked up by the gun commander, or as the infantry ask for particular targets to be engaged.

They do not attempt to fire on the move, but advance from fire position to fire position.

---

3. Perhaps best defined in the context as 'the point of main effort'.

On arrival on the final objective, they are normally withdrawn into reserve, however, as the support artillery has had to change position as a result of the advance, the role of the assault gun is to fill in the '*Feuerpause*', i.e. bridge the gap in the supporting fire, until the artillery is in position again.

PW often wondered why the Allies did not use assault guns and had come to the conclusion that the British Army had no tradition of infantry close-support artillery (such as the 13 (IC) Coy in the German infantry regiment), and the greater number of guns in the British divisional artillery enabled adequate fire support to be given, even when the artillery was advancing in leap-frog fashion.

(iv) Employment in Defence

The normal role of the assault gun in defence is to assist the immediate counter-attack. The aim of the assault gun commander is to remain concealed until the enemy infantry attack has been launched, and then to emerge and engage the advancing infantry before they reach the Forward Defence Lines.

Only in rare circumstances will assault guns be dug in as pillboxes. PW considers that this procedure nullifies the great advantage conferred by the mobility of the gun. He states, however, that his gun has been put in, in a purely Anti tank role on occasion, and in such cases he has in fact dug the gun in.

(v) Fire control and engagement of targets

While all gun detachments are trained both in direct and indirect shooting, the latter is normally only practiced by the howitzers, as the flat trajectory of the guns presents crest clearance problems.

Indirect fire: The line is laid out by director method, and an indicator round is fired from the pivot gun. The remaining guns lay on the airburst and the range is given by a Forward Observation Officer by R/T.

Direct Fire: This is by far the most normal method of engaging targets. Method of fire is always gun control, gun commanders picking up and engaging their own targets independently. Ranging is carried down to an unverified bracket only, and PW states that he can guarantee to go to fire for effect in three rounds, which, he claims, is no mean achievement when the fall of shot has to be observed by scissors telescope from behind the shelter of the assault gun armour. A minor point of some interest is that correction for drift is not automatically applied in the assault gun sight, and must be separately calculated.

After some experience against British troops in Normandy, PW revised his normal ammunition proportions, which were based on his experiences in Russia, increasing the proportion of armour piercing at the expense of HE. Against Sherman tanks, PW states that he always used armour piercing, as he has found the HE does not have sufficient effect. Against lighter tanks of the Cromwell type, PW states that armour piercing is liable to go straight through, and he therefore orders it.

Engagement of Anti Tank guns: Prisoner stated that there was no co-operation between assault guns of the same platoon. He had not heard of any such manoeuvre as the pinning of the Anti tank gun by fire from the front, while the other assault guns made a flanking movement. On being fired on by an Anti tank gun, he simply chose a fire position and shot it out independently.

(vi) Co-operation with other arms

The fire of an assault gun unit was never co-ordinated with that of an artillery unit.

PW had never directly co-operated with tanks.

Co-operation with infantry was effected by a liaison officer at the Headquarters of the unit supported, and frequently an NCO with pack wireless set was sent to accompany the commander of the actual assaulting infantry.

The Assault gun is very vulnerable to infantry close combat methods, and as a consequence is invariably given a 'bodyguard' of 4-6 infantry to deal with short-range Anti tank weapons, such as the bazooka. Engineers are sometimes called upon for the task, used mainly as infantry, but their technical knowledge proves very valuable in the clearance of obstacles such as minefields.

(vii) Miscellaneous

(a) Employment at night: PW has operated at night by the light of star shell, shot from the assault howitzers.

(b) Ammunition supply: The armoured ammunition carriers (1 per platoon) are fitted with wireless, and are called forward by R/T when required.

Document 6/3[4]

German Tiger Tank Tactics

An intelligent and observant PW of an independent Tiger Tank Battalion has given some detailed information about present-day Tiger tank tactics.

Since PW was in action only between 19 September and 2 October, his battle experience is not extensive, and in some cases his information is based on theoretical teaching rather than practice, but it is considered a reliable guide.

Throughout their training, and in action, crews were constantly told that the Tiger is the best and safest tank in existence, that no other tank can hit so hard or take so much punishment. This principle governs their training and employment, for crews are trained not to rely on support from infantry or other weapons, but to make the most of the range and performance of their gun and the thickness of their armour.

The company, which in this case is the Independent Tiger Company Hummel, has three platoons of four tanks sub-divided into half-platoons. The commander of the first half-platoon, consisting of tanks Nos. 1 and 2, is also the platoon commander, and is usually a *Leutnant*, sometimes an *Oberleutnant*. The commander of the second half-platoon with tanks 3 and 4, may be a *Leutnant*, but is generally a senior NCO. The other two tank commanders are normally NCOs. The company commander's spare tank, when it is available, normally carries only a driver and one other replacement. In practice the spare tank is often used to replace a non-running fighting tank.

Whenever PW's company moved by road behind the front line it moved by platoons, with an interval between the tanks by day to 1 km, at 15 kms per hour. Intervals between platoons varied, since the company's soft-skinned vehicles, including some 30 trucks and three petrol tankers, sometimes moved together ahead of the tanks, sometimes after the whole company and sometimes distributed along the column. PW could not remember any factors which decided the procedure for any one move. In any case the main armoured column was never immediately preceded by other transport, but was always led by the platoon commander of the leading platoon, which varied on each move. There was no settled place in the column for the company commander, but he normally travelled

---

4. ISUM 152, 1 December 1944 from *Second Army Intelligence Summary* 167.

behind the leading platoon, with his spare tank either ahead of him with the platoon, or behind with the second platoon. On some occasions the company commander travelled in a staff car to maintain control more easily.

Column control and communications were normally the job of MG DRs belonging to company headquarters. Radio was not used.

Owing to the comparative unreliability of the 600 hp Maybach engine of the Tiger 'A', convoy discipline was very hard to maintain, and the intervals between tanks varied between ½ km and 3 kms on even short runs.

When moving into action in Holland the nature of the ground made it necessary always to keep to the roads. A similar procedure was followed – one platoon going ahead followed after a variable interval by the other two platoons, generally together.

NOTES:

(i) There is no settled place for the company commander. He normally travels with the second platoon, but if he is forward with the leading platoon, he almost invariably moves in the position normally occupied by the platoon commander who then travels behind him. PW therefore suggests that the third tank should be a priority target, since it will contain at least a platoon commander, possibly the company commander.

(ii) There is no observation toward the rear, the forward platoon relying for rear protection on the following platoons.

(iii) All guns are normally carried at the twelve o'clock position. Sometimes the platoon may order tanks 3 and 4 to carry their guns at the half-left and half-right positions respectively, but only when the sides of the road are clear from trees and buildings.

(iv) Communication while on the move is normally visual or by Motor Cycle Dispatch Rider. Radio is not normally used, since its employment is frequently followed in a very few minutes by heavy artillery concentrations, but operators must be listening in case the company commander, or, in rare cases, the platoon commander gives an urgent emergency order .

(v) When moving over open country, the platoon methods, of which the first is the more normal. PW thinks the second method (by bounds) is used in fairly close country.

The smallest unit employed as a fighting unit is the platoon of four tanks. Normally the company acts as a single unit. The Tiger is considered too blind to work alone and is always used in the largest concentration possible.

Fire with main armament is opened at 1600 m where possible. In Russia the opening range is normally greater, up to 2,000 m. At 1600 m it is considered that the second shot should be a direct hit on a target 2 m high. In PW's company HE formed some 65% of the total ammunition carried, since 'only two AP rounds are necessary to knock out an enemy tank, but lots of HE is needed to destroy transportation columns or infantry positions.' A few rounds of smoke (6-8) were also carried. Fire is never opened on the move. Even if attacked, Tigers normally move on to a firing position preferably hull down, before replying, except with MGs. If attacked by an anti-tank gun the usual procedure is to turn towards it and move forward, relying on the thick frontal armour, until the exact position is located, when HE is fired to kill the crew, or, if close enough MG fire is opened. If this involves too great a deviation from the axis of advance the tank will stop, preferably in a hull-down position, and 'shoot it out' with the anti-tank gun. When the need to continue the advance rules out this delay the anti-tank gun will if possible be blinded by smoke and left for the following platoons to deal with. PW had never practised or employed indirect fire.

All tanks in the company use the same radio frequency. In theory only the company commander may send, and platoon commanders in an emergency, all tanks hearing every message that is sent. In practice, according to PW, 'everybody talks all the time, except the company commander, who can hardly get a word in edgeways.' This may be the result of lax control by PW's commander, but he states that even in training it was very difficult to stop operators talking to one another.

Crews are taught that the 'one unforgiveable crime' is to abandon a disabled Tiger either in attack or defence. They must stay inside and use their guns as long as the enemy is in range. If there is an enemy counter-attack, the tank becomes a pillbox of great strength which must not be abandoned until it is on fire or in imminent danger of being captured, in which case it must be blown up. PW saw one crew, which had abandoned a crippled Tiger in the Arnhem area, which was forced to re-enter it by MG fire from their company commander's tank. Afterwards they had a lecture from their platoon commander, who told them to remember that a wounded Tiger can be as dangerous and savage as an unwounded one.

When co-operating with the infantry, the following tactics are used. In Holland and in country where the going cross-country is unsuitable, the tanks keep to roads while the infantry moves at the sides, giving flank protection against anti-tank weapons. In good tank country the infantry normally followed closely behind the leading tanks. Reaction to opposition varied with the type of ground. Anti-tank weapons in open country were normally taken on by tanks, in close country by infantry with fire support from tanks. Infantry opposition was normally dealt with by tanks, leaving the infantry to do the mopping up. Against determined resistance from infantry in prepared positions or with anti-tank support, the Tigers would take up fire positions and neutralize enemy fire while infantry went forward for close assault. In close country or bad visibility tanks would commonly advance with infantry acting as close reconnaissance and giving warning of concealed positions. Communication with infantry was visual only. There was never any radio contact with infantry, and indication of a target by infantry to tanks generally took the form of waving and pointing until a tank could pick it up with its periscope.

PW had not taken part in any action with assault gun cooperation, but had had some instruction on the subject while in training. In such an attack the assault guns would take up fire positions and engage the enemy at the *Schwerpunkt* while the attacking force of tanks and infantry went forward. Assault guns would leapfrog forward behind the attack, but would always fire from fire positions, never on the move, and would never go far enough forward to risk being caught in a tank battle. It was emphasised that the assault gun was primarily a support weapon for infantry and had little direct contact with the tanks, although the tank unit and the assault gun unit might be in radio contact, and an observer from the guns might go forward in a commander's tank.

PW had had no experience at all of working with other types of tanks. He believed that heavy tank battalions and companies had formerly had an allotment of medium tanks (Pz Kw IV) which gave flank protection, but was fairly sure that this was no longer the case. His own company had never had any such allotment, and the availability of such support had never been considered in their training. This was also true of such heavy tank battalions as he knew in the training period (501, 503, 509, 510).

Heavy tank battalions had a reconnaissance platoon as part of the Headquarters Company, whose chief task is ground reconnaissance, but PW's company had no reconnaissance element at all, and had to rely mainly on infantry for its reports. Since infantry had little idea what constituted safe ground for a Tiger; this occasionally led to mishaps, but in general, in PW's experience, the Tiger was almost completely road-bound in Holland, and moves were normally planned from the map.

PW gave the following details about the employment of tanks in defence.

Tanks represent now almost the only generally mobile arm in the German Army, and this mobility is always borne in mind. Tigers are regarded as the commander's main counter-attack force where available, to be used en masse at the main point of resistance. Therefore, anything which might reduce their mobility is avoided.

Digging in is very rarely done with Tigers. PW has seen it carried out with other types of tank, but Tigers are only dug in in special cases. For example, if a river bank were being defended, positions might be prepared to enable the tanks to act as a sort of miniature coastal defence gun, but always with an exit and with the understanding that the tank shall not stay there if it can be more useful elsewhere.

In defence, Tigers are commonly (always in PW's brief experience) sited well forward, some 100 metres behind the infantry's foremost defended localities. Behind them are the main infantry positions and anti-tank guns. Tigers being considered proof against any infantry attack and almost unaffected by artillery fire, are kept thus forward to repel any armoured attack before it can reach the main infantry positions. Enemy infantry are engaged with MGs, but are mainly left to the care of their own infantry behind them, who are also entrusted with the rear defence of the Tigers.

In such positions, Tigers are normally hull-down and carefully camouflaged. If the attack, or the infantry part of the attack, seems to be on such a scale that it can be adequately dealt with by their own infantry, the Tigers do not betray their position by opening fire, but wait for what they now regard as the inevitable armoured support, when they gain the advantage of surprise from their undisclosed positions.

These positions are always carefully reconnoitred beforehand, if time permits, and are so arranged that every tank can receive supporting fire from at least two others if necessary.

There is no question of withdrawing in the face of a superior enemy – Tigers are expected and ordered to stay and fight it out, with the provision already mentioned, that no Tiger must ever be captured undestroyed.

Document 6/4[5]

German Battlefield Recovery of Armoured Vehicles

(i) Organisation

Each German tank battalion has a repair platoon. This platoon has a strength of either 110 men or 125 men depending on the number of tanks in the battalion. The division has a repair battalion. Both the platoon and the divisional battalion were originally equipped with an 18-ton recovery half-track. Now, however, equipment is so scarce that in most cases only the repair battalion still has the half-tracks. There are now, ordinarily, two to a division. The repair battalion also has a trailer to transport tanks. However, this trailer was only usable on roads and even here its performance was not satisfactory. Its use has been discontinued.

(ii) Recovery

If a tank other than the Tiger has been disabled on the battlefield and the crew is not able to repair it, the recovery vehicle is called up to remove the tank out of range of enemy fire.

The tank is pulled off by the half-track. It is attached to the half-track by two long rods, employed either parallel to each other or to form an angle:

either: tank [====] half-track, or: tank |◁===| Half-track

depending on how severely and where the tank was hit.

Tiger tanks cannot be pulled by these half-tracks and must be dragged off by another tank or pushed out and pulled by two half-tracks.

(iii) Equipment

Repair platoons were equipped at one time with set of spare parts including motors and gun barrels. Now, however, this is no longer possible and worn out equipment has to be exchanged for new equipment at a depot. The only thing carried along now is one spare motor.

---

5. ISUM 166, 1 December 1944, from First US Army.

Document 6/5[6]

Use of the 88mm Pak 43 Anti-Tank Gun

Wartime Intelligence Officer's Comments

The following has been extracted from a captured document:

Experiences at the front show that the 8.8 cm Pak 43 Anti-Tank gun is not unconditionally suitable for certain types of mobile warfare, e.g. for counter-attacks, temporary defence, and especially for covering disengaging movements.

This is due to the fact that the gun's weight (4½ tons), height (over 6 ft) and the fact that it is towed by a large unarmoured vehicle, limit its mobility on the battlefield. Furthermore there is not always time to complete gun positions and the gun is difficult to camouflage, especially from the air.

Its heavy traversing arrangements make defence against close quarter infantry attack particularly difficult.

The gun is therefore especially suitable for employment on a static front. In mobile warfare it is only to be employed for the defence of vital positions and orders must be given in sufficient time to enable gun positions to be completed.

The pamphlet 18/9 'Guiding principles for the employment and use of the 8.8 cm Anti-Tank gun' dated 27 June 1943 is being amended.

Document 6/6[7]

Using the Panzerfaust as a Flying Mine

This weapon was recently found in the role of a formidable trip wire trap for both armoured and unarmoured vehicles. The German name for the arrangement is *'Panzerfaust als automatische Sperre'* (Panzerfaust as automatic obstacle).

---

6. ISUM 174, 22 December 1944.
7. ISUM 148, 27 November 1944.

The tube of the Panzerfaust is secured to a fence or by stakes driven into the ground, and suitably sighted. A trip-wire is then led from the firing mechanism of the weapon across the path of the vehicle to an anchoring point on the opposite side of the road. It is reported that the trip wire is usually found suspended two feet above the road, and that it can be seen easily in the daytime.

PANZER FAUST 30 AS FLYING MINE

(COPY OF A GERMAN TRAINING INSTRUCTION)

The German instructions point out that a greater zone can be effectively blocked than with a number of T-mines and that every unit possesses Panzerfaust weapons, while T-mines are only available to the engineers in a limited quantity.

The weapons found were *Panzerfäuste* 30 which, in order to fire, require modifications to the sight, but it should be noted that the Panzerfaust 60 with its simplified trigger mechanism and lever could be used almost without alteration.

Modifications Necessary

(a) The back sight of the Panzerfaust 30 acts as a release lever and is reinforced by a steel plate.

(b) A wire loop is rivetted to the top of the modified sight to hold the trip wire attachment.

(c) A flat piece of metal is inserted under the modified sight to form a spring and keep it clear of the release button when surplus weather loads bear on the trip wire.

Chapter 7

Infantry Tactics and Weapons

Editor's Comments

Despite the problems experienced by the Wehrmacht in the autumn of 1944, many German officers exhibited a thoroughly professional attitude toward fighting. The critique by Oberst Heinrich von Bahr of an attack made by a panzer grenadier regiment in Italy (Document 7/3) is a classic case of attention to detail, even at this late stage of the war. German defensive tactics incorporated counter-attacks as a matter of course and forces were always assigned to this task, even at the lowest levels, as illustrated by these orders (Document 7/2) from a battalion commander. Allied superiority in materiel resulted in an emphasis on better defensive positions (Document 7/1) and night fighting, (Document 7/4) and encouragement for snipers (Document 7/5).

Document 7/1[1]

Defensive Position of 858th Grenadier Regiment

Wartime Intelligence Officer's Comments

The following order dated 18 October 1944 deals with the improvement of the defensive positions of 858th Grenadier Regiment of 346th Infantry Division

---

1. ISUM 113, 21 October 1944, from *1 Corps Intelligence Summary* 81.

in the area of Wüstwesel. The identification of Lais[2] as Commander of 858th Grenadier Regiment confirms the fact that this regiment and Kampfgruppe Lais are now the same formation. The line established here no longer exists since the rear boundary of the main defensive position, as outlined, was reached even before these plans had been completed.

Infantry Regiment 858   Regimental HQ 18 October 1944
G (Ops)

(i) Improvement of positions

Battalions will work out a programme for the building of positions on the basis of which the main defence line can be constructed. The constructions must be planned so that communications by runner can quickly be established within platoons. Approach and communication trenches must be planned so that they conform to natural camouflage such as hedges, picket fences or clumps of bush etc. Spoil must be camouflaged at once.

The coming of autumn makes the construction of approach trenches to the forward positions necessary. In the construction of all types of approach and fighting trenches thought must be given to drainage, which can be maintained by digging water holes in drainage trenches.

(ii) Battle Positions

Through observation and continuous patrolling, the enemy, in the past few days, has been unable to determine the course of our main defended lines and has not located our machine gun and heavy weapons positions. In order to give a false picture of the strength of our positions, a Divisional order states that by 20 October 1944 all machine guns and heavy weapons will prepare alternative positions sufficiently far away. The present positions are to be maintained as dummy and alternative positions and by occasional manning must give the enemy the impression that they are actually held.

The course of our main defence line may not thereby be altered. The rear body of the main defence position will be laid down by the Regiment on the general line (Map 1/50,000) KP11 (1500 m SE Wüstwesel E8214) – Stapelheide E8513 (the northern one) – Kruisstraat. The responsibility for this area rests on battalions according to their sectors. Machine guns will occasionally be fired from dummy and alternative positions. Positions and outposts occupied by night can be safeguarded from surprise by use of grenades set off by trip wires. It rests on the sense of responsibility of the Company Commander and the ingenuity of the Company to lay small

2. Major Otto Lais, commanding 858 *Grenadierregiment.*

115

minefields and set up other devilment such as tripwire, hand grenade booby traps etc in the forward area to make the approach of the enemy against our main defended line more difficult.

The casualties and capture by surprise of entire sections reflect a terrible laxity and lack of junior leaders entrusted with the task of organizing a defensive position.

In the next day or so I shall satisfy myself in the building of the main defence line as carried out by the company commanders. I order that the work plans are firm by 21 October in the order of priority according to the urgency of this work.

(iii)   Shelters

For sections which are occupying houses and are using the cellars, wherever possible an exit leading directly to the trenches must be made. Thereby losses can be avoided which occur when the section makes for its alarm post under artillery or tank gun fire, through the open door.

I recall our habit in Russia which was to make a tunnel direct from the cellar to the communication trenches. In this manner it is definitely quicker to take up alarm positions than to run across a yard or garden where no cover is available. For those who are positioned in the open it is possible to gather material from damaged houses or farms and build small shelters so that when the cold sets in the troops have some protection against it.

Units who are partly in houses and partly in the open will insure that frequent reliefs are carried out.

(iv)   State of Readiness

Recent experiences repeatedly show the unpreparedness of our troops who in many cases have allowed themselves to be taken by surprise by enemy assault sections.

Warning of increased enemy artillery, mortar or machine gun fire will immediately be given by all commanders down to section commanders and if positions are not immediately manned by the entire section an observation post of at least a double post per section will be manned. The remainder of the section will stand to with all weapons ready. Section Commanders who fail in their duty to have their section in a state of readiness will suffer severely. The junior leaders must be informed that I have passed on two recently reported instances of shocking examples of cowardice in the face of the enemy. Their sentences must be brought to the attention of all.

The saddest case, which I have encountered in my entire military career, is the latest one reported to me, in which a sergeant and section commander remained in a cellar with his entire section and anxiously asked his men what he should do while a weak British assault detachment took the platoon position without a shot being fired. I have instituted proceedings against both the NCOs and Platoon Commander for desertion and cowardice, and the section commander for neglect of duty and cowardice in the face of the enemy.

The establishment of greater alertness at a time of enemy artillery fire and noise of battle, combined with machine gun fire, will be ordered for all support weapons and HQs in the main defended area.

(Signed) *Lau*
Distribution:
Down to Companies

Wartime Intelligence Officer's Comments

A pencilled note states that plans are to be handed in to the Battalion by 1600 hours 20 October 1944 and that posts will be shown as follows:

Existing posts	blue
Proposed posts	red
Posts under construction	green

Document 7/2 [3]

Employment of Company and Battalion Reserves

Wartime Intelligence Officer's Comments

The following Order of I/857th Grenadier Regiment of 346th Infantry Division dated 12 October 1944 indicates the methods now employed by some formations in organizing company and battalion reserves for local counter-attacks. Since available forces do not permit of a strong occupation

---

3. ISUM 116, 24 October 1944.

of the Main Defence Line (HKL) the chief form of defence seems to be centred upon an immediate counter-attack. Each company is to organize its own reserve force and employ it against a local break-in. The reserves of the companies whose positions are not immediately threatened, may be used by the battalion commander against any serious penetration of the HKL.

I Battalion, 857th Grenadier Regiment   12 October 1944

Subject: Establishment of Reserves

The order to hold the HKL (Main Defence Line) at all costs and to clean up immediately any break-in that occurs, through counter-attacks, is well-known. There may be no doubt about this order which comes from highest authority. The available forces permit only a weak occupation of the HKL and hence facilitate an easy break-in by the enemy. They make it more difficult to form local reserves for the immediate elimination of such break-ins. Strong enemy attacks could hitherto not be halted because of the shortage of immediately available reserves. The danger of continuous dentings and a gradual push-back of the HKL must be checked. In order to get a complete picture of enemy dispositions on the battalion front and thus avoid surprises, the following is ordered:

(i)   A close reconnaissance of the entire sector will be conducted by all companies every night.

(ii) Companies will procure information about bridges, communications, strength and disposition of the enemy through nightly reconnaissance deep into enemy lines. The area to be reconnoitred is left to the discretion of the Company Commander (consult with neighbour). A well trained patrol leader soon learns to determine the difference between the movement of fighting troops and supply columns. The extent of supply columns permits deductions of enemy strength. The picture may be supplemented by questioning civilians but this information must be treated with greatest caution.

(iii) The companies will provide the following reserves. These will also be considered Battalion reserves:

1 Coy	2 NCOs & 16 men
2 Coy	1 NCO & 8 men
3 Coy	1 NCO & 8 men
4 Coy	1 NCO & 16 men for Battalion HQ

These sections are to be made up of old and new soldiers and each must have a trained No. 1 and No. 2 MG man. The cohesion of the section must not be endangered by constant changes of personnel. Sections may be replaced by others equally well trained but the strength must remain unchanged under all circumstances. Casualties will be replaced by front line troops. Equipment will be at Company Commander's discretion.

(iv)   Employment of Reserves

In order to eliminate local break-ins Company Commanders, after notifying Battalion HQ, may make use of their own reserves. In the case of serious break-ins the reserves of companies whose HKL is not seriously threatened will counter-attack at the command of the Battalion along with the Battalion reserve under the command of Lt Schmidt. The forming up point for this counter-attack force will be announced in each case.

For action outside of the Battalion sector the reserves from 1, 4 and 5 Coys and the reserve force will form up at Battalion HQ and will go into action as a company under Lt Protmann. These reserves will stand to on receipt of code word 'Minimax'. Thereupon Lt Schmidt will report to 1 Coy and take over the platoon from Lt Protmann.

For this task sections are to be equipped as follows:

    1 Coy: 1 sec with MG and three cases of ammunition
              1 sec without MG
    4 Coy: 1 sec with MG and three cases of ammunition
    5 Coy: 1 sec with MG and three cases of ammunition
    HQ: Both sections without MG
    Each section will carry one *Faustpatrone*.[4]

Weapons and ammunition will be supplied by the front line whenever sections are not thus equipped. These reserves must be ready to march one hour after receipt of code word.

Completion of preparations by 1800 hours 13 October 1944.

Signed: MÖLLE

---

4. An early name for the *Panzerfaust* anti-tank weapon.

Document 7/3[5]

A German Regimental Commander's Critique, 91st Light Infantry Division

Wartime Intelligence Officer's Comments

An interesting document captured in the Italian theatre contains a detailed analysis by the commander of 200th Panzer Grenadier Regiment of 91st Light Infantry Division on the reasons for the failure of the regiment's attack on 9 December. The commander spares no one in his criticism. Two factors are significant. First, the most elementary mistakes were made by junior officers and NCOs, a reflection on the current training and experience of these leaders. Second, however, and more important, it is an indication of how a vigorous and thorough senior commander acts to correct this, and it is a fair guess that many of these same mistakes did not occur in the next attack.

The attack did not achieve the success which was expected. The regiment was unable to gain any ground of importance, suffered severe and bloody casualties and became so disorganized that about 12 hours were necessary to regroup. This would have enabled a more energetic opponent to have broken through and threatened Faenza from the rear, if not actually to have captured the town, and bring about the annihilation of the regiment. The 'enemy's' casualties were not heavy. He appears to have retained his fighting spirit and will undoubtedly continue his attempts to break through.

The following points demonstrate specifically the reasons for the failure of the attacks:

(1) Insufficient time was given to companies to put themselves properly in the tactical picture and in fact they never were.
(2) No timings were laid down, or, if they were, they were not adhered to.
(3) Companies allowed themselves to become scattered by enemy artillery fire.
(4) They were drawn off by the enemy in a flanking sector and attacked where they had no right to be.

---

5. ISUM 200, 7 January 1945, from *SHAEF Intelligence Notes*, 13 January 1945.

(5) Scattered elements pushed on without bothering to keep contact and maintain communications, or stayed where they were and took no further action, thus allowing themselves to be shot up by artillery and heavy infantry weapons.

(6) Company commanders obviously had not detailed contact platoons, if in fact they gave any orders at all – as a result of which considerable sorting out was necessary.

(7) LMGs were not so sited as to enable the attack to be pushed home.

(8) No Verey lights were put up, so that battalion commanders, artillery and support units did not know the whereabouts of forward troops.

(9) Company commanders failed to rally their assault sections, or at any rate did not muster the remaining elements for further attack, but wandered about without plan or objective.

(10) Battalion commanders went forward in the proper way to sort out the confusion, but left behind the means to command and deprived companies of their wireless sections and LMGs. They did not order regardless 'Hang on – dig in – regroup, until fresh positions have been prepared.'

To a certain extent they were prevented from doing this by the break-down of communications forward.

(Marginal comment here – probably by Captain Michej, CO I Battalion, who was later killed. Referring to von Behr's orders he writes, 'I did!')

(11) Battalion commanders changed their HQ far too soon and far too often, so that subsequent action taken by the artillery and SP weapons lacked orders and co-ordination.

(12) Officers commanding heavy companies were not at battalion HQ in order to ensure that there was co-ordination of fire at all times and, above all, to take command in the absence of the battalion commander.

(13) Insufficient use was made of the artillery; forward observers, who should have been forward, were back at battalion HQ. Individual forward observers had failed to exchange frequencies.

(14) Executives were either completely clueless (*schimmerlos*) – even as regards their own commanders' intentions – or they were left without communication with their commanders and could neither report, nor take action, nor even get into contact with companies.

(15) Communications nets were quite inadequate and poorly organized.

(16) The troops didn't shoot but ran into enemy fire.

(17) Owing to the bad state of communications the heavy weapons were unable either to concentrate their fire or support individual forward thrusts.

(18) Due to inadequate means of inter-communication, direct and indirect fire were in no way related to each other.

(19) Companies which were echeloned to the rear came forward into the operational lines much too soon without any orders from the battalion commander. As a result, battalion commanders had nothing in hand and were obliged to commit their assault platoons much too early, in order to achieve even the smallest gain.

(20) Defence areas in front of the two objectives were not laid down beforehand with the gunners and supporting infantry weapons as a protection against counter-attacks, and, during the time supporting fire was being given, these areas were not engaged.

(21) One battalion reported repeatedly that the second objective had been reached. This report was based entirely on observation through binoculars and not on actual reporting by the companies. In fact, the battalion was not firmly established on the first objective, but was merely scattered over the area.

(22) No report was made at any time when report lines were reached or passed.

(23) Neither executives nor company commanders, let alone platoon commanders or squad leaders, can read a map. At best only a rough or an incorrect check is made on the ground, but generally none at all. In this way reporting, which in any case is poor enough, becames damnably inaccurate.

(24) In cases where there is no land line communication, battalion and company commanders do not avail themselves of the lateral radio link, but rather make inquiries first at regiment or battalion. Many an officer is without a clue as to the technical aids at his disposal, their capabilities and their potential in action, and even goes so far as to admit it

(*Marginal Note: 'Fatal'*)

This is to the detriment of combat efficiency.

(25) Only in most exceptional cases can commanders be called leaders, at best they may be found stuck out in front.

In the present engagement and in all future actions the following lessons will be learned from the above mistakes:

The shorter the time allowed for the preparation of an attack or operation and the weaker the forces at your disposal, the more accurately must the information, briefing and preparatory orders be given and carried out.

At the very least the following instructions and orders must of necessity be given and applied to all operations:

(1) From the old MLR all commanders must acquaint themselves with the country over which they are to attack. At the same time definite bearings must be taken for finding direction and check points laid down. Exact orientation must be carried out previously by each company. Should there be no time for this, exact points for direction finding and reference points must be worked out from the map, the latter being applicable to D Day.

(2) Routes up to the objectives or report lines must be laid down by Battalion and must take into consideration the opposition expected and the difficulties likely to be encountered in covering the ground. Regimental objectives and report lines should not be disclosed to companies, but only to battalions. The latter should then judge from company reports when regimental objectives and report lines have been reached.

(3) Orders must make it quite clear what action is to be taken when:
       companies run into enemy defences
       enemy fire is opened from the flank
       enemy counter-attack is mounted
       objectives are reached
       companies appear to be becoming scattered
       part of a company pushes on too far or gets held up

(4) For each expected phase of the battle a fire concentration and co-ordination of heavy infantry weapons and artillery must be previously planned.

(5) Weapons must be detailed to deal with enemy flanking fire; that is, the HMGs of the rearward company and part of the mortars or heavy mortars.

(6) According to what enemy resistance is expected, a fire plan must be fixed to assist companies and assault squads in their advance. In the event of the battle's taking an unforeseen turn, such as the right platoon of the forward company getting on faster than the left, heavy weapons and artillery must be sufficiently manageable and in hand so as to be able to switch their fire immediately.

123

(7) Contact companies and platoons must be detailed.

(8) In the event that communications break down, detailed orders will be given for companies to put up Verey lights.

(9) Location of the heavy company commander must be laid down, and only in exceptional circumstances will he not be at battalion HQ.

Document 7/4[6]

German Night Fighting Tactics

Wartime Intelligence Officer's Comments

Evidence of increased German emphasis on night fighting and rules of night tactics are found in an undated document, recently captured, which contains excerpts from a manual 'Night Movements and Night Attack', under preparation. Pertinent extracts from the document follow:

(i)   General

At night the enemy's superiority is least effective. Therefore, night is our best ally. It must be used for daring attacks and all marches. Attacking at night reduces losses and may bring great success to units under courageous leadership. Particularly, an enemy who feels helpless without tank and air support and who spends rainy nights in buildings, must be beaten at night.

Orders for night attacks must be given early to permit careful preparation. The larger the unit, the earlier should the order be issued.

Irregular timing of the beginning of the attack increases surprise, which is of the greatest importance. Therefore, the following measures should be taken:

Inconspicuous reconnoitring and registering of fire distributed over several nights.

Continue normal combat activities. No noises, no light, no shifting of units before nightfall.

Conditions are favourable when the target can be seen at 50 metres distance. Pitch-black nights usually cause failure.

---

6. ISUM 206, 23 January 1945, from *12 Army Group Weekly Intelligence Summary* 23.

Spotlights facilitate aimed firing and blind the enemy. When several spotlights are directed against a low-hanging bank of clouds, the reflected light will produce the brightness of a half-moon.

It may be a great help to set on fire barns and buildings located on the flanks or in the rear of the enemy.

Parachute flares should not be used, because their long burning time and short range provide the enemy with light to get his own units prepared. If the enemy lights up the forefield, smoke candles should be released quickly.

The attack will rigidly follow the direction previously ordered. No change in direction can take place once an attack is under way.

The target of the attack must be reached one to two hours before daybreak to allow time for organizing for defence under the cover of darkness.

(ii) Infantry Night Attacks

Individual hand-to-hand combat is decisive. Therefore, attack in deeply staggered wedge formation with a strong point.

Use few but daring men and many weapons.

Assault squads and platoons should lead. Try to overcome the heavy weapons of the enemy with light weapons.

The attack should be launched from positions which are as close as possible to the enemy.

Leave these final assault positions on a whistle signal or visual signal. The foremost assault squads and platoons throw themselves upon the enemy with loud yelling and destroy him in individual hand-to-hand combat.

The attack may take place with or without artillery support.

Where complete surprise of the enemy may be anticipated, that is on dark nights, attack without artillery support promises greater success.

Artillery fire at night follows special rules, because aimed single shots are not feasible as a rule. Fire should be directed against probable strongpoints and area targets. A bell-shaped cover should be provided against enemy counter-thrusts, according to a determined fire plan.

(iii) Infantry and Tanks

Night attacks by armoured units or armoured *Kampfgruppe* may be extraordinarily successful. Tanks, however, should not be used without infantry.

The following conditions are necessary for a successful night attack with tanks:

Sufficient vision. Targets must be visible from a distance of 150 to 200 metres.

Suitable terrain and favourable ground conditions.

Night attacks by tanks with armoured infantry riding on vehicles promise great success. The tanks attack first, the infantry follow closely behind or accompany the attack on the flanks. After reaching the target, the infantry take up defensive positions. The vehicles are pulled back while it is still dark and then put into readiness as a reserve against counter-attack.

Motor noises of approaching tanks should be drowned by low flying raiders, by artillery fire and loudspeaker broadcasts. These noises must not be made for the first time during the night of the attack, but should also be produced during several previous nights.

Document 7/5[7]

Enemy Sniping Methods

Wartime Intelligence Officer's Comments

A Yugoslavian PW, who volunteered for a sniper's course so that his arrival at the front could be postponed, nevertheless picked up considerable information on the present enemy methods of training snipers.

(i) Training

The course began on 20 July and lasted four weeks. The first week consisted mainly of theoretical instruction on the carbine (Model 98) and the telescopic sights (marked H4 x 60). Target practice followed on ring targets of 40 cm diameter, first at 150 metres and then at extra 50-metre intervals up to 500 metres. In the third week shooting practice at cardboard figures took place.

---

7. ISUM 111, 19 October 1944.

(ii)   Snipers' Methods

Although he was not employed as a sniper when he finally did reach the front, PW was able to describe in some detail the methods of operation as taught on the course.

Snipers were to operate invariably in pairs. They are each equipped with a rifle with telescopic sights, and a minimum of other equipment. One man carries a pair of binoculars, and each moves with a maximum of sixty rounds of ammunition.

Camouflage precautions included the well-known brown and green camouflage jacket, blackened hands and faces and helmets with attached foliage if necessary. The team was to work its way as far forward as possible looking for a position which offered (a) good observation and (b) cover. One of the pair then took over the role of observer.

Particularly valuable targets were said to be: artillery observers, officers and runners, in that order. When a target was seen it was not to be engaged unless a hit was certain (*der Schuss muss sitzen*). The observer reported whether the aim was accurate or not, and no more than three shots were to be fired from the same position. Frequent change of position was advisable.

In a withdrawal, snipers were also to withdraw and there was no question of their remaining behind our lines to engage in desultory sniping.

(iii)   Daily Propaganda Diet

The course included at least half an hour of hate propaganda daily. This consisted of a kind of frenzied oration by one of the NCO instructors and was along the following lines:

NCO:	'Every shot must kill a Jewish Bolshevik'
Chorus:	'Every shot'
NCO:	'Kill the British swine'
Chorus:	'Every shot must kill'

Chapter 8

Recruiting, Replacements and Training

Editor's Comments

The desperate shortage of manpower experienced in the last months of 1944 and the extreme measures taken to alleviate it are well illustrated in Documents 8/1 and 8/2. An analysis of the quality of the replacements being provided to the better formations in Italy (Document 8/3) is indicative of the problems facing the Wehrmacht. Recruiting began to verge on impressment by force (Documents 8/4 and 8/7) and the results were not productive. Nonetheless, there seems, even in the autumn of 1944, to have been a lessening of the standards of officer selection and training (Documents 8/5 and 8/6).

Document 8/1[1]

Manpower in the German Army

The problem of manpower to meet the coming battles for Germany becomes daily one of the most pressing facing the High Command. Three years of intensive fighting in Russia, coupled with the permanent loss of almost one million men in the battle of France, has dangerously depleted the vast resources of manpower once available to the Reich. Up until now

---

1. ISUM 100, 8 October 1944.

the maintenance of production of both military and consumer goods has been made possible by drawing upon the huge pool of civilians available in the occupied countries. With the loss of France and the Low Countries, Finland, Rumania, Bulgaria and the Baltic States, additional foreigners can no longer be found in large quantities to man either the factories or the fortifications of Germany. This task must now be accomplished by the *Herrenvolk* themselves.

As the Allied advance threatened the frontiers of Germany, a total mobilization of all available persons was undertaken. To meet the ever-worsening situation in the west new divisions were organized, and early in August four new series of divisions were already evident: the new 500 series, the 'leave' divisions culled from men home from Russia or Norway, the converted training divisions, and the utilization of divisional staffs to carry out an operational role.

The retreat across France, with its staggering loss of men at Falaise, Mortain, the Midi and those bottled up in ports like Brest, Le Havre and Dunkirk, resulted in the destruction of so many divisions as fighting entities, that even the waves of newly-formed divisions did not provide sufficient organized manpower to defend the frontiers of Germany. The 'total' mobilization of Himmler thereupon became a 'super-total' mobilization. Every man in the Reich was to be flung into battle to halt the invaders, be he trained or untrained, fit or unfit, organized or unorganized.

In this way, since no time was available to organize fully-fledged fighting divisions, troops were found to stand along the Siegfried Line and the Waal and halt the onrushing Allies, already hampered by an ever-lengthening supply route. Training schools, static staffs, pilots and ground crews, sailors without ships, police units and even the ARP were all impressed into the line, and usually equipped with rifles and some MGs and mortars.

With the airborne invasion this picture of last-ditch mobilization was revealed with still more clarity. The result was like lifting a rather large rock from moist soil. The most startling conglomeration of units crawled out to defend the bridges at Arnhem, Nijmegen and Eindhoven. The identifications obtained in Holland, together with others found on the borders of Germany, indicate that the defence of Germany was undertaken by the utilization of various units and formations which can roughly be classified as follows:

> *Volksgrenadier* Divisions
> Battle Groups

Wehrmacht Units
Luftwaffe Units
Marine Units
Parachute Military Units

An exhaustive list of identified units is at this time impracticable. However an illustration of these various categories of units will be attempted by a short description of the type of personnel found chiefly on the 21 Army Group front. The kind of formation listed here is, for the most part, the quickly-assembled groups of bodies whose chief tactical purpose was to hold and delay. If necessary they could be ruthlessly sacrificed so long as their intended purpose was fulfilled. The need for the utilization of these categories of the national population is a measure of the desperation that governed the High Command in its efforts to stabilize the situation.

It must be remembered in studying these units, that they do not comprise the bulk of the German Army in the field. There are still available the remnants of SS and Wehrmacht divisions to provide the backbone of leadership and manpower for the defence of Germany. It is also extremely likely that subsequent call-up groups will be utilized chiefly for the reinforcing of fighting divisional formations.

(a)   Volksgrenadier Divisions

These last-ditch formations were to receive the bulk of available manpower still left in Germany. Of the divisions promised by Himmler, thirteen in the 500 series have been identified by contact and documents, with another seven probably in the offing. The 'leave' divisions (59th, 64th, 226th) and the administrative staffs (136th, 176th, 406th, 462nd) have absorbed a good many of the potential military personnel in the country. Now a new group of divisions (36th, 180th, 183rd, 190th, 246th) seem to have been achieved by scraping hard along the bottom of Germany's manpower barrel. The Reich's normal call-up groups have been mortgaged so far in advance that to bring new divisions to the west, battered divisions from Russia (36th, 183rd, 246th) had to be refitted and reinforced, while training units were assembled to form others (180th, 190th). These two latter groups and the 500 series probably constitute the bulk of the *Volksgrenadier* Divisions.

Of the latter type 180th Infantry Division is typical. The reconnaissance element was composed of men who had served for a few weeks earlier in the war, but had been discharged as medically unfit. Thirteen PW of this unit claimed it was 'criminal folly' to put them in the line, since they could not fire a rifle and their LMGs (Czech) could not be persuaded to fire bursts. A sitrep dated 23 September from this formation asks: 'Where can Lance-Corporal Hapel, who has totally collapsed from former wounds and Trooper Eichhorn, blind in the left eye and his right eye damaged, see an MO?' The Grenadier Regiments of the division consisted of a large group of men called up in September 1944, and brought direct from their training battalions into battle, many of the gunners had less than six weeks' training, while four men from the Engineer Battalion had been called up on 25 August 1944, after having served for years as Luftwaffe gun crews.

Representative of the personnel used for the reforming of divisions from Russia is 246th Infantry Division. After suffering heavy casualties on the Central Front in Russia, it was reformed in the vicinity of Prague during the months of August and September. Given the name '*Volksgrenadier*' it now contains 40% Naval personnel, 20% convalescent and 40% defence workers. By these means they were able to bring the regimental strength up to between 1500-1700 men.

Volksgrenadier divisions represent the final sifting out of the manpower pool to produce divisional formations for both the eastern and western fronts. In them the non-essential factory workers, the small shopkeepers, the petty officials have finally taken their place in the Wehrmacht after managing for five years to convince the Nazi government of their indispensability elsewhere.

Within the fortifications of the Siegfried Line these divisions have effectively stopped the American advance. That this success will continue against a full-scale offensive, and when out of the protection of their concrete bunkers, is most unlikely.

(b)   Battle Groups (Kampfgruppen)

Severely handled during their headlong rush from the Seine to Holland and Germany, few of the divisional staffs were able to retain complete control of the units under their command. In an attempt to get as many troops as possible through the continuous encirclements that waylaid them, units were split into tiny groups and told to make their way back to allotted meeting-points as best they could. The method adopted to organise these small bodies of men was the time-honoured battle group system. Starting off with such men as were available, these ad hoc units, calling themselves by the name of their senior officer, picked up stragglers and isolated groups in their retreat back, and with these fought off any attacks that came their way until they had reached the temporary safety of the waterways of Holland or the Siegfried Line. These men constituted the first type of battle group that was met on the frontiers of Germany.

The second type of battle group was formed in early August or later, when the breakthrough in Normandy became evident. Hastily assembled, for the most part from training battalions and schools, these units ranged from battalion to brigade size and lacked both training and heavy weapons.

(i)   Battle Groups formed from divisions in Normandy

Kampfgruppe Prehm: This group was formed in Capelle about 6 September 1944 and is typical of the units created from the remnants of the divisions that escaped across the Seine. Personnel were from 17 Luftwaffe Field Division, 272nd Infantry Division, 331st Infantry Division, 363rd Infantry Division, 16 Sicherungs Regiment, 624 Cossack Battalion and HQ of Seventh Army, amongst others. It is now an integral part of 346th Infantry Division forming II Battalion of 858th Regiment.

Kampfgruppe Pohl: About a battalion strong this battle group was formed in Turnhout 2-4 September, and presented another confusion of souls and paybooks from the 9th SS Panzer Division, 719th Infantry Division, 17th Luftwaffe Field Division, *Landeschütz* Battalions 484 and 737, *Marsch* Battalion 501, Marine *Ersatz Abteilungen* Kiel and Wilhelmshaven, not to mention a couple of Russians.

(ii)   Battle Groups formed in Germany

Kampfgruppe Wilhelm: This unit was formed at Oldenburg between 1 and 10 September from stragglers, convalescents and odds and ends. PW taken included a man of 38 with a glass eye, a man of 45 with a still unhealed wound received in Russia, one of 44 with stomach ulcers, and a Dutch civilian lorry driver who was included when his truck was filled with ammunition at the barracks. This latter trick was done by suddenly announcing to the Dutchman that he had been 'accepted' as a 'voluntary Auxiliary', and he was then promptly sent off to the front, truck and all.

Kampfgruppe Ewald: This consisted of 2 Battalion (Pioneer) *Ersatz* Regiment 1, formerly located at Stendal. Personnel came from all branches of the service and included air gunners, air crews, infantry and orderly room clerks. Most of them were sent to Stendal on approximately 22 August. Nearly all of them were medically unfit for parachute jumping, and they were told they were to train as air-landing troops. The battalion moved to Schijndel on 1 September to continue training. It was forced to become a fighting unit and received its new name when Allied paratroops landed almost on top of its training area.

(c)   Army Units

(i)   *Landesschützen Battalion 8B*: This unit has been stationed in the Lille and Tournai areas guarding railway lines. Most of the PW were between 40 and 50 years of age and had had no training beyond basic infantry drill. Being veterans of the last war they stated they did their duty to the last, but saw no future in fighting tanks with rifles.

(ii)   *Werfer Regiment 1*: This regiment was formed from *Werfer Ersatz* Battalions 2 and 3 in Bremen following the air landings of 17 September. They left Bremen on 19/20 September and began to support troops three days later in the region of Deurne. All PW but one had been casualties in Russia, and were at the Convalescent Troop of their *ersatz* battalion when reorganised. The one exception was a civilian MT driver who had been employed in a chemical factory in Bremen. His firm received a telephone message on 17 September, as a result of which he reported with his lorry to the unit barracks. There he was given an armband with *'Deutscher Wehrmacht'* printed on it. A *Nebelwerfer* 41 was pitched on to his truck, and he was sent to Holland with the regiment. He stated that 7 or 8 civilian drivers (including French and Dutch nationals) were recruited in the same way.

(iii)   *Ohren Battalion 286 and Magen Battalion 136*: These two units were specially organised for men physically unfit for normal service. The necessity of special food for men suffering from stomach ulcers and stomach wounds led to the organisation of *Magen* (stomach) battalions. But this logic hardly seems to apply to the *Ohren* (Ear) Battalion which consisted entirely, except for the NCOs and officers, of men who were hard of hearing. The difficulties of this latter unit were manifold. Officers could only give orders to their men by gestures, and guards were unable to hear anyone approaching, so that they fired immediately when suddenly confronted by someone. Two sergeants of the guard had already been killed in this way.

(iv)   *198 Sicherungs Regiment*: This unit was composed of men from high age groups and *Naurentage*. These latter were men who had lost their fathers in the 1914–18 war, or were the only surviving son of a family which had already lost its sons in this war. Both of these classes had been exempt from military service until recently.

(v)   *1409 Fortress Infantry Battalion*: This unit was formed in St Polten, Vienna, about 14 August and was composed of drafts from 138 Infantry *Ersatz* Battalion, 130 Grenadier *Ersatz* Battalion, D17 Battalion, 482 Grenadier *Ersatz* Battalion, 462 Grenadier *Ersatz* Battalion, 9 Field

Division Luftwaffe, and this list is by no means exhaustive. PW were Austrians and south Germans, and all had served on the Russian front, had been wounded and returned to their *Ersatz* units.

(d) Luftwaffe Units

The best resistance to the advance in Holland has been put up by elements of the Luftwaffe now converted into an infantry role. Young, enthusiastic, but disappointed at the abrupt halt put to their technical training, they have displayed an unusual dash in both defence and counter-attack, that has been remarkably absent from German tactics during the past month. This was achieved despite a woeful lack of training in an infantry role.

(i) *20 Luftwaffe Fortress Battalion*: One of five similar units identified in the west, this battalion was formed early in September from the Luftwaffe Interpreters Training and Replacement School at Olmütz in Germany. The battalion of about 400 men had done one infantry exercise the day before they went into battle, and during the course of it their commanding officer was killed.

(ii) *51 Luftwaffe Training Regiment*: A training unit designed for the training of pilots and air crews, it has been identified as part of Battle Group Seidel in an infantry role. The men are young and eager, and have fought well despite a lack of heavy weapons and the necessity for using aircraft machine guns in the field. Ten of these regiments have already been identified in the west.

(iii) *Parachute Regiment Hoffman*: Organised early in September this unit was composed predominantly of Luftwaffe personnel. The regiment included no genuine paratroops; none had received paratroop training, nor was such training intended. Other men were ex-crews from Russia, members of Luftwaffe field units wounded in Italy, and some Wehrmacht personnel from Finland and Russia.

(iv) *Luftwaffe Jaeger Ersatz Battalion z.b.V.*[2] 6: This battalion consisted entirely of men who had served military sentences in the Luftwaffe, and were being given a chance to regain their previous rank by proving themselves in action. It was originally formed in Poland in April 1944 and its personnel were all ex-criminals of the Luftwaffe from *Luftflotte* 4. It fought in Russia, Rumania, was flown to Italy, and finally was sent to area Hasselt in Belgium on 7 September 1944. It is a 'suicide battalion' from which men never expect to return, and it is always put in where the fighting is bitterest.

---

2. *Zur besonderen Verwendung* meaning unattached or detailed for special work.

(e) Marine Units

The garrisons of ports like Le Havre, Brest, Boulogne and Calais have consisted of almost 30% naval personnel. By utilizing these marines in an infantry and artillery role, the German Army has been able to use its regular divisions for other tasks, and leave the defence of the coastal cities largely to the Navy. In addition to those marines comprising the coastal garrisons, other marine units have been milked to provide manpower for the *Volksgrenadier* Divisions and to stand in the line and hold until these divisions are ready to take over. With the inability of German ships to leave the safety of their ports without quick and heavy losses, it seems as if the Navy has shared with the Luftwaffe and the Wehrmacht the honour of defending Germany on its flat feet.

(i) *Marine Flakschule 3*: This unit had originally been located at Mistroy where it gave instructions on 3.7 cm and 2 cm flak. After invasion it contributed its students and part of its permanent staff for guard duties in the Lille area, and was subsequently turned into infantry in September 1944.

(ii) *Marine Bau Kompanie*: Despite its name, this company had nothing to do with construction, but was used as a guard company in a naval ammunition dump. Personnel was largely old *G.v.H.*[3] category or politically unreliable, and aged between 35-40. It was given an infantry role early in September.

(f) Police and Auxiliary Units

These units, with their older age groups and little infantry training, have been thrown into the line in ever-increasing numbers. No attempt has as yet been made to absorb them into normal divisional formations, and the chain of command governing them is very vague. They are probably controlled by the senior military formation in closest geographical proximity to them.

(i) *3 Police Regiment*: The use of civil police in an Army role may be expected in any area of operations in the Reich itself. The personnel of this unit were in their early 40s and had been in the Police service since September 39 or early 40. Previous to that they had been independent shopkeepers or tradesmen. None of the PW had been police before that time. Their infantry training was begun in May of this year, and

---

3. G.v.H. or *Garnisonsverwendungsfähig Heimat*. A soldier only physically capable of garrison duty in Germany.

they were first put into action against the Allied airborne landing forces at Best.

(ii) *Reichsluftschützdienst*[4] (ARP Service): Of the 40 PW captured the youngest was 40 and had been discharged from the Army with lung trouble in 1940. Others were as old as 67 and only a few were under 60. On 7 September all the ARP services of Waltrop and surrounding district were combed out for foreign service. The remainder, which contained this group, were sent to Wyler and set to digging an anti-tank ditch across the road Nijmegen-Wyler, where they were captured.

(iii) *160 Gruppe RAD* (German Labour Service): This unit left Rheine, Westphalia, by train 10 September and travelled to Nijmegen. The 8th Company consisted of 4 platoons each of 50 youths of 17 years of age. More than half of these were Poles. The personnel had each been issued with a rifle and ten rounds of ammunition for his own protection and military training. They were employed in digging an anti-tank ditch when captured.

The units here listed are merely representative of scores like them now stretched from Belfort to Breskens. A study of over 300 PW reports shows that the majority of personnel now manning the western fortresses of the Reich have been hastily drafted in their present formations in the Army during the past two months. Their age groups and state of training have already been described. That this force has succeeded in holding the Allies is largely a testimony to the recuperative power of the German General Staff, as well as to a patriotism born of a fight on the frontier of one's homeland. But equal to, if not greater than both these explanations of the German stand, is the great administrative problem now facing the Allied armies in the west.

Yet even to acquire these troops, the German High Command had to abandon the already largely abandoned German Navy; it had to give up its hopes for a mighty Luftwaffe, and finally it had to sacrifice part of its dwindling resources of industrial manpower. When these are gone, there is little else to draw upon – only still older age groups and still more essential skilled workers.

That these strategems have achieved tactical success cannot be denied, but that this pauper's policy is bound to fail in the long run, is just as obvious. It is hardly likely that this makeshift force, with its lack of training and scarcity of heavy equipment, will succeed where the SS and panzer divisions of Normandy failed.

---

4. German air raid protection service, a civil defence organization.

Document 8/2[5]

The Formation of New German Divisions

At the beginning of 1944 Germany found herself with three hundred and twenty five divisions of all sorts, to fight the battles in the east and prepare for the coming invasion in the west. Reinforcements for depleted and reforming divisions in Russia were obtained from the new call-ups and the balance of available manpower was organized into new divisions. So well did the normal call-up of age groups supply the army in the field, that not only were normal casualties replaced, but the total of divisions within the Wehrmacht increased steadily as the war progressed.

With the invasion of France and the new Russian offensive of 22 June 1944, the manpower resources of Germany and her satellites were unable to meet the new demands created by the staggering losses inflicted on both fronts. Not even the conscription of the peoples of the occupied countries could offset the losses of dead, wounded and prisoners. New divisions formed after D-Day to replace those destroyed were manned, not by the normal age-class of the year, but by dipping deep into the emptying barrel of German manpower, and scraping out such dregs as had remained safely ensconced there for five years.

Men on leave and convalescing in German hospitals, recruits waiting to complete their training, personnel of training and demonstration units, ex-policemen, retired regulars, and all the non-essential manpower that industry in the Reich could afford to disgorge, were hastily assembled to form the divisions destined to stop the threats from both the east and the west.

Captured documents and PW statements indicate that during 1944 the new infantry divisions of the Wehrmacht have come from the following five groups:

(a) 25th wave formed January–February
(b) the conversion of training divisions to operational status from April–August
(c) the 'leave' group formed June–July
(d) the 26th wave formed July–August

---

5. ISUM 78, 10 September 1944.

(e) the conversion of divisional staffs to operational roles (*z.b.V.* divisions) beginning in August

(a) Twenty-fifth Wave[6]

This group of divisions formed in January-February of 1944 obtained its personnel from the normal residue of the year's call-up, after reinforcements and replacements in the east had been met. Given available numbers below 100, these divisions were organized as the new 'pocket-type' division, designed to conserve manpower. The six divisions, 77th, 84th, 85th, 89th, 91st and 92nd, contained two regiments of three battalions each, with regimental numbers over 1000. Committed against the Allied bridgehead, the first five are now virtually destroyed, and 92nd Infantry Division's existence in Italy is now uncertain.

(b) Training Divisions converted to Operational Role

These divisions, designed to train and supply reinforcements for formations in the field, became the next logical candidates for an operational role. Located near the battle zone, and having on hand suitable personnel, as well as a cadre of trained officers and NCOs, the process of conversion of them was begun in April and was being completed late in August, as the battle moved north to take in the area occupied by the training divisions still left in Holland and even Denmark.

These divisions also took on numbers below 100, but the regimental numbers attained no definite pattern with most of them being below 300 but 70th Infantry Division returning to the 1000 regimental numbers. This latter may be explained by a captured map which shows that on Walcheren Island both 165th Infantry Division and its three reserve regiments, and 1018 Grenadier Regiment and 1019 Grenadier Regiment, all existed at one and the same time. It is probable that a 70th Infantry Division was to be formed independently, but that the shortage of manpower forced 165th Infantry Training Division to provide the balance of personnel.

Amongst this group of converted divisions are 47th from 156th Training Division, 48th from 171st Training Division, 49th from 191st Training Division, 16th from 158th Training Division, 70th from 165th Training Division and 19th possibly from 166th Training Division. It is probable that 160th Training Division in Denmark may soon turn up in a new uniform.

---

6. The German army of the Second World War was raised in a number of *Wellen* or waves, all of which were equipped and organized identically. The first wave consisted of the pre-August 1939 regular force, the second wave of divisions mobilized in August 1939 and so on. In all, the army mobilized thirty-five waves by the late spring of 1945 but the new formations were, after 1943, progressively weaker and less well equipped.

(c) The 'Leave' Divisions

A large percentage of the personnel of this group of divisions was recruited while on leave from Russia, Norway and Finland. Desperately needing new formations in the west, all available manpower in Germany in June and July was shoved into these hastily assembled formations and flung into action with barely any training as a divisional unit.

With regimental numbers over 1000, three divisions of this group have already been identified, 59th, 64th and 226th, while the existence of two others, 232nd and 237th, is attested to by a captured document.

(d) Twenty-sixth Wave

This wave is designed to provide the bulk of new divisions this year, and information about them is given in the G-2 Reports of First and Third US Armies. Captured documents reveal the identity of thirteen divisions in the '500' series, all apparently products of the total mobilization programme that followed the abortive assassination attempt on Hitler.

These divisions in this new twenty-sixth wave must represent the final scrapings of the Reich's desperate manpower resources. They are what may aptly be labelled the *Götterdämmerung* Wave, created in his extremity to strengthen Hitler's last ditch stand against extinction as Allied drives in the east and west thrust ever closer to Germany's borders.

The documents, dated 1 August 1944, are orders of the German Army Personnel Office for transfer and promotion of General Staff officers. The following Divisions are mentioned: 541st, 542nd, 544th, 547th, 548th, 549th, 551st, 553rd, 558th, 559th, 560th, 561st, and 562nd Grenadier Divisions.

It is significant in view of the admittedly low morale in the Wehrmacht that these units should all be designated Grenadier Divisions instead of Infantry Divisions. Of course, the two words are synonymous, but Grenadier Division is a more imposing title than Infantry Division. It was noted previously that the Nazis prefer to form new Divisions from remnants rather than rebuild old Divisions which have suffered defeat in battle. The reason for this is psychological, i.e. the old soldier will fight better for a new unit than for an old unit which has already been defeated and decimated in battle. Similarly, with these *Götterdämmerung* Divisions, the Nazis have used the title 'Grenadier' to impress upon the soldier that these units are superior to ordinary Infantry Divisions.

There is no clear indication why Himmler chose to begin numbering these *Götterdämmerung* Divisions with 541. However, 537th, 538th, 539th and 540th are the numbers of *Grenzwacht*[7] or Frontier Guard Divisions. These Divisions of the twenty-sixth wave are in a sense *Grenzwacht* Divisions too, for they were formed with the express purpose of manning Germany's last lines of defence. Therefore, it is not unreasonable to assume that the *Götterdämmerung* series is an extension of the *Grenzwacht* Divisions.

Most of these Divisions are still in the process of formation in Germany or occupied territories, but two of them (553rd and 559th) have been identified opposing Third US Army. 553rd Grenadier Division is reported to contain three Grenadier Regiments, numbers 1119, 1120, and 1121. 559th Grenadier Division likewise has three regiments. They are numbered 1125, 1126, and 1127. Judging from these regimental affiliations, 558th Grenadier Division, the only one known between 553rd and 559th, should have 1122, 1123, and 1124 Grenadier Regiments. The number of the regiments within the other divisions of this new wave is as yet uncertain, but a Russian report identifies 1082, 1083, and 1084 Infantry Regiments as belonging to 544th Infantry Division.

The detailed organization of these divisions has not yet been established but it is likely that each of the three regiments will contain three battalions instead of two. Nine battalions is an unusual divisional organization for new formations. All previous waves of divisions formed in 1944 were organized on a six-battalion War Establishment, either two regiments-three battalions or three regiments-two battalions. A civilian source reports the further unusual feature of 88mm AA anti-tank guns in the 13th Infantry Gun Coy of each regiment. With the need for protection against our superior armour, this is a reasonable possibility.

(e) Divisional Staff Converted to Field Divisions

The final source for new identifications can be produced by mobilizing divisional staffs and providing them with troops to enable them to carry out an operational role. 136th *z.b.V.* and 176th *z.b.V.* Divisions have already been identified on Second Army Front, and 462nd Depot Division may be expected. The problem of converting these depots to an operational role is, that while the staff is available, it is like a head without a body until troops have been found for the staff to command.

---

7. The *Grenzwacht* ('Border Patrol') was the pre-war paramilitary frontier security service. In 1939 its regiments were militarized as part of the army.

Document 8/3[8]

Reinforcement Situation in Italy, Autumn 1944

An analysis of over 4000 PW received at 1st Canadian Corps Cage during the months of September and October 1944 shows the type of reinforcements now being received on the Italian front. The same low standard of men and morale is evident amongst the recent recruits to this theatre as is now found manning the Siegfried Line and the Rhine. The youngest and best personnel are, as usual, given to parachute units with second priority going to the panzer formations.

(i)   1st Parachute Division

This always has received the very highest quality of reinforcements to maintain its standard as the 'elite' division in this theatre. The two very large groups of reinforcements received, usually referred to as the 'Gardelegen' and the 'Verdun'[9] reinforcements, were up to standard, except that they had no field experience. Most were very young – 17–19 – but there were also a fair percentage from A A units and former flying personnel. The latter do not take too kindly to being put in as infantrymen albeit with a high-sounding name. Most of these reinforcements have been absorbed and a large number of them are now 'good Germans':[10] or in a PW cage. Since the middle of October a new type of paratroop has been observed and deserters have not been uncommon. Some of these new reinforcements are Poles, but there are also *Reichsdeutsche*[11] deserters, who are thoroughly disgusted with everything. It can be safely said that morale in this division has taken a very decided drop since the beginning of October.

(ii)   26th Panzer Division

Still the same sort of reinforcements have been dished out as Panzer Grenadiers, with one noticeable exception. This was in 26th Reconnaissance Battalion at the beginning of October when a very large number of infants had the most astonishingly high morale and professed

---

8. ISUM 145, 24 November 1944, from *1st Canadian Corps Intelligence Summary*, 30 October 1944.
9. The Luftwaffe established airborne training centres at Gardelegen in Germany and Verdun in France.
10. That is, dead Germans. There was a saying in the wartime British army: 'The only good German is a dead German – if you meet a live one, kill him quick before he goes bad.'
11. German nationals resident within the pre-1939 boundaries of Germany.

complete faith in final victory, etc. Just what the cause of this was, was never ascertainable as the reinforcements they came with from Germany who were sent to other units, were anything but confident. The main reinforcements received were all 17-18 years old, and several were under 5 feet tall. Many had deficient vision and other physical defects and the general attitude was that they were glad that they did not have to stay out in the rifle-pits any longer. Most had been called up in April or May and they were usually taken PW on their first or second day in the line. The percentage of *Volksdeutsch*[12] was fairly low. The other source of reinforcements has been the further weeding out of the administrative area of the division and these are between 35 and 42, mostly married men and mostly very bitter against the present regime. Most are only too anxious to help us to bring the war to a close as soon as possible.

(iii)   162nd Turcoman Division

Infantry fighting value very low. All, including Germans, desert when opportunity offers. Turcomen still keep coming in from various hiding places. One Polish deserter, who left 329th Grenadier Regiment two or three months ago, claimed that they did not dare put it into the line on account of its low fighting value.

(iv)   90th Panzer Grenadier Division

As this had already had a fairly heavy beating before we came into contact with it, the picture is possibly biased. Many are in the 35-45-year-old classes and these are particularly 'browned off'. Reinforcements received have been of the convalescent type, with which we have become so familiar, and their main theme was 'better today than tomorrow' when referring to the end of the war.

(v)   General

In general, PW seem to be much better informed about world conditions than a month ago. Few cases of absolute ignorance of what has happened in the Balkans are encountered. A general impression received is that in spite of all Nazi propaganda about Air-Gangsters and Terror-Raids, most of them hold the Regime responsible for the state Germany finds itself in at present. The usual impression is that it will be finished early in 1945 at the latest.

---

12. German-speaking persons resident outside the 1939 borders of Germany, in Eastern Europe and the Balkans.

Document 8/4[13]

The Sad Story of Battle Group Gobel

The most bedraggled members of the Wehrmacht to show up in the cage in some time were 12 prisoners from Battle Group Gobel. They were equipped with a very dismal story. Seven weeks ago proclamations were posted on the walls of Alsdorf (north of Aachen), requiring all men aged between 17 and 50 to assemble at the city hall. 1200 innocents showed up, whereupon they were drafted into the German Army on the spot. A new order was then read, allowing all men over forty and those with more than five children to return home. This cut the eligibles down to 300, who were shipped over to Merzenhausen K9860 that very afternoon.

At Merzenhausen the men were divided into groups and, still clad in civilian clothes and without weapons, given infantry training. After two weeks of this kind of training they were sent to Hasseltsweiler F0566 where they were issued *Soldbuchs*[14] and christened '149th Field Replacement Battalion'. (This outfit is possibly now the replacement battalion of the 149th Grenadier Regiment of 49th Infantry Division). After three more weeks of 'infantry training' they were sent to Mersch FO463 where, at last, uniforms were issued. The uniforms, however, were apparently German Army rejects for the last five years, and no shoes at all were given out.

Thus outfitted, the battalion was moved to Julich, where it was quartered appropriately enough, in the city jail. After the bombing of 16 November, during which the unit sustained no casualties, since the Jail was a new one, the men were turned into the street as debris cleaners and received more 'infantry training' on the side. On 28 November, 80 of the men were taken under control by a Lieutenant Gobel, who told them they were now 'the defenders of Julich'. At Kirchberg, the next stop of Battle Group Gobel, the men were finally given a rifle each and as much ammunition as they could stow in their pockets, since no web equipment or gas masks were issued. They were put in the line against the 16 US Infantry Regiment early in the morning of 24 November.

13. ISUM 151, 30 November 1944, from *1st US Infantry Division G-2 Report*.
14. *Soldbuch* or paybook, the prime source of identification for a German soldier, which contained details of his military record.

Document 8/5[15]

Recruiting and Training of Officers in the German Army

A considerable number of PW have recently been interrogated as to the methods by which new officers are being recruited in the German forces today, and as to the relations which exist between officers and OR. Both classes have contributed their views, though the bulk of the information obtained comes from the latter.

Normally it appears that the selection of officers is made by recommendation, and COs are frequently reminded to keep their eyes open for promising material. It is possible also for OR to apply for consideration as officer candidates, either on enlistment or at a later stage, but this is far less common than selection by recommendation. It is interesting to note that in one instance an appeal was made for volunteers to come forward as officer candidates in infantry, but it was not possible either to confirm or to disprove that similar appeals had been made in other arms. Two PW from 1051 Grenadier Regiment of 84th Infantry Division stated that between 20 and 25 September an appeal was read out on two mornings in succession to their battalion and that one Corporal and one Lance Corporal volunteered. Both were selected after filling in application forms and producing references for their good conduct in civil life.

Apart from technical qualifications peculiar to each arm, the following general considerations apply:

(i)   PW opinion was unanimous that influence of any sort, whether through highly placed friends or through the party, has no effect on a candidate's chance of selection if he does not possess the necessary qualifications.

(ii) No special medical examination is held before a candidate is commissioned or sent away for officer training.

(iii) As regards educational standards, matriculation and university training seem to make a man almost automatically a prospective candidate, provided that his military record is satisfactory. Men have, however, been selected with a grade 8 public school education.

---

15. ISUM 157, 6 December 1944.

(iv) A clean conduct sheet is essential and an unblemished civilian record. No information could be obtained as to the weight attached to political views.

(v) Perhaps the most important factor is a smart military bearing and the possession of military horse-sense.

(vi) Every candidate must have had normal infantry and basic training, and a minimum of two months' front line experience.

It appears that the majority of new officers come from the lower ranks. Ambition and the desire for prestige play their part with senior NCOs who otherwise are not generally anxious to become officers. Financially a commission has little attraction for a Sergeant Major although clothing and other allowances are higher for a Lieutenant, and RSMs do not generally desire to exchange their kingdoms for a lieutenancy.

When a CO picks out a likely candidate, he usually goes as a Corporal to an NCOs course in his own arm lasting from three to six months. He then normally returns to regimental duty and is formally recommended by his CO, being promoted *Fähnrich* and later *Oberfähnrich*. During this period a candidate attends further courses according to his needs, but it does not appear that all candidates have to attend a course specifically designed for potential officers before being commissioned. One lieutenant, captured at Dunkirk, became an officer after the siege had begun and did not consider there was anything unusual in the fact nor complained of the absence of OCTUs[16] in the fortress. He had had a university training but had done no courses since he had been recommended as an officer candidate.

A medical *Oberfähnrich*, called up in 1939, with two university terms studying medicine to his credit, received further training as a medical orderly and assistant to the Medical Officer and was sent on two separate occasions to Heidelberg University for one term. On capture he also was awaiting promotion to officer's rank. It was not, however, found possible to establish any standard period of waiting for an *Oberfähnrich* before becoming a lieutenant, nor any specific reason or condition which terminated such a period.

Relations between officers and OR were described by representatives of both classes as cordial, but disciplined, and old soldiers claim a marked difference between the war of 1914–18 and today. Officers and senior NCOs were said to look after themselves first, but OR did not complain of this.

---

16. Officer Candidate Training Unit, a Commonwealth military term.

Off parade there was a spirit of camaraderie between the two. There was no question of OR, for example, having to frequent different cafes from those used by officers, except where financial limitations made this inevitable, but relations here were maintained usually on an official footing. On entering an officer would give the Hitler salute and OR, if seated, would 'sit to attention' but would not rise. The PW from 1051 Grenadier Regiment said that on one such occasion the company commander came over and asked if they were enjoying themselves but he omitted to stand a round of drinks. Such things, they added, do not happen very frequently.

In the line all shared a similar lot, and food and fox-holes were the same for both. There was little confirmation forthcoming from the PW interrogated of the accusations sometimes made in the past that officers are apt to leave their men when the situation becomes unusually difficult. From all accounts the welfare of the men was well looked after by their officers, some PW saying that during quiet periods they were better entertained as soldiers than they had been as civilians. Most entertainment was provided by civilians, organized by *'Kraft durch Freude'*[17] but the army provided some from its own resources.

The above symposium, then, generally reflects the OR point of view, which is probably more concerned with the system prevailing under peaceful conditions. No evidence was forthcoming of any recently-introduced emergency procedure for building up officer strengths rapidly, nor was it apparent that any shortage of officers was generally felt. It was unfortunate that the selection of PW available did not include any representatives of the newly-formed or reconditioned divisions, where such problems might have been expected to show themselves.

17. The *KdF* or *Kraft durch Freude* began as the Nazi regime's attempt to provide affordable holidays and leisure activities for workers and their families. During the war, it functioned in a similar fashion to the ENSA and NAAFI service organizations in the British armed forces and the USO in the American armed forces, providing leave centres, films and entertainment for military personnel.

Document 8/6[18]

Training of Officer Candidates

A PW from 1 Parachute Reserve and Training Regiment captured in the Breskens bridgehead has supplied a comprehensive picture of enemy methods of training prospective officer candidates.

In July 1942, after having volunteered previously for flying duties with the Luftwaffe, he was mobilized into 33 *Flieger* Regiment in Westphalia. The first stages of training covered infantry subjects common to all arms, including MGs (42 and 15, the latter an aircraft version), rifles, pistols, grenades, intensive fieldcraft and camouflage methods, wood and street fighting and range practices. Unarmed combat was not included.

Early in the 13-week infantry training course, instructional officers began to look out for prospective officer material. Personnel of good physique who were above the average in education and intelligence were registered as cadets, and volunteers for cadet courses were also interviewed. Thereafter approximately twice weekly throughout the term of infantry training, extra-curricular interviews were held with an officer (*Studienassessor*) who took stock of the material for officer training. Generally, former teachers and active officers made up the interviewing and selection cadre.

As the course progressed, subjects of a wide range were discussed, among which the Nazi philosophy of life (*Weltanschauung*) figured largely. Musical subjects and literature (notably Schiller and Goethe) comprised a proportion of the timetable, while study of, and written essays on, such subjects as war, war in Russia, money, England, colonies, provided a suitable means of inculcating Nazi precepts into impressionable minds. Considerable time was given to map reading on scales of 1:100,000, 1:25,000 and 1:10,000 (not 1:50,000) and even during the infantry training, a period on Luftwaffe maps of 1:1,000,000 and 1:4,000,000.

Sport was conducted along vigorous competitive lines, under the close supervision of officers. PW suffered a knee accident early in the course, however, was immediately hospitalized, and apparently never received an opportunity to complete his training. He thus can supply no further information on the remaining highlights of the course.

---

18. ISUM 114, 22 October 1944.

On being discharged from the hospital, the PW entered a pilot's school, but as his eyesight was discovered to be defective he was required to leave on physical grounds. After some months of inactivity in *ersatz* units, PW joined I Battalion, 1 Parachute Training Regiment and accompanied it to the Pas de Calais area, whence he participated in the retreat to the Leopold Canal.

Document 8/7[19]

German Recruiting Methods 1944

Two 18-year-old former members of the Hermann Goering Reinforcement and Training Regiment who deserted to the Dutch Patriotic forces, have recounted their experiences and impressions since being called up in May of this year. It would be difficult to find a brace of more unwilling upholders of the enemy cause, or two more willing informers than these young stalwarts, one from Vienna the other from Lorraine, who have been cared for by the Dutch underground since 10 September.

Both were called up to report to the above-mentioned unit in Utrecht on 25 May 1944. The man from Lorraine made a stern effort to evade the draft, hiding in the woods for three weeks until his parents began to receive visits from the SS or Gestapo. On this latter account, he gave himself up to the authorities on 12 June and arrived at Utrecht the next day. On the 14th, together with 1000 recruits, he entrained for Berlin because of the danger of air invasion, only to return to Hilversum on 1 July. The Viennese managed to avoid joining the draft to Berlin, but was temporarily attached as a driver to a petrol column, and, after recovering from appendicitis, spent a few weeks on the dunes at Katwick D7204 with HQ Company in a coastal defence role.

Training occupied the summer months in various parts of Holland. It consisted of the usual infantry training, rifle, MG 15 and 42, pistol, MP 38/40 and a heavy diet of fieldcraft. Much time was spent on fire and movement tactics in pairs, by sub-sections and pairs. 'Abrollen' or 'rolling sideways' was practised with the idea of learning to deceive the enemy as to

---

19. ISUM 136, 13 November 1944.

where the individual would pop up next. After a short advance, the soldier would drop to the ground, roll over, usually to the right from one to three paces, wait, and then rise again for the next bout.

Gas training was thorough and the instructors remarked that although at present the Luftwaffe was in no position to start a gas war, it must be expected that towards the close of the war gas might be used.

A vivid picture was drawn of recruiting activities in Lorraine. The first pronouncement on the subject by the local *Gauleiter* stated that no one would have to do forced labour. This was later qualified considerably and volunteers were called for. As the manpower situation worsened, young men were forced into the Army by fair means and foul, and were made to sign on the dotted line that they were volunteers. They were ironically enough, shipped off on a train with 'volunteers' written all over the cars. The means used to force young men to report for military service ranged from warnings and menaces to deportation of the parents of sons who were in hiding nearby or who had escaped.

On one occasion at the beginning of June 1944, the number of dodgers who hid away in the woods had risen to over 300 in a certain district. Their parents had been warned several times, but as this did not lead to surrender, SS troops surrounded the wood and attacked with MGs and automatics. The evaders tried vainly to defend themselves with some French MGs, rifles and pistols which they had acquired, but could not hold out against the superior weapons of the SS and were mostly killed in battle. The survivors are reported to have been shot out of hand. The parents of the youths involved were either deported to Holland or sent to concentration camps at a few minutes' notice. Trucks for their deportation must have been held in readiness, according to PW, as they arrived punctually immediately the battle was over.

Chapter 9

Problems

Desertion, Discipline, Transport and Food

Editor's Comments

By the autumn of 1944 the Wehrmacht was experiencing serious problems with desertion and discipline, despite a fairly rigorous system of military courts-martial (Document 9/3). Stern measures were instigated (Document 9/1) but problems remained although the poor state of discipline in the 606th Division (Document 9/2) may not have been typical. Other problems included a lack of motor transport and a scarcity of spare parts for those that did exist (Document 9/4), as well as a reduction in rations (Documents 9/5) despite an efficient supply service (Document 9/6).

Document 9/1[1]

Desertion in the German Army

(a) General

Following the debacle at Falaise and the Seine and the disintegration of Seventh Army, as well as a large part of Fifteenth Army, desertion in the Wehrmacht became a problem calling for the most drastic measures. Cut off from their units, or fed up with constant harassing from the air and artillery, many of these men decided it was far simpler to stay put and await the advancing Allied troops, rather than attempt a difficult and hazardous flight back to the Reich. This type of desertion was easily accomplished

---

1. ISUM 149, 27 November 1944.

amidst the chaos and disorder that prevailed in the chase from the Seine to the Siegfried Line. When the momentum of our attack was forced to ebb due to a long and difficult supply route, the High Command, with efficiency born of a history of withdrawals, assembled this disorganized mass of units and sub-units into a semblance of order and by the middle of September the vague outlines of a unified front and command began to emerge.

Desertion, however, had become so common a practice, that the habit continued on even after a new line had finally been formed. It had been so easy before to proceed through the German lines to the front and beyond, by merely asserting that one was a straggler trying to get back to one's unit, that not only was the potential deserter allowed to proceed, but in many cases was provided with transport warrants and pay besides.

(b)   Types of Desertion

It was thus possible for an infantryman in Russia on 21 August 1944 to travel from the Eastern Front to Eindhoven on a warrant destined for the village of Malozw Mac, because he had convinced his company commander that the village was in Belgium rather than Poland. Or a Czech who left his unit in the vicinity of Warsaw on 5 September 1944 to travel by train via Berlin to Hamburg. A forged paybook and a story enabled him to get from the Transport Rail Officer a ticket and rations to Apeldoorn in Holland, from whence he proceeded to the south side of the Moerdijk bridge where he hid until 7 November 1944 when he gave himself up to the Dutch police.

The ease with which desertion could take place is most strikingly illustrated by the member of 79th Reserve Grenadier Regiment who at the end of August decided to give up, and with the help of a Dutch civilian received clothes, work and his keep, until the fall of Tilburg. Despite his absence from the Army for over a month, in October he donned his uniform, slung his rifle over his shoulder and cycled to Bergen, and by telling the Naval authorities that he was a straggler, received an advance of twenty-four florins. 'Well, I had to have money', he said, when the interrogator asked him for an explanation. 'My Dutch friends treated me well, but a man needs money.'

With the firming up of the front, wholesale desertions tapered off, but the art had not been forgotten and during October a continuous flow of deserters turned up. The devices used to cross the lines were varied and ingenious. Three PW of a Hermann Goering unit set off on bicycles taking with them enough rations for two days. During their entire journey of three weeks they were never asked for any papers. German troops gave them directions without hesitation and whenever they were short of food they would go to the first artillery unit they saw and ask for rations, saying that they were a rear party rejoining their unit. They were never refused.

Another chap from 957th Grenadier Regiment of 363rd Infantry Division hid himself for nearly a week in the hope of getting through to our lines. Much to his embarassment, he bumped into his own Regimental HQ. He was brought up before the Adjutant who obviously disbelieved the story he told of wanting to rejoin his company. Suddenly the Adjutant with a shrug called a runner whom he ordered to conduct the PW back to his unit. They set off together and both gave themselves up to Allied troops.

A man from a Luftwaffe regiment was found in a house in an advanced position waiting to surrender. Since he was a pure German he was given a second chance and detailed to go out and bring in two Allied PW to redeem himself or else be shot. He used this opportunity to escape from his escort into Allied lines. His escort fired but missed.

(c)   Reasons for Desertion

Poles, Czechs, Russians and other non-Germans form the largest category of deserters. These men, for the most part, are constantly on the look-out for a suitable occasion to make a get-away. When the rigours of the field become too unbearable, they will take the most incredible chances to come over. Walking through minefields. swimming wide rivers and killing their own sentries are some of the actions taken to enable them to desert.

The reasons for Germans deserting are more varied than those of the non-German group. One PW has suggested the following six reasons:

(i)   Inability to put up with conditions in the field.
(ii)   Recognition of the fact that Germany has lost the war.
(iii) Dissatisfaction with the medical treatment received and the fact that as personnel of a low medical category they have been upgraded.
(iv) Dissatisfaction with their officers (there are stories of a platoon commander 'getting sick' as soon as the unit was committed, and of other officers leaving their troops to get back to safety).
(v)   'Horror' at finding their unit under SS command.
(vi) Lack of news from home.

To this far from exhaustive list, may be added long periods of unbroken fighting without rest, inadequate equipment, bad food and personal resentment at some unfair treatment. A few desertions have been the result of an ideological disagreement with Naziism, but for the most part this reason has only been advanced after one of the other causes has made itself felt. It is a measure of the success of Goebbels's propaganda that very few German deserters blame Hitler for their plight. The SS, the Party and the High Command come in for their share of condemnation but the Führer is usually left alone.

(d)   Recent measures against Desertion

So bad had the situation become that items such as these could frequently be found in unit orders:

> By 1600 hrs 20 October 1944 the number of deserters, General Courts-Martial, Regimental Courts-Martial and a list of those shot through the head for cowardice, since 13 September 1944 is to be forwarded. NCOs and OR by number, Officers by name.

And in a captured file of daily orders of 64th Infantry Division, hardly a day went by when at least one, two or three items of the following kind did not appear.

> Private Alfred Schreinert of Battle Group Kuhn on 9 September 1944, while in a defensive position at Bruges, tied a white handkerchief to his carbine and raised same. He acted cowardly and in fear of sustaining personal harm hoping that the enemy would cease firing. On 24 September 1944 he was sentenced to death by a Court Martial for cowardice in the face of the enemy. This sentence will be made known to the troops.

To prevent this rot in the framework of the Wehrmacht from developing to disastrous proportions, drastic and immediate steps had to be taken. These counter-measures are of two types. The first is designed either to catch the potential deserter before he makes good his escape or to deprive him of aid which will help him carry out his plans. The following devices employed at unit level are only some of those reported by PW.

Party members are always liberally scattered among frontline companies about which there is any suspicion. These are usually trusted old timers of 35 years of age and over, drawn from other units and posted as officer cadets with the rank of sergeant or corporal.

A more ambitious attempt to discourage desertion was reported by 2nd US Infantry Division:

> In PW's platoon there are twelve foxholes and one man stands guard at each. At night all twelve sentries are connected by a wire tied to their left wrists. From this wire another wire leads to a Sergeant in a dugout.

The wire is given a jerk when sentries change, going from one jerk to the next, thus informing the Sergeant that all is well. Main purpose of the wire is to keep the sentries from deserting. If a sentry unties the wire and slips away without jerking it and arousing the Sergeant, he is classified as a deserter and not as a victim of our patrols.

Another far-fetched method of discouraging premature surrender was conceived in Battle Group Hahn in Holland, where all personnel were searched for white handkerchiefs before going into the line. If found, these were confiscated by their zealous officers, since they might be used to signal surrender.

But the most effective and far-reaching counter-measure now practised does not rely on the ingenuity of the unit commander for its success. The High Command has stepped into the picture, and it is now laid down that reprisals will be taken against the families of all men considered to be deserters. Thus on 5 October an Order of Battle Group Aretz, based on a directive from 64th Infantry Division, stated:

A new law has been passed according to which all members of a soldier's family who deserts or shows cowardice in battle are to be arrested and held responsible in lieu of this soldier.

I know for sure that in his deepest heart every decent soldier agrees with this hard decision which at last assures that not only every good deed receives its due reward, but also that every evil deed receives its just retribution.

On this occasion I wish to state that during my rounds of the Battalion's positions I was at all times deeply pleased by the soldierly bearing and attitude of all ranks and I, therefore, do not assume that the above Division instruction was necessary for us. Nevertheless, every one who might still weaken must know that he may possibly save his own life but, simultaneously, will destroy all that he loves and holds dear. Therefore, every one who still is not quite sure of his courage, should examine himself and ponder the consequences of one moment of weakness. This examination should help him to become one with his comrades of the front line and to obey his leaders unconditionally.

Document 9/2[2]

Discipline in 606 Division

The following document issued by 606th Infantry Division (*z.b.V.*) indicates the shocking state of discipline present in some of the hastily-assembled divisions now manning the western front.

606 Infantry Division (z.b.V.) Division Quartiergeneral (Main)

General Officer Commanding   4 December 1944

In recent days there have been in the Division several incidents which give grounds for the utmost concern regarding discipline.

(i)   An extraordinary occurrence took place in the billeting area of one company. An *Oberjäger*[3] and a Dutch woman were found murdered. When the Judge Advocate General arrived to investigate the facts the company commander had to be fetched from his bed: he was sleeping in his billet together with the sister of the murdered woman. The investigation revealed that the company commander had been celebrating on the previous evening with the murdered *Oberjäger*'s section, in the company of the two Dutch women. There was no question of suspecting jealousy as a motive, since both women were described as having been procurable by all who took part in the celebration, including the company commander. The company commander displayed no interest in the investigation. When the Deputy Judge Advocate General was about to leave, an attempt was made to present him with a case of wine.

(ii) An *Oberjäger* with several paratroops appeared in Roermond and commandeered foodstuffs and canteen goods. On being pulled up by an artillery officer from a survey unit, he refused to obey orders and declared that his company commander had ordered him to 'organize some grub and booze'. The men at the front were the real jolly good fellows, everybody else was a nobody to him, and so forth.

He was arrested with difficulty by the artillery officer.

---

2. ISUM 212, 28 January 1945, from *Second Army Intelligence Summary*, 27 January 1945.
3. A senior private in the mountain troops.

(iii) A large number of NCOs absented themselves from the Division Battle School, when it was about to be engaged in an offensive action, and although it is stated that they returned to their regiments, up until now no report or statement has been forwarded to the Division by any unit.

(iv) A doctor from Brueggen reported to Division that a quantity of foodstuffs and other articles had been stolen from Diesgareshof (which is situated in Germany).

These examples constitute a serious threat to the discipline and consequently to the fighting capacity of the troops. Company commanders have no longer in every instance got their men well in hand and do not set a personal example of bearing and mode of life to their men. They constitute a danger to their units.

The supervision exercised by battalion commanders has not been keen and strict enough to maintain control over men or remove them in good time from their posts.

I order regiments to take energetic action in this matter forthwith. Here, any sort of leniency is out of place. If it does occur, company commanders will be relieved of their commands. Regular checks are essential, especially checks of supply columns.

Discipline can not be acquired merely from the repetition of drilling, but every commander must be vigilant to see that it is maintained at all times and at all places.

I order that authorizations of all sort will be issued from now only by battalion commanders in person.

> (Sgd) Goltzsch[4]
> *Generalmajor*
> in temporary command

---

4. *Generalmajor* Rudolf Goltzsch (1897–1974), who took over 606th Division three days before he issued this order.

Document 9/3[5]

German Courts-Martial

The following information on Crime and Punishment in the German Army, with special reference to Courts-Martial, was obtained by PW interrogation.

Minor offences are dealt with by company or battalion commander. Such offences are:

(i)   Late rising at reveille, being late on parade or being out after tattoo without permission.
(ii) Improper dress or disorderly conduct in or out of barracks.
(iii) Neglect of clothing, equipment, weapons or fatigue duties.
(iv) Debt, gambling, lying, drunkenness, improper retention of money or valuables (as opposed to stealing) and offences against comrades.

Such offences may be punished by reprimand, by imposition of extra duties (e.g. drill, guards, fatigues or other parades) and by reduction or stoppages of pay up to two months.

Alternatively, any of four grades of confinement (*Arrest*) may be ordered:

(1) *Quartier – or Kasernen Arrest*: Confined to Barracks
(2) *Gelinder Arrest*: Confined to a room
     This may last up to 2 weeks; food in this case remains normal.
(3) *Geschärfter Arrest*: Detention
     This may last up to 3 weeks – the prisoner sleeps on a plank bed and gets only 2 meals a day.
(4) *Strenger Arrest*: Detention in a detention camp
     This involves solitary confinement, usually underground on a bread-and-water diet, with no bed or blankets.

Thirdly, reduction in rank may be awarded to various grades of *Gefreiter*[6] as an alternative to other punishments. One night's stay pending appeal is given. No appeal is entertained after the beginning of the sentence.

---

5. ISUM 182, from *Second Army Intelligence Summary*, 27 December 1944.
6. German rank roughly equivalent to the Commonwealth lance-corporal or the American private first class.

A *Kriegsgericht* is a court-martial proper and can deal either with minor offences if they are referred by OC to a court-martial, or with major offences such as:

Cowardice or desertion
Thieving
Betraying military secrets
Abuse of authority by NCO or above
Deliberate absence of more than 7 days overstaying leave
Disobedience in emergency

The normal sentence for these offences is 3-10 years detention or posting to a *Strafabteilung*.[7]

The court is composed of:

Oberkriegsgerichtrat – who functions as president and pronounces judgement
Kriegsgerichtrat – who is prosecuting officer
Verteidiger – who is defending officer

In addition there are two or more *Staatsanwalt* who do not form part of the court and do not interfere except on points of military law and procedure. These, together with officers studying procedure, are referred to as *Beisitzender*.

Before the trial a summary of evidence is taken by an officer who normally does not appear at court (referred to by one PW as a *Kriegsgerichtrat* and by another as *Kriegsgerichtinspektor*). He collects the evidence and makes sure that the prisoner's statements broadly agree with his witnesses; for this up to 9 days may be allowed. The defence statement is signed by the officer and countersigned by the accused, and forwarded to the court-martial together with evidence of the accused's character from his unit, and a copy of his record with the civil police at his home.

According to normal court procedure the accused is marched in wearing parade dress without side-arms and bare-headed under escort of two *Feldgendarmerie*[8] (or SS), after the court have taken their places, and remains standing to attention until otherwise ordered.

The charge is read by the *Oberkriegsgerichtrat*. Witnesses for the prosecution are marshalled by the *Kriegsgerichtrat* and evidence given for the prosecution is followed in turn by defence witnesses.

---

7. Punishment unit, given the most dangerous tasks in the front.
8. Military Police.

Questions may be asked of witnesses by either *Kriegsgerichtrat* or *Verteidiger.*

When all witnesses have been called the evidence is reviewed by the *Oberkriegsgerichtrat*, who gives judgement verbally and pronounces sentence after consideration of the record of the accused.

If judgement is accepted, execution of sentence proceeds forthwith and reports are sent via regiment to the man's company; copies go to the division for record purposes and to the 'Reich Records.'

In the event of an appeal the case is referred to the divisional commander who may intervene or order a trial by higher court (*Oberkriegsgericht*) or, on further appeal, to the *Reichkriegsgericht*, which is final.

Officers appointed to *Kriegsgericht* were usually older men or *Beamte* and were lawyers in civil life; during the last year these courts are said to have been almost entirely conducted by SS.

Summary Justice is apparently recognized in the German manual of Military Law. In the field any soldier has the right to shoot on the spot any rank guilty of cowardice or attempted desertion. If this has not been done any officer not present may hear evidence on the spot, constituting in himself a court of summary justice, and deliver and execute sentence including the death penalty.

Document 9/4[9]

The Supply Transport of a German Division

A prisoner, captured on 29 October 1944 near Goes, was employed with a Heavy MT (Motor Transport) Column of 70th Infantry Division, in the Zeeland islands. According to his report, 70th Division had only one heavy Motor Transport column – 21 vehicles and 51 all ranks at the end of October, with an overall capacity of 60 tons. It is to be noted that the textbook design of a German heavy MT column is to carry 60 tons, and it is in keeping with enemy practice to adhere to the 60 tons, no matter how makeshift the means.

The column had the following vehicles on 16 October 1944:

---

9. ISUM 125, 2 November 1944.

Motor Cycle Solo	Victoria	1
Staff Cars	Citroen	2
Mobile Workshop	Chevrolet	1
Tanker	Ford	1
Omnibus (30 men)	Opal-Blitz	1
Medium Lorry	International	1
Lorry 3½ tons	Renault	1
Lorry 1½ tons	Ford	2
Lorry 2½ tons	Chevrolet	2
Lorry 3 tons	Renault	1
Lorry 2 tons	Chevrolet	1
Lorry 2 tons	Citroen	1
Lorry 2 tons	Ford	3
Lorry 1½ tons	Chevrolet	1
Lorry 1½ tons	Citroen	1
Lorry 2½ tons	Ford	1

All had 4-cylinder engines. Of these, ten were lorries confiscated from civilian sources. This motley array of vehicles carried everything for the divisional supply services: ammunition, petrol, construction materials, soldiers. It took the supplies, arriving by sea from Holland, from the harbour to the island supply depots. The men were even responsible for loading and unloading the ferries between Flushing and Breskens, and for getting the supplies unloaded south of the Scheldt forward to units!

Petrol for this gypsy caravan arrived by sea, and in sufficient quantities. A small petrol point, holding 10,000 litres (2,200 gallons) was maintained at Goes, and a GHQ petrol point also existed at the other end of the town with 60,000 litres (13,200 gallons).

The maintenance problems facing such a column must have been immense. A prisoner, formerly employed in an MT Repair Depot in eastern Germany and captured on the American front, gives some idea of the spare parts problems involved. According to him, the situation as regards spare parts for various types of German Army vehicles is as follows:

Borgward trucks (3 ton): almost no parts for this model since bombing of Hansa-Lloyd plant in Bremen. If gears go, vehicle is abandoned.
Buessing trucks (3½ and 4½ tons) – only 30% of spare parts requirements available, owing to bombing of the plant in Brunswick X90. Renault – no parts available.

RSO (*Rauppenschlepper*) tractor – adequate supply.
Horch and Steyr vehicles – great shortage.
Maultier (3½ ton) half-track – two models:

(a) Ford V8 – sufficient parts from Ford plant in Cologne
(b) Opel-Blitz – scant supply, and lack of one or more parts frequently exists. The plant is in Russelheim M45 (in Mainz).

The vehicles in use in a front-line division, and the spare parts situation as outlined above by an experienced transport NCO, give some idea of the transport problems faced by the German Army. The cause: the loss to the Reich of factories in conquered territory, and of raw materials due to the blockade, the bombing of factories, and more recently, the intensive disturbance to industry caused by the campaign to find more men for the Army. More and more, the Germans are unable even to carry things back with them as they retreat. The Supply Services of the Allied Armies can be thankful that they are able to enjoy the prospect of a column of vehicles of the same make and capacity on any of our supply routes.

Document 9/5[10]

German Rations and Messing

Recent interrogation has shown that despite the large stocks of foodstuffs captured by the Allies the Germans are maintaining a very close approximate to their three standard ration scales for front line, Lines of Communication and home-service personnel respectively. The various ration scales as given by PW are given below.

The normal system of messing appears to be to issue to each man every evening the components of his supper and breakfast meals, consisting mainly of bread, cheese or sausage, butter, etc., and to provide from the unit kitchen only one hot meal a day at noon and hot drinks at breakfast and dinner times. In the case of field units the main meal is normally provided by the usual mobile field kitchen and is usually considered very

---

10. From ISUM 112, from *Second Army Intelligence Report* 136.

good and sufficient by the troops. The ration as a whole, however, is not thought to be more than barely adequate.

A definite attempt appears to be made to see that forward troops are fed as well as possible but PW complained that when out of the line the food is insufficient and normally very badly cooked.

Fresh vegetables and potatoes are not normally included in the issue (one PW states however that in Norway where he had served previously dried potatoes had been an issue) but they can be obtained by local purchase. No provision is made for the issue of milk but personnel on ration scale I occasionally get a special issue.

Front-line troops sometimes receive an additional 'Kampfzulage' consisting of a 'Grosskampfpäckchen' containing one tin of Schok-a-Cola (concentrated chocolate) and one cube of oatmeal (similar to that in our 24-hour ration).

'Marketenden' (NAAFI) goods are usually available weekly against payment but some PW stated that they seldom saw them. There is an occasional free issue of similar goods.

Daily Ration Scales as reported by PW:

NB: Only one PW had any idea of the ration for the midday meal (7 ounces meat, 1¼ ounces noodles, etc. ¾ ounce lentils, peas, etc. For ration scales II and III the meat ration is 5¼ and 3½ ounces respectively.)

The tables below therefore exclude this meal. PW stated that in ration scale III the ration was only sufficient to make up into a stew every day.

Quantities given by different PW often vary slightly and where this is the case the figure given represents the most likely ration:

SCALE I

(For fighting troops and flying personnel resting)
About one loaf of bread
2.1 ounces of butter or lard
5¼ ounces sausage and/or cheese
1.05 ounces sugar
⅓ ounce ersatz coffee
7 cigarettes

SCALE II

(For L of C Tps, troops under training and front-line troops)
About half a loaf of bread
1.4 ounces butter
4⅕ ounces sausage and/or cheese
¾ ounce sugar
⅓ ounce ersatz coffee
6 cigarettes

SCALE III

(For home-service and sedentary   *Notes:*
L of C Troops)

About one-third of a loaf of bread   1. Jam is sometimes issued in lieu of
                                           cheese

1.05 ounces of butter   2. The bread ration appears to be
                                           very flexible, figures given by various
                                           PWs differ widely

2.8 ounces of sausage and/or cheese   A loaf of bread weighs
                                           approximately 3 lbs.

⅓ ounce sugar
⅓ ounce ersatz coffee
3 cigarettes

Document 9/6[11]

German Army Rations

The following interrogation report published by the 9th US Infantry Division, answers many questions concerning enemy rations.

The present method of obtaining food and getting it to the front lines of 277th *Volksgrenadier* Division is explained by a PW who, until recently, worked in the I Battalion rear echelon. The most significant aspect of the procedure is that all food for the division is purchased no more than 50 miles from the front lines.

Two organic units of a German infantry division are the Butchery Company and the Bakery Company. Both companies are together responsible for the food supply of the entire division. This may be a large responsibility for two units consisting of no more than 50-80 men each, but the following method simplified the routine. Upon the arrival of the division in a general area, an officer of the Butchery Company has the job of procuring meat and vegetables. This is done by requesting all farmers in the Divisional area to turn in a certain amount of their livestock and vegetables once a week at the slaughter house of the Butchery Company.

---

11. ISUM 200, 27 January 1945, from *9th U.S. Division Intelligence Notes*.

The same procedure is followed by the Bakery Company in order to obtain flour.

The Butchery Company of 277th Division is at Drei Mühlen 240167, 15 kms east of Schleiden. The place is only a small group of farms; yet all the fresh and canned meat for the division is prepared and stored there. The Butchery Company has its own cannery, and much of the prepared food is like Compo rations.

At Drei Mühlen the rations are picked up by trucks belonging to the divisional trucking company. When a battalion kitchen unit, which is always at the rear echelon, runs low on food, trucks bring the rations from the Butchery Company down to battalion rear, by-passing regiment completely. On a run of this kind the trucks usually carry ammunition at the same time, which, of course, is picked up at another place. The Bakery Company distributes its products in the same manner except that it uses horse-drawn transportation. This company is located at Zingsheim 2431 south of Drei Mühlen.

As the battalion kitchen unit, the food is prepared and put into large cans to be sent to the battalion HQ. This is also transported by horse and wagon. According to the PW, the supply train is supposed to leave I Battalion Rear – located at Ettelscheid 0816 every day at approximately 1330; but lately many of these transports never reached their destination because of our artillery fire on the German main supply routes. In fact, several PW from 1 and 2 Coys of 990 *Volksgrenadier* Regiment state that their food has not come through to the front lines for six days and the men had to forage for something to eat.

Another point brought out by the PW indicates that the Germans take care of their available equipment. The use of horses is still important enough for 277th Division to create a rest camp for them. At this camp, the horses are well fed and given no work. The camp has one possible disadvantage for the horses – it is at Drei Mühlen – the location of the Butchery Company.

Chapter 10

Propaganda

Editor's Comments

Propaganda was both utilized by the Nazi state and feared by it. Appeals were made through patriotic exhortations (Document 10/1) and through seemingly commonsense assessments (Document 10/2) with frequent references to the new generation of 'Vengeance weapons' that would shortly appear. Yet, so bad was the general situation that effort was made to both counteract Allied propaganda (Document 10/5) and prevent it being widely distributed among the frontline troops (Documents 10/3 and 10/4).

Document 10/1[1]

The Watch on the Rhine

Wartime Intelligence Officer's Comments

A further example of a leaflet printed by the enemy for distribution to his own troops has just been captured. It is printed in black, with a lavish use of a variety of display types, over a lightly-printed reproduction in red of a Germanic warrior keeping watch over the Rhine. This figure wears a flowing cloak over what appears to be a suit of medieval chain-armour, and he grasps the hilt of an enormous sword. He has, however, a steel helmet very like that

---

1. ISUM 100, 10 October 1944, from *Second Army Intelligence Summary* 122, 4 October 1944.

of the modern German soldier, and his cloak is fastened at the neck by a brooch bearing a swastika. In the background the Rhine appears complete with symbolical castle, Meuse Tower, and steel-arched bridge.

What do you say about it?
For four years our fathers' generation kept
THE WATCH ON THE RHINE
'STEADFASTLY AND LOYALLY'

Had not the other side a tremendous superiority in material over them?

No enemy set foot on the bank of our sacred German river so long as the front held firm – the front that was manned by warriors hardened in fires of every kind and steeled by every possible sacrifice and hardship!

Our enemies advanced only when the front was forced to yield by the collapse of the home country, and

WITH THEM CAME SHAME AND CORRUPTION,
MISERY, DISHONOUR AND EXPLOITATION!

Comrade,

The enemy means to outflank the west wall at the very point where we are and to cross the Rhine into Germany!

Shall our people, shall our families, have suffered five years in vain? Shall they suffer misery and starvation amid the ruins of our cities in a conquered Germany?

Do you wish to go to Siberia to work as a slave?

WHAT DO YOU SAY ABOUT IT?
NEVER shall this happen!
NEVER shall the enemy subdue Germany!
NEVER shall the heroic sacrifices of our people prove in vain!

Therefore, everything depends now on your courage! The struggle against an enemy who at the moment is still superior, is tremendously hard. But for all of us there is no other way out than to fight on, with knives if need be!

If you all do your duty, we shall hold the Rhine until the present danger has been overcome. Then the enemy, who is not obliged to fight for his life as we are, will have to give up this struggle before us.

We, however, will enjoy rapid reconstruction and a happy future in a strong, free Germany!

For this it is worth while to give your all!

IT IS BETTER TO DIE THAN TO ACCEPT
DISHONOUR AND SLAVERY!
IT IS BETTER TO BE DEAD THAN A SLAVE!

Therefore keep the watch on the Rhine steadfastly and loyally!

Document 10/2[2]

Skorpion Tells All

Wartime Intelligence Officer's Comments

The following 'straight from the shoulder' talk for German troops is a translation of a captured propaganda leaflet. While no mention of the SS is made anywhere in the document, 'Skorpion' is known to be the propaganda organization working very closely with SS Standarte Kurt Eggers, the Corps of SS war correspondents. A branch of the organization, known as 'Skorpion West', which came to this theatre from Italy, was identified some months ago. It was known to include a printing press, a film projector and an amplifier unit for the entertainment and instruction of German troops. The document is translated as follows:

If you want to know the truth, comrade, ask 'Skorpion'!

How does the war stand?

We are engaged in a very heavy defensive battle against the British and Americans. The enemy has still today absolute air supriority. He has more tanks and artillery than we have. We have not been able to prevent him landing in the south of France. We have also not been able to prevent his advancing in Italy as far as Florence, and reaching Poland in the east. For the fighting German soldier who does not know anything else and does not hear anything else these things look bad. We have reached a point now that we need no longer conceal this.

The truth looks entirely different!

---

2. ISUM 114, 22 October 1944, *Second Army Intelligence Summary* 136, 18 October 1944.

We must soberly examine the developments during recent years, which are now clearly discernible, in order to recognise the inevitability of events.

After the entry of the USA into the war the German command recognised that it would be merely a question of time until the American industry with their practically inexhaustible reserves of raw materials would catch up with the German lead in armaments and finally exceed it. Especially in the field of aircraft production there was no question that in the long run we could not maintain the equilibrium against the American production. The only possible conclusion for the German armament industry, therefore, was total reorganization and the construction of completely new types of weapons, the effect of which would be able to counter-balance the mass of enemy weapons. Such reorganization naturally required time and if it were as simple as it would appear, the enemy would have probably acted similarly in the meantime.

What has happened in the interim can only be termed – as specialists in the opposing camp repeatedly point out – a revolution of the greatest dimension in war history.

We are not quite ready yet!

It is in the nature of things and every soldier knows it – no matter how hard the moral burden may affect him – that no details of these things can be disclosed until the actual mass employment can take place. As surely, as against all doubts which are still in everyone's mind, one day the V1 weapon arrived and has since been employed without pause, so surely the new weapons will also materialize for the development and production of which we have taken upon ourselves for over two years the most rigid defensive measures. We shall experience in a very short period why that had to be so.

One can openly admit now that the enemy bombardments of the Reich territory spread over the recent years have hampered the development. We can admit this because we have overcome all the difficulties caused thereby and because developments can no longer be impeded no matter how severe the air attacks may be.

Churchill and Roosevelt knew of the construction of the V1 long ago. They have also knowledge of the weapons of which the German population has as yet no idea. Even the best counter-espionage could unfortunately not prevent this. But they could neither prevent the VI nor produce a defence against it. This failure depresses the enemy terribly. They hoped and made every effort to win the war against Germany before now and they are still trying to. Their greatest hope lies therein that we ourselves may not know the situation and that we may give up the fight.

Churchill has expressed the opinion at General Eisenhower's HQ that if this 'last blow' does not lead to Germany's capitulation, the war has been finally lost for him. If it requires a further confirmation that these thoughts are not theory but sober facts, then this confirmation has been provided by the American Minister of War Stinson himself, in that he told Churchill 'if the war is not ended within a few weeks, America will reserve the right to take all further steps.' Thus far are our enemies!

It is up to us now to resist the enemy with the utmost tenacity in order to hold the space which we require for the employment of the new weapons and in order to gain time.

We must learn to recognize the true picture of the situation. Our position is very difficult. On the other hand, that of the enemy is at present apparently excellent. But we know better.

Churchill himself it was who during the recent memorable debate in the House of Commons said: 'We must finish the war by the autumn otherwise we have lost it.'

Address your enquiries to 'Skorpion' FPN 00020. If they are questions of special importance which occupy the soldier seriously, 'Skorpion' will answer them. It will always tell the unvarnished truth.

Document 10/3[3]

German Counter-Propaganda Measures

German anxiety as regards leaflet propaganda is neatly summed up in an unidentified company order dated 18 October 1944 which runs as follows:

In the Field 18 October 1944   *Company Order*
Enemy Leaflet Propaganda
The great increase of the enemy's demoralising leaflet propaganda demands strict obedience to orders previously issued, especially:

---

3. ISUM 127, 4 November 1944.

(i) Enemy leaflets in German, as well as in foreign languages, of a demoralising nature, which are addressed to foreign speaking members of the Wehrmacht (*Osttruppen* etc). are to be given immediately to the unit commander and forwarded through the usual channels to Army HQ, if possible four copies, with the location where they were found.

(ii) The number of people handling the leaflet is to be kept as small as possible.

(iii) Severe punishment will be awarded for unauthorised passing on or distribution.

Document 10/4[4]

The Power of the Written Word

Wartime Intelligence Officer's Comments

There is increasing evidence that the enemy is disturbed by our leaflet and general psychological warfare campaign. In recent weeks the enemy has found it necessary to reply to our arguments to his own troops. Some time ago a leaflet: '5 Minuten nach 12 – Wir bitten um Auskunft' (It's 5 minutes after 12 – give us some information please'), was fired by First Army units. The translation below, made from a document found on a captured German NCO, indicates what happened on the receiving end. The Germans evidently feel that leaflets are putting too many ideas into the heads of men who are supposed to have discipline, not thoughts.

1st Battalion, Grenadier Regiment 330 (183rd Division)
Battalion OP   *23 October 1944*
Subject: Leaflets
To: 1st, 2nd, 3rd, 4th Co.
Before the day is over all company commanders will take action regarding the leaflet which was dropped today under the title 'Five Minutes Past Twelve'. Reference must be made to the following: Back page – 'Information please.'

---

4. ISUM 157, 6 December 1944, from *First US Army G-2 Periodic Report*, 2 December 1944.

Here is the information:

It is true that among us there are men who are not 100% fit and who are committed in the front lines. But in these critical moments of the war the immediate safety of our homeland and the protection of our women and children are at stake.

It is also true that air force and naval personnel, not fully employed at present in their respective branches of service, have joined us in order to protect the Fatherland. However, it is not true that these troops have not had any training in handling the simplest infantry weapons. According to army tradition infantry training precedes any specialized schooling in all branches of the service. This does not seem to be the case in other countries.

It is true that every unit commander who apprehends or recognizes a saboteur, a traitor to our Fatherland and thereby to our women and children as well as to innumerable comrades, has the right to bring him to well-deserved justice.

It is not true that we claim that Americans shoot their prisoners. However, it is true that Americans are using prisoners of war and civilians not evacuated from occupied places for construction of defence positions in their front lines.

It is not true that the SS is 'guarding' us from the rear, as the Russian GPU does, because we ourselves belong to an SS unit by being under the command of Himmler, commander of the replacement army and all *Volksgrenadier* divisions.

Regular mail delivery proves that our lines of communication and supplies are not interrupted.

The German soldier does not consider captivity as 'honourable'. No doubt the same attitude prevails among the Americans.

To ward off the present crisis in this war, it is paramount that each one of us gives his all in the firm belief in our Führer and in full faith that a turn in this critical moment will come. The Führer has predicted that turn and we faithfully believe in it.

It is easy to be faithful in good times; it is when the going is tough that our belief in the Führer and in our final victory is really tested.

Signed 'Illegible'
Captain and Battalion Commander

Document 10/5[5]

Don't Listen, Friends – It's Treason

Wartime Intelligence Officer's Comments

The excerpt below was translated from a leaflet taken from a prisoner in the First US Division cage.

The Secret Weapon of the Enemy At Work!

Naturally the enemy is not really capable of matching our V1 and V2, but he is trying to harm us by his vicious propaganda over many radio stations.

Friends, let's not forget that listening to enemy stations is treason and that long-term jail sentences await you if you don't abide by this order. It is not, however, that we have anything to conceal from you. That is silly! Most of our people don't realize that the people in England, France and Belgium are not allowed to listen to foreign broadcasts either. Our measure is simply designed to stop gossip, or rather not to start any.

Here is an example of an enemy method of propaganda:

September 9.
OKW: We shot down 12 enemy planes last night.
Enemy station: We lost not 12 but 14 of our planes!

September 10.
OKW: We shot down 26 enemy planes over the western approaches to the Reich.
Enemy station: We didn't lose 26, but 31 of our planes!

September 11.
OKW: The enemy lost 148 machines yesterday.
Enemy station: We only lost 8 planes yesterday!

So you see for yourself how the enemy operates. He generously allows us seven extra planes in two days to gain our confidence. The next day he has the nerve to cheat you out of 140 planes. That is typical of the methods of these American Jews and British capitalists!

---

5. ISUM 157, 6 December 1944, from *1st US Infantry Division Periodic Report* 160.

Chapter 11

German Assessments of Allied Troops

Editor's Comments

Despite their serious defeats on the Western Front during the summer of 1944, the Wehrmacht retained a somewhat arrogant belief in the inferiority of the Allied soldier, particularly the American soldier. German assessments of the American army were generally dismissive (Documents 11/2, 11/3 and 11/5). The German opinion of the British soldiers was somewhat better (Document 11/1) and Wehrmacht intelligence officers were fascinated by a talkative British NCO who criticized their weapons and tactics (Document 11/4).

Document 11/1[1]

German Intelligence Notes on the Arnhem Operation

Wartime Intelligence Officer's Comments

PW was formerly confidential clerk to the commodore of Jagdgeschwader 3, stationed near Erfurt. He is young, intelligent and co-operative. The information can be considered reliable.

---

1. ISUM 241, 26 February 1945.

PW has given the points which he remembers from an OKL[2] Intelligence Bericht[3] 'Luftlandung Holland' which Jagdgeschwader 3 received at the end of October 1944. PW does not remember the exact title of the document or the signature. The report was classified 'Geheim'; it consisted of 10 mimeographed pages, single-spaced, and several photographs (landing areas at Arnhem, British gliders, captured British soldiers, etc.)

German Analysis of Operation

Plan

(i) The mission of the combined airborne operations was to seize intact the principal crossings of the Maas, the Waal and the Rhine.

(ii) These crossings would then have facilitated a rapid thrust into middle Holland.

(iii) From Holland the Allies could then have broken out on to the north German plain.

Had the airborne operation succeeded, it would have been extremely difficult to forestall steps (ii) and (iii) of the plan.

Reasons for Failure

While the Allied operations on the Maas and Waal were successful, final failure came because the crucial Arnhem landing was overpowered by the Germans. The reasons for the Allied defeat at Arnhem were:

(i) The landings were not concentrated enough; since the landings were spread over a period of three days the Germans never faced the entire strength of the British 1st Parachute Division at one time.

(ii) Allied intelligence was not aware of the location of the SS Panzer Korps which was refitting north of Arnhem. Or, if the Allies were aware of this force, they did not make proper dispositions to meet it. The former view is more likely.

(iii) Arnhem was too far from the front; the airborne troops could not hold out long enough for the Allies to break through from the south to link up with them.

(iv) The bad flying weather following the landings prevented effective re-supply from the air. It also prevented the necessary 'isolation of the battlefield', and direct support of ground operations. If German

---

2. OKL, *Oberkommando der Luftwaffe*.
3. *Bericht*, a report.

supply and transport routes could have been effectively broken, the Allied force might have been successful.

Allied Successes

(i)   *Surprise.* The Germans considered the operation to have been successful as regards the element of surprise. The degree of surprise was especially heightened by the fact that the bombing preparation (attacks on flak positions, etc) was on a normal scale. If an unusually heavy bombing raid had preceded the operation, the German defenders would have been better prepared.

(ii) *Flexibility.* The Germans believe that the air commander of the operation temporarily surrendered tactical control over a part of the air fleet to the commander of the entire operation. This flexibility was considered noteworthy.

(iii) *Dropping Zones.* In German opinion, these were well chosen. No alternatives were proposed.

(iv) *Assembly after Landing.* No criticism.

(v)   *Quality of Troops.* The British 1st Parachute Division was rated as elite troops.

Conclusions

(i)   As a result of Arnhem the German staff now definitely feels that 3–4 days is the absolute maximum that airborne units can operate without being relieved by ground forces.

(ii) Objectives for airborne troops must not be as far from the front lines as Arnhem was.

(iii) Instead of spreading a landing over three days, it should preferably be completed in one day, with forces concentrated as much as possible. (The American operation in Normandy, where an entire parachute regiment was dropped at the Orne railway bridge, is regarded by the Germans as a model operation, according to PW.)

(iv) Airborne operations can still surprise to a high degree.

General
Order of Battle

PW states that the Order of Battle information in the OKL report was very full.

Future Attacks

The Germans considered the Holland operations unprecedented in magnitude and conception. They expect another such full-scale assault, and expect that the lessons of Arnhem will be utilized to produce more concentrated landings. The time or place of such an assault was not indicated.

Use of Dummies

The Germans do not feel that the deception achieved by the use of dummy parachutists is commensurate with the expenditure of air power etc., involved in dropping them.

The German method for dealing with any landing is first to send a small mobile reconnaissance party to the place where enemy landings have been reported. Thus, when dummies are found, full German dispositions will not have been made on a false basis.

Document 11/2[4]

The German High Command Discusses the American Soldier

Wartime Intelligence Officer's Comments

From the Seventh US Army G-2 Periodic Report of 12 October 1944, comes the following translation of an article in the Wacht, newspaper of the German Nineteenth Army. Written on 1 October it attempts to assess the fighting qualities of the American soldier. As usual, it attributes all success of the American Armies in the west to their overwhelming superiority of equipment.

It is typical of the Teutonic mind to belittle material superiority when he himself hasn't got it. The Nazi has forgotten his victories in Poland, Belgium, Holland, Greece, Yugoslavia and France when it was the overwhelming numbers of planes and tanks that enabled the Wehrmacht to smash the unprepared peoples in its path.

The reasoning of this Goebellesque effort becomes still more inexplicable when one considers that it is the constant hope and promise of a V-weapon

---

4. ISUM 112, 20 October 1944, from *Seventh US Army G-2 Periodic Report*, 12 October 1944.

that maintains in the German people such faith in victory as they might still have. All future plans of both the High Command and Nazi Party are based largely on a secret weapon that will give them not equality, but superiority in materiel. Yet to the average, opaque German mind this frantic hope for technical and industrial superiority apparently does not seem to be inconsistent with deriding their enemies just because they happen to have that self-same superiority – and effectively use it.

The US Military High Command Has Never Taken Risks

One of the prerequisites for military success, in addition to a knowledge of one's own means and capabilities, is a correct estimate of the enemy, of all his capabilities and of all his weaknesses. Apart from the available materiel, general human qualities and psychological intangibles play an important role, and only the sum of all these determines the military value and efficiency of an army. The latter factors, however, are more difficult to evaluate than the others, and are usually recognized only after the test of battle.

The experiences of this war in particular have proved that one cannot judge one's enemy on the basis of his performance in previous wars. The Frenchman, for example, generally recognized as possessing extremely admirable military qualities, demonstrated himself to be, in general, a rather weak enemy in 1940, while the Russian's perseverance and his adaptability to the requirements of modern warfare often resulted in great surprise or frequent severe consequences.

As far as the American soldier is concerned, we were even more dependent on more presumptions. In the last World War, the Americans did not make their appearance until the last phase, while in the African and Italian campaigns only a small proportion of the troops employed were Americans.

It has only been during the past weeks in France that the German soldier has come to grips with the bulk of the American Army, and even this applies only to a limited extent, since the main burden on the part of the Americans is not borne by the infantry element of the army but almost exclusively by planes, tanks and heavy weapons which are employed in great numbers.

This fact, however, cannot be regarded merely as the basis of enemy successes but – and this seems more important during the present phase of the war – it is also characteristic of the enemy's method of employing the means at his command.

The English, and even more so the Americans, have been afraid of and avoided any large sacrifice of men during the entire course of the war. And even when they were forced to buy certain successes with heavy losses, they still shrank from the all-out, the true soldierly sacrifice. The majority of cases, however, in which they met with success – as particularly during the past week in France – are to be traced to the quantitative superiority of materiel at their disposal.

Wherever the American soldier had to fight the German soldier under conditions that at least approached equality, the German's spirit and his training always proved to be infinitely superior to his enemy's. There are enough examples to show that the fighting quality of the German soldier can make up for even considerable superiority in materiel. Just think of the heroes of Cassino or the Combat School in Metz when it broke up – by itself at first – the dangerous tank thrust directed at the industrial Saar territory.

It is no secret that the USA was dragged into this war against her own will by Roosevelt and his Jewish supporters. And through unscrupulous agitation over a period of time a state of war-preparedness was arrived at, but always under the condition that no great sacrifices would have to be made. The people were then told that the technical and industrial superiority of the United States alone would win the war. And with this feeling – as if he were, so to speak, under the protection of the technical achievements of the New World – the American soldier goes to battle. He is completely dependent on his materiel, and he falters at the moment when he is no longer certain of the effectiveness of that materiel.

Past campaigns have proved this, time and time again. Never has American infantry attacked without a great armoured spearhead, never has it assaulted positions until they have been covered with a hail of shells or bombs. And, if the attackers nevertheless met resistance and drew fire from German infantry weapons, the attack would be broken off immediately and they would try again the next day to force a decision with their superiority of materiel. This method of attack does not only lack initiative and imagination, but it also slowly kills every natural fighting instinct. Similarly, in the statement of American prisoners of war an almost unanimous war weariness is apparent, which is only balanced by the hope of a speedy victory by the Anglo-Americans.

In other words, the same thing which has helped the American Army to its great successes, will become a deadly danger to the same army the moment the picture of materiel undergoes any decisive change.

This is true of the fighting morale of not only the American soldier, but even of his leaders who, including the top man, placed their full confidence in the superiority of materiel. Even during the critical days of the battle for France, the enemy high command could not make up its mind to take any great risks and could therefore not prevent the formation of a new defensive system along the borders of the Reich.

The US High Command missed this opportunity and again based its new plan of attack on the effectiveness of materiel. Although the Anglo-American army commanders understood well enough to imitate, even in the smallest details, the mechanics of the strategy used by Germany in 1940, the inspiration, the spirit, and the powerful creative forces were lacking. And nothing but a mere imitation was the result, which denied not only the boldness in decision but also the magnitude of the success – else, where could have been the justice of history? What is required now is to gain time for our leaders to create a new strategic original plan (*strategischen Original*).

Document 11/3[5]

What Germans Think of American Soldiers

Wartime Intelligence Officer's Comments

The following is a translation of a captured document discussing the recent battle experiences of 183rd Volksgrenadier Division.

183rd Division has been in contact with the enemy on a large scale from 2 October to 6 October 1944. During this period, the enemy launched only a holding attack against the sector northwest of Beilenkirchen. Since 7 October, only local attacks have occurred in the division sector.

In contact so far have been the 2nd US Armoured Division, the 29th and 30th Infantry Divisions.

A considerable number of battle-experienced replacements were found in the enemy units, due to their casualties during the invasion and the Battle

---

5. ISUM 155, 4 December 1944, from *2nd US Armoured Division G-2 Report*.

of France. Greatest caution and a measure of uncertainty was noticeable in all battles. A spirit of brave and daring enterprise was practically always lacking. Although clear numerical and material superiority existed, favourable conditions leading to quick successes were not utilized.

During their one month in contact in the Geilenkirchen area, the division has gathered the following experiences:

(a) Infantry
(i) Infantry in the Attack

The enemy does not launch a major attack without air or tank support. The main job during the penetration of the west wall was left to armoured units. Infantry was motorized or on foot, followed the armour and had the job of holding territory taken by the armoured elements. It was easy to separate infantry and armour with light fire from the heavy infantry weapons and the artillery. The enemy stayed away from areas with no observation, as well as from wooded and underbrush areas. During combat in wooded areas, the American showed himself completely unfit.

Hardly any light infantry weapons were committed by the enemy. The firefight was carried out primarily with artillery and tanks.

(ii) Attack with Limited Objective

Several such attacks were launched by the enemy in the division area, some with and some without tank support.

Artillery and mortars fired concentrated preparations in the penetration area. Smoke is used liberally. When tanks supported the action they were lined up in two waves. The second wave was charged with the security, in which the infantry was carried by the tanks of the first wave. The infantry was committed only when the tanks had broken the main line of resistance and then rolled up the flanks to the right and left with the tanks.

In the main battle area, the fight is carried practically entirely by the infantry. They showed great sensitivity against counter-attacks because, after reaching the objective, the preparations for defence were lacking.

Infantry attacks with tank support were carried out without any power and were easily dispersed with concentrated defensive fire.

In villages, the enemy split up into battle groups of 2 to 30 men who are equipped with explosives for the destruction of houses and cellars.

(iii) Patrols and Combat Patrols

All patrol activity was carried out at night. Strength of patrols is up to 15 men, combat patrols up to 30 men. They are not always supported by heavy infantry weapons and artillery. The enemy attempted in some cases, especially where the terrain did not afford observation, to penetrate the main line of resistance by surprise. All patrols could be stopped and dispersed in all cases very easily. The Americans leave wounded, dead and pieces of equipment, and many prisoners of war could be brought in.

Prisoners state that the preparation of patrols is poor. It was observed that the enemy tries to deceive in some cases by acting loudly and away from the planned penetration points.

American patrols with the mission of bringing in German prisoners of war have been successful.

(iv) Defence

The American defence is characterised by its deployment around strong-points. Large areas are without control and therefore our own patrols are able to penetrate deep into enemy territory. Light infantry weapons are not used very much. Sharpshooters are used very seldom. Mortars are very often placed in poor positions and very easily spotted.

However, enemy mortars are extremely effective, due mainly to their concentrated employment on our forward trenches. (Up to 12 mortars). White phosphorus is also used with the mortars. The effect of the mortar shell is equal to the German ammunition. Enemy anti-tank weapons have appeared occasionally. The defence is primarily carried by artillery and dug-in tanks, which are covered by infantry.

(b) Tanks
(i) Tanks in Large Scale Attack

Tanks are the main weapons of the attack. The enemy uses Sherman tanks, light tanks (M5), also Flamethrower tanks, tanks with dozer blades and tanks with bridging equipment. In the attack tanks are used in groups of up to 15. They advance with greatest caution. A daring attack was observed on only one occasion. The teamwork among the tanks is good. In the attack against pillboxes, 2 to 4 tanks work together and fire first from a distance of 200–300 metres against the apertures. Following this, the tanks – with flamethrowers – advance and knock out the pillbox. The pillboxes were bypassed in some instances. However, the enemy always avoided terrain which didn't allow observation. Whenever the tanks received fire from our own anti-tank weapons or from armoured vehicles, they immediately started to fire for five to ten minutes on the suspected positions. They were supported in such an operation by artillery and fighter-bombers. Afterwards they started to advance again slowly. Whenever one tank was shot in flames, the group of enemy tanks withdrew most of the time. Sometimes the enemy gave up a penetration, or took it up again after considerable artillery preparation. Our own artillery and mortar fire – when well placed – always forced the American tanks to stop and in most cases to turn back. Even fire poorly placed sometimes had effect. At dusk the enemy tanks always stopped their attack.

(ii)   Defence

Tank strongpoints in strength – up to 25 tanks form the backbone of the enemy defence. Tanks are dug in 400 to 1000 metres in front of the main line of resistance. They are dug in up to the turret. Sometimes the tanks are dug in parallel instead of facing to front. They shoot immediately at anything that moves. Whenever no connecting trenches exist between tanks, the crews stay completely under cover during daytime. The 76.2 mm gun on the Sherman is exceptionally accurate. This is probably due to an excellent sight. Normally the frontal plate of the light tank destroyer (38T)[6] will not be penetrated by this gun. Dug-in Sherman tanks are difficult to fight. The 75 mm anti-tank gun is ineffective against the turret over 600 metres. Light or heavy artillery fire does not do any damage. Only the use of 210 mm howitzers was effective. The replacement of tank units in the line is mostly carried out under smoke protection.

(c)   Artillery
(i)   Artillery in Attack

Increased artillery fire (up to 5000 rounds daily) preceded the large scale attack of 2 October. Targets were the positions of heavy infantry weapons, of artillery batteries as well as of villages in the primary battle areas. Batteries fired on main supply routes and villages in rear areas. Very heavy artillery fire prepared the attack itself. Targets were the planned location of the penetration as well as all heavy weapons. During the attack artillery fire was placed in front of the advancing tanks. In addition, the enemy placed harassing fire on roads leading to the main battle area. He also fired heavy concentrations on these targets. Artillery expenditure was increased up to 12,000 rounds within 24 hours. As a rule, artillery planes are used both in attack and defence. Fire direction from tanks must also be taken into consideration.

---

6. The *Jagdpanzer 38T* or Hetzer was a late-war German tank destroyer armed with a 75mm gun on the chassis of a 38t Skoda tank. It was issued to the tank destroyer units of infantry divisions.

(ii)   Defence

Enemy artillery supported combat patrols and small scale attacks. It fired on locations of our own heavy weapons and artillery as well as observation points. It placed harassing fire and concentrations on supply routes and villages in the battle area. Daily ammunition expenditure was between 1000 and 2800 rounds. Concentrations reached up to 60 rounds.

Enemy observation points are located in trees, chimneys, in houses and any other high point. Forward observers tried to get positions close to our main line of resistance in attacks and combat patrols in order to direct fire from there by either telephone or radio. For adjustment, the enemy used smoke shells (white and red-purple smoke). In some instances the infantry fired a pink flare which came down as smoke over the positions of the heavy infantry weapons. Enemy artillery fires for effect by concentrating several batteries. Single self-propelled guns are pushed forward sometimes to fire on suspected and located observation points. Enemy artillery fires on specific points and on any of our movements. When firing according to a fire plan on roads and villages far into rear areas, enemy fire is most of the time accurate. Observation batteries operate with ingenuity. In spite of this, deception was effective with our own roving guns and dummy installations. In counter-battery fire ammunition expenditure reaches a maximum of 60 rounds. Fragmentation of American ammunition is about equal to our own. Duds are not a rarity. Up to 80 per cent duds were observed in short concentrations. The enemy uses shells with very sensitive fuses as well as double-fuses and also cement shells with great depth of penetration. Smoke shells have an effect of 1 to 2 minutes and cause coughing. When phosphorus shells hit close, burns are caused and eyes are affected. Whenever phosphorus got in wires, they could not be fixed again.

(d)   Air Force

No saturation bombing took place in the division sector. However, fighter-bombers had complete superiority of the air in good weather. Up to 25 planes circle over our positions and attack with bombs and machine gun the main line of resistance, fire positions, roads and villages. The co-operation with ground troops is good, the accuracy of the guns not too good. The damage done by bombs is in no comparison to the number of planes and the expenditures. A few German fighters caused the immediate turning away of the enemy fighter-bombers. They manage very cleverly to stay out of AA fire. Whenever the weather is good, artillery planes are practically always in the air. Using the wind to their advantage and with their engines cut, they stay in the air almost motionless and successfully direct artillery and heavy infantry weapons fire. When fired on, they usually take off.

Document 11/4[7]

Enemy Interrogation Report of a Talkative Allied Soldier

Wartime Intelligence Officer's Comments

An English sergeant, captured 29 October 1944, was interrogated at 94 Infantry Division where the results were compiled into a report which was passed on to Tenth Army.

The PW had apparently talked so profusely and convincingly about our tactics and methods, adding his own comments, that the GOC Tenth Army decided to have the report mimeographed in toto and distributed to battalion level for all to note.

As most of the information contained in the document is very basic, only a few more interesting and perhaps unintentionally amusing extracts have been reproduced.

94th Infantry Division   *Division HQ 6 November 1944*
G Int   *Nr 1031/44 SECRET*

Enemy Tactical Principles and Our Methods

I Infantry
(PW describes Allied reconnaissance patrol and infantry tactics in great detail, from which such conclusions are drawn, as for example that Germans open fire too readily, bunch or straggle too much or make too much noise.)

---

7. ISUM 191, 8 January 1945, from *1st Canadian Corps Intelligence Summary*, 21 December 1944.

The Attack

(i)   No Allied attack is made without artillery preparation.

(ii) *The German Counter-attack*

PW believes that on the whole, German counter-attacks are poorly launched. Our (German) troops bunch together too much. Concentrating our attack enables the enemy to concentrate his defensive weapons. PW suggests flanking thrusts to dissipate the enemy defence. Crowding troops close together interferes with mutual fire support.

(iii) *Recognition of Officer in the Field*

Officers are not recognized as much from their shoulder tabs as by their smarter bearing and better fitting uniform. In clear weather and with the aid of field glasses it is sometimes easier to pick out the Iron Cross Class II and the Assault Badge than the man who wears them.

(iv) *Evaluation of the MG 42*

PW says the MG 42 which the enemy calls 'Spandau' always fires high through the tree branches. Nevertheless, the moral effect should not be underestimated and is considered one of the most unpleasant of weapons.

(v) *Spotting our Weapons*

The enemy uses 'Flash Spotters' to locate our artillery, mortar and MG positions. MGs are spotted through their tracer ammunition.

II   Artillery

(a) *Ranging*

(i) *Ranging with Air Bursts*

A comprehensive list of target points are compiled before the attack goes in. On these the artillery registers with air bursts (*hochgezogenem Sprengpunkt*), usually in the morning although the time may vary.

(ii) *Ranging by means of tanks*

This method is more accurate (than bracketing?) and therefore preferred. A tank fires directly into the artillery target point. The position of the tank and the artillery is known and the distance of the target point from the tank can be calculated from the rangefinder and aiming circle. From those the firing table can be compiled. Usually one round is sufficient for each target point. Ranging varies from 3 hours to several days before the attack.

(b) *Effect of Own Artillery*

The effect of our shelling has lessened because:

(i) The enemy avoids houses and built-up areas except perhaps in cold weather

(ii) Ridges and depressions are usually not occupied as these are categorically under our shellfire

(iii) Our Harassing Fire is overcome by the use of cross-country vehicles for bringing up supplies.

III   Signals

The usual methods of line and wireless communication within the batteries are described with a note on Allied emphasis on security and line tapping.

IV   Engineers

Here again the information is very routine. The usual methods of mine detection and lifting are mentioned as well as the steps in the erection of Bailey bridges and a note on railway tunnel repairs.

(a)   *Mines*

PW has a knowledge of:

Teller Mines

Schützen Mines

Box Mines

'Shoe Mines' (?)

(*The query was inserted by the German Intelligence Staff, not by us, as they apparently had no knowledge of this type of mine!*)

(b)   *Bridging*

New Methods

New equipment for assault crossings has been developed which was intended for use on the Arno. It was not used thanks to our rapid withdrawal. Although PW has no further details, he believes the equipment is in use in Holland and will be used in Italy over the next big river obstacle.

Document 11/5[8]

What The Enemy Thinks of Americans

Wartime Intelligence Officer's Comments

The following document, translated by XVIII US Airborne Corps, was issued by 18th Volksgrenadier Division on 5 November 1944 deriding Americans and their combat tactics. After four weeks of fighting in the Ardennes 18th Volksgrenadier Division should just about be ready to start whistling another tune:

Grenadier Regiment 294   Regimental HQ, 5 November 1944

SUBJECT: Extracts of a report about American combat methods

(i)   Infantry

Recent fighting on the West Wall has proven that the average American infantry soldier is a long way from being a good fighter. We do not want to go so far as to call him yellow, but numerous observations have shown that he will attack only when definitely superior in material, tanks, artillery and airpower. He will avoid close combat whenever possible, and is extremely sensitive to immediate counter-attacks. Frequently he flees from a village when his own artillery opens up in the vicinity.

With some exceptions, the Americans will avoid night fighting; we found in Normandy that they hated it, and they have not changed. They will even go so far as to light the battlefield at night. Security is pulled in at night or otherwise considerably enforced. Reconnaissance groups usually consist of 10 to 20 men, very heavily equipped with explosives, flamethrowers, and phosphorus grenades. In contrast, they do not carry heavy weapons on reconnaissance and when we attack them with coordinated fire they will flee and leave their heavy equipment behind. Occasionally we find a reconnaissance group of 2 to 3 men, and sometimes a single American infantry soldier is a good fighter – but both are exceptions rather than the rule.

The training of the American Infantry apparently produces many excellent hand-grenade throwers, mostly in their reconnaissance troops; also numerous expert riflemen who are mainly stationed in strongpoints

---

8. ISUM 201, 17 January 1945. from XVIIIth US Airborne Corps.

up to the outpost in order to safeguard communications.

The American soldier uses cover to good advantage, using any pause in the fighting to dig himself in. His foxholes are outstanding for their comfort. He uses plenty of camouflage – not always advantageously. His front-line behaviour is rather careless lately – but we can probably attribute that to our lack of heavy weapons and to the reluctance of the German soldier to take up the fire-fight.

American outpost security at night is systematically built up: a listening post in front, a chain of guards stretching 25 yards back and then another very close chain of guards for a further 25 yards.

When bunkers or strongpoints are taken they will either be demolished or mined. But our immediate counter-attack after a bunker-line has been breached is usually successful (short artillery preparation and strong use of hand grenades are necessary). The quicker the counter-attack the more successful and the less our own losses. And again the enemy will flee and leave everything behind.

(ii) Artillery

The American artillery has proven itself to be of a high standard and extremely effective, in Normandy as well as on the West Wall. The mobility of the enemy's artillery, which proved to be such an advantage in Normandy, is still noteworthy, although slightly diminished. Excellent coordination between artillery, tanks, and the Air Force – especially air reconnaissance – shows the existence of a good communication system.

The Americans have always made it a point to destroy our OPs whenever possible by knocking them out with fighter-bombers, or by using artillery smoke shells. This practice has slightly diminished on the west wall, but it will recur when they again take the offensive. At present they frequently try to knock our OPs out with a single, well-aimed heavy mortar or medium artillery rounds at irregular intervals; sometimes they fire directly on the cover around the OP in order to kill the observer with shrapnel.

We see from the maps and papers captured on PW that the American leaders have exact knowledge about our bunkers and the positions and even missions of our artillery. The few positions they have not yet plotted receive hardly any fire. In Normandy they frequently plotted our OP tanks by direction-finding equipment.

Besides all this, the American artillery is amazingly accurate and fast in its fire adjustment as well as in its indirect fire. Cub observation planes will give the direction for 2 or 3 rounds (sometimes by using red smoke) and in no time the fire will be adjusted. The accuracy of his indirect fire proves that he has excellent maps and fire data.

In Normandy whole artillery regiments or even larger units would lay down coordinated fire, but recently we have not observed that practice. But then and now they use an immense amount of ammunition. In general, they will not fire close to their own Main Line of Resistance (MLR) and if they do they use shells with low shrapnel effect in order to save their own troops.

At present most of the American indirect fire is concentrated on supply points; they seldom fire on high ground. Interdiction fire occurs mainly at night, slowing down in the early hours of the morning, to be resumed between 0900 and 1000.

Recently the slightest noise on our part, as close as 200 yards from the MLR, has drawn fire from their mortars or artillery. They may be using listening instruments.

(iii)   Tanks

According to all our observations American tanks will lose their aggressiveness and turn around as soon as they are attacked by close combat methods or artillery. When they become separated from their infantry they act the same way. Our 'L.F.H. explosive shell with AZ' is effective against all light models up to and including the Sherman tank. Well-aimed artillery fire will sometimes destroy them, but a good supply of ammunition has to be on hand in order to be able to keep up the fight.

(iv)   Air force

An attack by fast bombers is usually preceded by a feint-attack. They fly in close groups of six planes over their objective and when out of sight they change their course and return for the bomb-run or they come widely scattered and unite above their objective. They always attack out of the sun. When attacked by our AA they scatter immediately.

The fighter-bombers usually circle around the front and then dive one after the other towards their objective, also always out of the sun. Some-times 2 to 3 fighters attack together while the others keep circling above. When attacked by our AA they scatter and try to attack at very low altitude.

(Signed) Kahler
1st Lieutenant and Adjutant

Chapter 12

In Enemy Hands

The Experience of Allied and German Prisoners of War

Editor's Comments

The experience of Allied soldiers taken prisoner by the Wehrmacht could differ widely, as illustrated by Documents 12/1 and 12/2. The behaviour of German prisoners of war was generally exemplary, a matter of apparent pride (Document 12/3).

Document 12/1[1]

German Interrogation Methods

Wartime Intelligence Officer's Comments

A Canadian private recently released from an enemy PW cage gives a first-hand account of German interrogation methods. On 26 August 1944, being a fluent French speaker, he was ordered to help the French resistance round up some Germans in the vicinity of Rouen. Having completed this task he returned to his unit to find that it had pulled out in the direction of Le Havre. He managed to get a lift as far as St. Romain and continued the rest of the way on foot.

---

1. ISUM 81, 18 September 1944.

About midnight a gruff German voice challenged him, and he then realized, too late, that he had taken the wrong route. As a PW he was marched off to an underground defence post, where he was questioned by an officer of the Gestapo. His own words best describe the interrogation that followed.

He first of all asked me if I was crazy as I had unknowingly walked along a road which was sewn with mines. He threw a map at me and demanded to know the strengths and dispositions of our forces. I told him that I was lost myself and had no idea of where my unit was. He took me by the throat and held me up against the wall and said that as I had had a P.38 and a Schmeisser on me when I was taken prisoner I would be shot. He then asked how many tanks there were outside Harfleur and I replied 6,000. He then hit me on the mouth very hard, knocking my top teeth out.

This rough treatment apparently getting him nowhere, the Gestapo man called to the guard to take the PW away. Later on he was interrogated again, but this time by an intelligence officer who tried the gentle, I'm-sorry-old-man system of extracting information, but met with just as little success. He started a general and friendly conversation, asking the PW how he had been taken prisoner and ending off with the inevitable query 'How many troops have you got?' To this the Canadian would only reply that he did not know and that he had lost his way.

All further efforts proving fruitless he was put in a prison together with some German soldiers who were doing time. In the week that he was there the area was bombed three times, and on the last occasion the prison was nearly hit and all the Germans fled. Seeking cover during the raid he was again taken prisoner in an underground defence position.

Following this he was moved to Tourneville Fort at Le Havre, where he was put in a room with six other PW. When the Allied attack on the fortress was launched, the Commander of the Fort asked them to negotiate a surrender. The Canadian, waving a white flag and dodging a burst of Bren gun fire, finally got in touch with the attacking troops and turned in 200 Germans and 300 Italians who were waiting to surrender.

Document 12/2²

Interrogation at Aachen

Wartime Intelligence Officer's Comments

Two American soldiers, Staff Sergeant Ewart M. Padgett and Private First Class James B. Haswell, were held as prisoners-of-war in Aachen for four days from 17 October to 21 October 1944. On 17 October Staff Sergeant Padgett was ordered to take a combat patrol into Aachen, contact the enemy, capture a prisoner, if possible, and then return. Caught in a ditch by machine gun fire and mortar shells and injured by shrapnel, Haswell and Padgett were finally forced to surrender. The account of what followed subsequent to their capture was told by Staff Sergeant Padgett and appeared in First US Army G-2 Periodic Report dated 11 November 1944.

We were taken to the Company CP where we gave them our name, rank, and serial number and they searched us, taking our wallets, money, knives and paybook and sealing them in a large envelope. A medic then entered the room, who could speak fluent English, and asked that we sign a statement saying that we had received no serious injuries due to the previous action. This we did.

In searching us they had overlooked a hand grenade that I had in my back pocket, but in going through the door as we headed for the Battalion CP the guard's hand accidentally hit the grenade in my pocket, so he relieved me of it and at first he seemed angry but was soon smiling.

When we arrived at the Battalion CP, which was in a large bomb-proof shelter, we were put into a small room with two guards who could speak excellent English. We tried to talk the guards into hiding out with us and returning to our lines that night, but the guards told us that there wasn't anything that they could do to help us. We were never questioned while at the Battalion CP.

From here we started toward the Garrison CP, and when we were approximately 50 yards from the door of the Battalion CP we met an SS officer and an SS trooper; the officer halted us and evidently not trusting the two guards behind us, he put the trooper behind us as a guard also. We continued on toward the Garrison CP and as we made a right turn around

---

2. ISUM 136, 13 November 1944.

the corner of the building a young girl was knocking on the door – when she turned and saw us she jumped into the air laughing and shouting, 'American Swine, American Swine'. The SS trooper immediately quieted her, so then she turned her back to us, but the trooper made her turn around and face us again. We later found out that the German civilians are not allowed to mock, harass, or turn their backs on American prisoners of war.

Document 12/3[3]

The Pride of the Wehrmacht

Wartime Intelligence Officer's Comments

The following is a translation of an article which appeared in a recent copy of a well known German magazine Wille und Macht *(Will and Power), on the subject of PWs, published March/April 1944.*

There is no other problem so thoroughly silenced by the press than the problem of prisoners of war. It is difficult to explain why. The death of the battlefield has a clean-cut, heroic connotation, which is lacking in the fate of prisoners of war. How an honest man can allow himself to be captured without loss of face is a problem which must be treated individually. There are situations in war when giving up is a duty, and others when giving up is a crime. Let us quote in history: Friedrich Wilhelm von Seydlitz, the most courageous, and, undoubtedly the most capable cavalry general under Frederick the Great, started his splendid military career as a Hungarian prisoner of war. He gave up after offering, as ordered, stubborn resistance. He led thirty men on an isolated outpost against five hundred. All ammunition spent, he surrendered. The enemy, impressed by this heroic stand, offered honourable surrender as it was customary in this period. The courageous attitude of von Seydlitz became the topic of conversation in army circles, and his meteoric career began.

---

3. ISUM 127, 3 November 1944, from *V Corps Periodic Report 147.*

Whatever the case, the life of prisoners of war, even considering decent treatment by the captors which is not always the case, is by no means easy. Except for packages and bleak letters from home, prisoners of war are mentally and morally completely cut off from the Homeland. All the information they receive is from the enemy. It takes a lot not to forget in this situation one's obligation as a man and a member of a nation. The situation of a prisoner of war becomes, of course, more difficult when the enemy, as in the case of Soviet Russia, attempts to compel the captive to act against the Fatherland.

A couple of days ago I came across an article written by some writer, Alistair Cooke, in the *New York Times* – an enemy newspaper – quote:

I was one of the few newspapermen who visited the strongly-guarded camps for German PWs. I saw more than a thousand brawny young Nazis at work and play. I saw their comfortable living quarters and kitchens. I learned their attitude toward war. According to international law protecting PWs against public curiosity, visitors are not permitted to question them. But the camp officers told me that the Germans often volunteered information, and are rather eager to discuss the war, of course with the understanding that Germany is going to be the winner. Any remark on the part of the American indicating doubt, results in silence on the part of the Nazi. What strikes the visitor is the lack of a guardhouse. It was different before when the camp housed Italian prisoners. Their happy-go-lucky attitude brought them repeatedly into conflict with the camp administration, often so serious as to result in solitary confinement on bread and water over a period of three days. After the completion of the sentence, they emerged in a jolly mood, not holding a grudge against anybody.

The Germans are different. They are so deeply inculcated with discipline that they learned the camp rules and regulations by heart, and adhered to them to the letter. Since the Germans moved into the camp, not once has occurred the necessity for disciplinary action. The camp officers pointed out other differences between Italian and German PWs. The Italians, as a whole, have been rather likeable. Their gay spirit, love for music, and the inability to hate anyone, made it difficult for the camp officers to treat them sternly. The Italians spoke of relatives and friends in Brooklyn, bought U.S.A. war bonds, and did not show any interest in war. They wanted to be freed, get a job, and to become citizens. In contrast, the Germans are tough,

194

sometimes aloof. They have no time for play. They continue their education, studying English, geography, chemistry, mathematics. They are quiet and respectful, but on the other hand, spiteful and sinister. Most of them are sure that Germany is bound to win the war.

Comments are unnecessary. We are proud of such soldiers.

Chapter 13

Humour (Such as it Was)

Editor's Comments

By the autumn of 1944, there was not much to laugh about in the Third Reich although Allied intelligence officers thought the guidelines on etiquette for prospective artillery officers amusing (Document 13/1). The 'League of Lonely War Women' (Document 13/2) could at best only be termed black humour and the behaviour of rather poor officers on the Italian front (Document 13/3) probably more funny to Allied readers than to the German soldiers forced to serve under them.

Document 13/1[1]

Sieg Heil by Numbers

Wartime Intelligence Officer's Comments

Extracts from order of German School for Artillery Cadets published April 1943.

---

1. ISUM 81, 18 September 1944.

Behaviour in Society

Paying a Visit

(a) Visiting hrs 1130–1300 hrs on Sundays, 1700–1800 hrs on weekdays. Never later, and never in the afternoon.

(b) Visiting card must be of a plain and simple design. Unmarried officers should leave a separate card for the householder, his wife and each grown-up daughter.

(c) Dress: Service Dress jacket, long trousers, small type badges of rank, sword, stiff peaked cap and white gloves.

   In the hall: remove cloak but retain belt. Take sword and hat with you, and wear gloves.
   Entering a room: carry hat in left hand. On taking a seat, lay hat down.
   Gloves: when paying a visit, walking in street, or on official business, both gloves must always be worn. It is impolite, when a superior officer stretches out his arm to shake hands, to keep him waiting while a glove is removed.

(d) Coming and going: length of visit should be about ten minutes. Do not look at your watch. No reason should be given for terminating the visit. On leaving, do not turn your back on the company when opening the door.

(e) Conversation: avoid any mention of your superior in conversation. Relatives should be referred to as 'Herr Vater', 'Fraulein Schwester' etc. (i.e. Never 'my wife').

Introductions

When introducing two ladies to one another, use the phrase 'May I make the ladies known to one another: Frau X – Frau Y'. The title of their husbands should be omitted (exception 'Excellency'). The hand of elderly women should be kissed, but never in public.

Forms of Address

Unmarried women:

(a) in general – '*Gnädiges Fräulein*'
(b) Baronesses – '*Gnädiges Fräulein*'
(c) Countesses – '*Gräfin, not 'Fräulein Gräfin*' (*Komtess* in Southern Germany)

Entertainments

(a) Wine: white wine to be drunk from tall glasses, red wine from short glasses.

(b) Dances: first dance and quadrilles always with dinner partner. Never dance continually with one and the same lady. As a matter of principle dance as soon as possible with the lady of the house and her daughters.

(c) Flowers: to be unwrapped in the hall, never presented with the paper round them. In presenting flowers, hold the stalks downwards.

(d) At large scale entertainments, be very careful to preserve a correct demeanour even at a late hour.

Written Communications

(a) Form of address: always choose the form of address to which the recipient is accustomed, and that which he has a right to expect from a well-bred young man, i.e. *'Hochverehrter Herr'* or *'Hochzuverehrender Herr* (plus Title)'.

(b) Contents of letter: must conform to *H.Dv.30*[2] paragraph 8.

(c) Ending: in correspondence with officials or untitled persons, long conventional polite formulas should be avoided, and the phrase 'Heil Hitler' used.

General

No flowers to be worn on uniforms or carried on vehicles.

For troops returning to the Fatherland from campaigns, permission for the use of flowers may be obtained from Higher Authority.

At races, the officer himself must not approach the Totalisator.[3]

Behaviour in public: The theatre may not be visited in riding boots. It is forbidden for officers in uniform to take part in Masked or Fancy Dress Balls.

---

2. *Heeres-Dienstvorschriften 30, Schrift-und-Geschäftsverkehr der Wehrmacht* (Berlin, 1939), the Wehrmacht manual for military writing, forms and correspondence.
3. Parimutual betting machine or wicket.

Document 13/2[4]

Let the People Speak – Quick, Herman, the Scissors

Wartime Intelligence Officer's Comments

The following circular, captured by 6 South African Armoured Division, was published by a Hamburg firm:

Dear Front Soldier:

When will you come back on leave?

When will you be able again to forget the hard duties of a soldier and exchange them for a few days of joy, happiness and love? Back at home we know of your heroic struggle; however, we do understand that even the bravest gets tired and that he needs a soft pillow, tenderness and healthy pleasure.

WE ARE WAITING FOR YOU:

For you who have been compelled to spend your leave in a foreign town; we are waiting for you whom the war has robbed of his home, waiting for you who stands alone in the world without a wife, without a fiancee, without a flirt.

WE ARE WAITING FOR YOU:

Cut out our badge on this letter. Display it visibly on your glass in every tea room, in every bar which is in the vicinity of a railway station; soon a member of our League of Lonely War Women will take charge of you, and the dreams you dreamt in the front line and the longings of lonely nights will find fulfillment. It is you we want, not your money, therefore ask for our membership card at once. There are members everywhere, since we German women understand our duties towards our country and towards those who defend it.

Naturally, we are not unselfish – for years and years we have been separated from our menfolk, surrounded by all these foreigners; naturally we long to have again a real German boy, to press him to our bosom. Don't be shy; your wife, your sister or your sweetheart is also one of us.

---

4. ISUM 113, 20 October 1944 from AFHQ Intelligence Notes 76.

We think of you but we also think of the future of our country. He who rests, rusts.

League of Lonely War Women
(*Verein Einsamer Kriegerfrauen*)

Document 13/3[5]

Martinets on the Italian Front

Wartime Intelligence Officer's Comments

Two recent accounts from Italy give an interesting sidelight into some types of German officers now leading the Wehrmacht to its Götterdämerung. With officers of this kind attempting to stem the Allied tide, it is little wonder that desertion has become a serious problem in the German Army.

It is not suggested that every German officer is a drunken Prussian beast, but that this type is not entirely a figment of the cartoonist's imagination is shown by these incidents.

Generalleutnant Hoppe[6]

Applause was not very loud when it was announced in an Order of the Day to 992 Grenadier Regiment on 1 or 2 October 1944 that their Divisional Commander was to become a Corps Commander, for the General enjoys an unenviable reputation for incompetence, eccentricity, and insobriety, and 278th Infantry Division has earned thereby the title of 'Hoppe's Circus'. (If Hoppe has a Corps, it must be '*zu äusserst besonderer Verwendung!*')

When new recruits are paraded for inspection, the GOC storms up and down before them, cutting a sorry figure and uttering such cliches as 'You are the cream of the Fatherland' and 'You will be the ones to win oak leaves for your beloved General', punctuated by an occasional hiccough.

---

5. ISUM 134, 11 November 1944, from *Allied Forces Headquarters Intelligence Notes*, 31 October 1944.
6. *Generalleutnant* Harry Hoppe (1894–1969), commander of 278th Infantry Division. Born Heinrich, he formally changed his name to Harry.

These recruits soon lose whatever military ardour they drew from this preparation, for the older hands in the division are usually outspoken in telling them that the firebrand General has already led three divisions to ruin in Russia and was doing the best he could to repeat the performance with the 278th Infantry Division in Italy.

Another occasion when the General distinguished himself was during an inspection of a military hospital.

With his trousers flapping against his spindly legs and his red tippler's nose aglow in the morning sunlight, the great one went to the first bed, played with his Knight's Cross, and asked, 'How are you, my man? What do they call me?' The answer came back pat – 'Wild Harry they call you, sir.'

Smirking at the racy manner in which the tour was going, the General benevolently rewarded the patient with fourteen days' leave. Further down the ward he asked the same question and the second patient, hoping also to benefit from his GOC's eccentricity, gave the same answer. Just to prove how eccentric he really was, Hoppe gave the unsuspecting wretch four days' detention.

Captain Buhrmann

When Captain Buhrmann reviewed near Imola a contingent of 592 *Marsch* Battalion destined to join his battlegroup, there occurred a scene reminiscent of Falstaff's recruiting drive in Henry IV.

Buhrmann started proceedings by haranguing the men as follows:

So far you haven't done much for Germany in this war, so now you're going to be made to. Until the Führer sends us the new weapons you'll have to defend yourselves with rifles. Italy is a secondary front, but the line must be held.

He then asked the men if there was anyone present who did not feel up to the job he'd have to tackle – fully expecting, so PW think, that no one would have the courage to present himself.

Two did, however – the first had a glass eye and could see very little with his good one. He explained this to Buhrmann who replied 'You ought to be glad you've got a glass eye – you don't have to close it.'

The other man then had his say. He pointed out that on one hand he had two fingers missing, and the remaining fingers were stiff. Buhrmann's answer to that one was 'Better stiff than off.'

About 14 others then stepped forward – PW say that sufferers from every ailment appeared except the deaf, who could not follow what was going on and probably thought that volunteers were being called for.

Buhrmann did not give these new incapacitates individual attention. He shouted '*Ab! Ab!*' (Get out! Get out!) and continued with violence 'I'll teach you! You'll see! You'll see!'

The incident was brought to an end by Buhrmann catching sight of an Italian civilian looking on. He reached for his pistol and the civilian disappeared like lightning.

PW said that on the morning of 10 October, when Lindenberg Coy came forward to the attack, the 'halt and the lame' who could not move fast enough were actually kicked up the hill by a sergeant.